Counseling Women

Counseling Women

A Narrative, Pastoral Approach

Christie Cozad Neuger

FORTRESS PRESS
MINNEAPOLIS

COUNSELING WOMEN
A Narrative, Pastoral Approach

Cover image: *Woman and Flowers,* Vicky Emptage,
© 2001 The Stock Illustration Source. Used by permission.

Cover design by Marti Naughton

Book design by Ann Delgehausen

Library of Congress Cataloging-in-Publication Data
Neuger, Christie Cozad
Counseling women: a narrative, pastoral approach /
Christie Cozad Neuger.
p. cm.
Includes bibliographical references and index.
ISBN 0-8006-3422-5 (alk. paper)

BV4012.2 .N48 2001
259'.082—dc21   2001023748

The paper used in this publication meets the minimum requirements
of American National Standard for Information Sciences—Permanence
of Paper for Printed Library Materials, ANSI Z329.48-1984.

Manufactured in the U.S.A.   AF 1-3422

05   04   03   02   01   1   2   3   4   5   6   7   8   9   10

This book is dedicated, with thanks,
to my sister of birth Laurie Cozad,
and to my sisters of choice, who have all been
conversation partners, reality testers, nurturers, and friends.

Contents

Preface

The problems and choices that bring many women to pastoral counseling are, at the very least, complicated by the layers of gender training, gender oppression, and the dynamics of racism, classism, heterosexism, and ableism. Pastors need to be equipped with pastoral counseling approaches that are informed by psychological, theological, and clinical methods that address the realities of women's lives. When religious leaders counsel with women who are struggling against depression, anxiety, abuse, exhaustion, and frustration, we need to be able to do more than listen and support. We need to be able to help women gain confidence about and language for the challenges they face. We need to be able to help women see their struggles in a way that exposes the cultural biases and distortions at their roots. And we need to be able to help women make the kinds of choices and connections that assist them to gain and maintain greater satisfaction and richer life options. The purpose of this book is to provide a set of resources for religious leaders who engage in pastoral counseling with women.

I became interested in the issues involved in counseling women when, after graduating from seminary, I engaged in two years of pastoral care and counseling training and then a doctoral program in pastoral counseling. During the two-year residency, I found myself primarily in counseling situations with women who presented descriptions of various problems they were facing. Those descriptions—of depression, of uncertainty, of weariness and frustration, of abuse—seemed to have many story strands in common. Yet the theories and approaches to pastoral counseling I was being trained in didn't lend themselves to exploring these commonalties. Instead, they encouraged me to look at each counselee's story through an isolating lens where cultural factors and issues of power and marginalization were less important than the particular developmental issues, with their intrapsychic and narrowly conceived systemic implications. My feminist consciousness resisted both the theological and psychological lenses that seemed to obscure and pathologize the real-life experiences of and consequences for these women who were seeking help. But that left me without adequate means to offer the kind of relevant and effective counseling that should have been available. I was able to offer affirmation, validation, and companionship, which were nurturing for women counselees, but my pastoral counseling theory and practice were missing a necessary integration.

Through a doctoral program and into many years of practice I continued to experience a lack of integration between theory, theology, and practice that could provide an effective means of taking culture and its layers of power and oppression, marginalization and entitlement, shared experience and unique life story, seriously. Feminist philosophy provided unifying threads but never adequate integration.

Two developments helped me to break through this stalemate. First, I was able to pull together my experiences in pastoral counseling with women to create a fourfold pastoral counseling framework that reflects my deepest theological commitments of empowerment, justice, grace, and interdependency. This framework gave me a way to bring consistency and integrity to my pastoral counseling work. *Counseling Women* is organized around this framework. Second was my discovery of and training in narrative counseling theory. This counseling approach, highly influenced by feminist and other liberation theories, reflects an attentiveness to both culture and person. It is deeply respectful, relies on a consultative rather than an expert model, and is elegant in both its simplicity and its thoroughness. It is efficient, effective, empowering, and deeply relational. The relationship of focus, however, is not that between counselor and counselee as much as it is between the counselee and the variety of relationships that form the warp and woof of her life story. It is a theory based on hope and on the foundational reality that human beings are makers of meaning at their deepest core and that reality is constructed as we make meaning out of our experience.

These theoretical dimensions are crucial for the practice of pastoral counseling. Narrative theory's efficient and effective qualities, as well as the de-centering of the counselor in the counseling process, make this approach well suited to parish pastors. Its respectful and advocative nature makes it well suited to a liberationist theological commitment. Its care for the particular story in the midst of dominant cultural discourses makes it well suited for working with women. Its focus on hope and possibility makes it well suited for all.

I am grateful for the opportunity to put these ideas into the public domain. I want to thank the editorial staff at Fortress Press who offered both opportunity and encouragement. I also want to express my deep appreciation to United Theological Seminary of the Twin Cities for the sabbatical time I received to complete this manuscript and for being a liberating and empowering place for faculty and students alike. The members of the Society for Pastoral Theology have provided a context in which to test ideas and engage in collegial conversation. It is a deep wellspring for me. The feminist pastoral supervision group in which I have participated for the past eight years read this manuscript and offered helpful ideas and powerful support.

My family is and always has been extraordinarily supportive and so my thanks go to my son Dan and his soon-to-be wife Chrissy and to my daughter Cathy and her new husband Gregg. And, as always, my deepest love and appreciation go to my life partner of thirty years, Win Neuger.

Finally, I want to express gratitude to all the women who have been willing to entrust their stories to me in a pastoral counseling relationship. This book has been woven from their narratives.

one

Setting the Scene

This is a book about pastoral counseling with women. It is a book intended to assist pastoral caregivers, male and female, in the church, in church-affiliated counseling centers, and in the variety of counseling contexts where the spiritual dimensions of people's lives are taken seriously. It is a book whose perspective is feminist-centered, which means that it unfolds within a set of assumptions based on the reality that women and men still live out their lives in a world that is profoundly sexist, racist, ageist, classist, and heterosexist and these harmful dynamics are at the heart of much of the distress and "pathology" that is brought to the pastoral counselor. This is a book that will offer resources to the pastoral caregiver and will make it more possible to care for women counselees in life-affirming and culture-changing ways.

There are many possible objections to a book that is focused on pastoral counseling with women. I will look at three of those. First, one might object to my use of what has become a "false generic"—the word *woman*.[1] I acknowledge that as problem and I think that it is one of the most serious risks in writing a book like this. There is no universal entity called woman that can be analyzed and "treated" in a book on counseling and care. The dynamics of race, class, and sexual orientation must always be seen as occurring alongside the dynamics of gender. The kinds of rules, norms, and assumptions by which the contemporary (dominant) United States culture operates are built upon dualistic categories and power hierarchies that order the value and worth of people. Maleness and femaleness make up one of those dualistic categories, as whiteness and darkness of skin, richness and poorness, heterosexuality and homosexuality, and so on. None of

1

these dynamics can be seen in isolation without false and overgeneralized claims being made. Nor are these dynamics or particularities additive. As Deborah King has said, "the relationships among race, class and gender [and I would add sexual orientation] are not simply additive as implied by such terms as double and triple jeopardy. Instead, these relationships are interactive and produce dissimilar results for women and men in particular circumstances."[2]

Consequently, there are grave risks in writing a book where the primary subject and focus is "women." The risk of making gender appear to be a dynamic that can be studied in isolation from these other powerful forces that interrelate with gender in every possible social situation is a significant one. Nonetheless, the focus of this book is on the dynamics of gender at cultural, institutional, familial, and personal levels and the correctives and constructions for pastoral care and counseling theory that emerge from this kind of analysis. In order to minimize the risks of this false generic I will be drawing from the experiences of and literature by people of various particularities so that we may begin to see both common patterns and significant dissimilarities in women's lives. It will be important to walk the fine line between paying attention to the particularities in women's lives and the way those particularities affect pastoral counseling theory, and finding points in common such that a meaningful set of theoretical premises and practices can be developed. The other issue is that these points in common must be found in order for there to be any kind of solidarity developed around gender—something I believe we need now more than ever as we attempt to support women and oppose backlash.

A second possible objection to the orientation of this book might be around the use of a feminist perspective. For many, the term *feminism* has polarizing and exclusivistic meanings. Some would say that we are in a postfeminist time and that, when looking at the dynamics of gender, we need to take a more inclusive approach that considers both women and men from either a nonbiased or a masculinist/feminist hybrid point of view.

This, I believe, misunderstands the nature of feminist scholarship. There are two responses to this kind of potential objection. First, my understanding of feminism is:[3]

- privileging women's experiences, voices, and perspectives in the building of theory and practice;

- critiquing theories, theologies, practices, and structures that exclusively or primarily reflect a dominant cultural exclusivistic point of view and that operate against the best interests of those marginalized because of race, class, gender, sexual orientation, or able-bodiedness;
- operating from a self-conscious standpoint of gender as a social construction and understanding the implications of that construction for the development of theory and practice.

One might set this in comparison to a definition of womanist thought, which would include the following:

- privileging African American women's (and other women of color) experiences, voices, and perspectives in the building of theory, theology, and practice;
- critiquing from the standpoint of race and gender (and usually class)— a standpoint that does not just add race and gender views together but forms a radical new lens from those views;
- focus on the harm that a fundamentally racist, sexist, and classist culture does to those who are marginalized by those particularities;
- belief in the necessity of racial solidarity between men and women, with appropriate gender critiques, for the dismantling of destructive racist structures.

Feminism and womanism share many things in common. For example, both have commitments to

- transforming all lives, relationships, systems, and cultures so that they are inclusive, life affirming, and just;
- believing that each individual life must be understood in the context of the power arrangements and rules of the dominant culture *and* that the construction of theory and practice must also listen carefully to each individual marginalized voice;
- certainty that theories and practices based on feminist and womanist perspectives are always inescapably and intentionally political;
- a non-neutral stance on the goals and practices of ministry—as Rebecca S. Chopp says, "Women and men engaged in feminist practices of theological education use feminist theory to persuade, to change, to open up, and to transform.[4]

The values listed above are, I hope, woven throughout this text. I write, however, from the perspective of a white, middle-class, heterosexual woman and the theory building I do must necessarily reflect that social location. Consequently, this book is from a feminist orientation.

Another point related to this potential objection about feminism is the limitation of feminist thought to exploring the lives of women. I do not understand feminism to be correlated exclusively to women's lives. Nor do I understand feminism to be a philosophical point of view limited to women theory builders. For example, much of the exciting new literature in the men's movement, which explores the dynamics of men's lives, is built on profeminist assumptions and many men writing in theology and pastoral counseling today do so from profeminist positions. Feminism and profeminism are ways of looking at the lives of people— men and women— in the context of a dualistic culture organized around power hierarchies related to race, class, gender, age, able-bodiedness, and sexual orientation. It is not only for the purpose of looking at women's lives even though it is about giving voice and power to women. It is also for the purpose of analyzing and challenging power dynamics that are destructive to all.

A third objection that might be raised in regard to the foci of this book is the project of pastoral counseling itself. In today's complex and litigious culture, many parish pastors are avoiding the work of pastoral counseling, fearful of the time and training needed to do responsible (and lawsuit-free) work. Yet, as we move toward more instances of managed care and more limitations on health insurance—especially around issues of mental health—and as spiritual concerns continue to be central in people's lives, pastors, I believe, will be called on to provide competent, effective, and well-boundaried forms of pastoral counseling. Pastors, who are able to look at the multiple dimensions of people's lives, often including their family contexts, their spiritual journeys, and their particular situations of life and work, have an enormous advantage in being able to help people today. The main task is to provide clergy with approaches that are reasonably short-term, that involve the resources of the congregation and community, and that allow adequate boundaries to remain between the pastoral counseling role and the other roles of ministry.

This book attempts to provide some of these tools and perspectives in the context of a pastoral counseling approach for women. In other words, although the focus is on the theoretical and theological deconstruction and reconstruction necessary in a sexist world, the creation of liberating and effective pastoral practices will be applicable for the counseling ministry in general. I will focus on some of the insights provided by theories and practices of narrative psychotherapy, intending that this counseling structure, which is usually short-term, contextually sensitive, and very teachable to both practitioners and counselees alike, will be useful for all pastoral counseling work. It is important for pastors to take up the challenge of providing effective pastoral counseling for their parishioners.

I have looked at three of the potential objections to a book like this. I wish now to explore the three reasons why I think it needed to be written. The first of those reasons is the radical reconstruction of knowledge that has happened in the context of both postmodernism and the various liberation movements of the late twentieth century. The massive investigations into gender have been a part of this reconstruction and it is there that I wish to focus. Gender studies gives us a lens through which to look at the revolution of knowledge and its affect on the building of new theory and practice for all pastoral counseling, and especially pastoral counseling with women.

Gender Studies and the Revolution of Knowledge

It is nearly impossible to be specific when we talk about the discipline of gender studies. It has become a huge and interdisciplinary field that covers investigations in anthropology, biology, sociology, psychology, theology, history, and more. As a working definition let us say, though, that gender study involves an investigation into the origins, meanings, and implications of the assignment of maleness (and masculinity) and femaleness (and femininity) to people based on biological, familiar, and social designations of sex—implications for people, relationships, families, institutions, cultures, and for knowing and knowledge itself. Male and female *sex* designations have been seen more as biological assignments, and masculinity and femininity, or *gender,* seen more as social assignments, though of course there are interrelationships. As mentioned earlier, a fundamental cultural principle that underlies the primary issues of gender is its basis in a binary, or dualistic, system: one is either male or female, masculine or feminine. This is a somewhat faulty dualism even when just looking at a biological assignment of sex (people are more or less female or male), but it is a dangerous and erroneous concept when assigning "innate" or "natural" characteristics as belonging to one or the other, but not both, of these sexes.

Contemporary studies about gender were initially motivated by two recognitions within feminism. The first was that women did not have the same access to resources in the public realm (particularly in the world of work, which women were entering in increasing numbers during and after World War II), and the second was that women's stories, to a large extent, had been left out of the public record of human society. Since these two realities were based on gender stereotypes that were recognized as normative and real, the field of gender studies was first directed toward exploring the validity of these stereotypes. These studies soon began to demonstrate—through a variety of disciplines—that the vast majority of sex differences were not primarily determined by "natural" forces. From this point gender studies splintered into numerous approaches with their own varieties of solutions—some exploring from the perspective that there were few to no differences between men and women except for the ones directly related to reproduction; some using the idea of androgyny to look at what "whole" people looked like with a variety of masculine and feminine traits; some looking at traditionally denigrated female or feminine traits and recasting them as valuable; some looking at gender through other marginalized particularities like class, race, sexual orientation, age, and physical ability; some looking at issues of justice and equality in the midst of sex differences; and so on. Beginning with the early studies about gender there were efforts to explore the impact of gender designations on individuals, families, institutions, and cultures as the social construction of gender became a dominant approach. Fairly recently, men's studies has joined the field of gender studies in a more significant way, making men visible in the exploration of gender, something that was only sporadically true in the early years. The field of gender studies has focused on individual development—how gender gets constructed (and processively reconstructed and reinforced) over the life cycle. It has also focused on what gender means for the social arrangements between people and the power implications of those social arrangements in the various hierarchies in which we live. Also, gender studies has looked at the symbolic, deep cultural structures that shape and define our knowledge base and our ways of knowing and invited us to question our most deeply held assumptions about truth.

Feminist-oriented gender studies has participated in the processes and methods of postmodernism—the shift from the belief that a fundamental truth exists and is knowable to the perspective that there are multiple and multifaceted angles on truth rather than a single organizing one. Consequently, postmodernism means that who we are, how we relate to various power systems in the culture, and what our past experiences have been all shape the way we understand reality and the way we construct it.[5] Some have said that feminism is one form of postmodernism. So, as Elaine Graham suggests, "Contemporary theories of gender are concerned not so much to identify or refute 'difference' as to offer a variety of conceptual processes by which all aspects of human culture—language, subjectivity, social structures, and symbolic representation—reflect and maintain 'gendered characteristics' and support gender as a form of social relations."[6]

For our purposes, it is important to recognize this shift in the discipline of gender studies from issues of identity and power relationships to epistemology and culture. It is in part this shift that further widens the gap between new knowledge about gender and its implications, and the practice of pastoral counseling that takes these insights to be foundational. This focus on the deeper structures that create and maintain gender distinctions is a critically important one. However, the three dimensions in the study of gender—gender identity, relationships developed around gender constructs, and these symbolic structural aspects—need to be kept together if we are going to be able to consistently put these radical insights into radical practice. The development of a theoretical and theological base that will stimulate and sustain radical and empowering pastoral practices is the goal of a feminist perspective in pastoral counseling.

Another important purpose of gender studies that is crucial for our development of radical pastoral practices is to recognize that the study of gender differences and their faulty foundations also allows us to see more clearly and give language to the variety of socially constructed differences that organize hierarchical power relationships within the culture. This has helped shift the meaning of the word *feminist,* which originally concerned itself primarily with the personal and political ramifications of gender distinctions and meanings, to a larger acknowledgment of the variety of power systems that organize the culture into systems of dominance and subordination. Each of these systems has tended to be built on a dualistic framework in American culture—race seen as black *or* white; sexual orientation as gay *or* straight; physicality as disabled *or* abled; and so on. Studies about gender have been and are being carried on within each of these previously dualistic categories and those categories are seen as crucial particularities in the study of gender. As Graham notes, "contemporary critical inquiries into gender—identity, relations, and representations—have moved from empirical studies of difference towards a broader analysis of social order and human behavior of which gender is an integral element."[7] Consequently, there has been much effort in recent years to develop feminist methods that would accomplish several purposes in the reorientation of knowledge and in the development of liberating practices. Deconstructive methods have emerged that bring a "hermeneutic of suspicion" to theories and practices previously held as truths. These deconstructive methods investigate theoretical points of view that have held dominant places in our perceptions of reality—points of view like God's maleness or women's lack of rationality, or innate empathic abilities—and look deeply into their assumptions.

Out of this deconstructive work has come the critical ability to take apart "truths" and see them as perspectives that, in many circumstances, privilege certain groups and disempower others. As Paula Rothenberg suggests, "While the people, places and things that make up our physical environment differ in a multitude of ways, only some of these differences are emphasized, treated as significant, and then employed by our society to justify and perpetuate inequality."[8] The deconstructive work of feminist and other liberation methodologies has been crucial in allowing enough critical distance to begin to do reclaiming and reconstructive work. Reclaiming methods are those that find ways to hear and record women's voices and women's experiences (both historical and contemporary) so that they are built into the meaning-making processes and theories of the culture. They work to undo the harm that has occurred through the missing and distorted perspectives of women and other marginalized groups. Reconstructive approaches look both at epistemological questions of how we know what we know and at providing content that has been missing. The three methods work together in processive, spiral ways to create feminist and womanist scholarship and to build liberating, effective, and empowering practices.[9]

It is obvious from this very brief summary that the study of gender done in its individual, relational, postmodern, and political contexts can take enormous amounts of theoretical energy. It has also done so in much of pastoral theology. Gender studies has provided a shift in the foundations for pastoral counseling that has potentially allowed much of pastoral counseling practice to shift from being harmful (especially to women and other marginalized groups as it unwittingly reinforced an oppressive status quo) to being radically life-giving and empowering for women, men, families, institutions, and the culture—that is if we can consistently move these new ideas into dialog with effective pastoral practice.

In some ways, pastoral counseling is especially amenable to a post-modern, liberationist milieu in that pastoral theological methods have always had to engage in multiple correlations between disciplines and perspectives that allowed for various and complex layers of meaning and interpretation. We have always had to try to understand the theological implications of people's lives as we have tried to offer pastoral care in their various crises. We have always had to allow people's lives to critique theological interpretations that did harm rather than good. We have always had to see the multiple meanings that exist within any pastoral situation and allow those various meanings to guide and reshape our practices. This ongoing correlational spiral that has always been a part of modern pastoral theology and pastoral counseling has been re-shaped many times as disciplines and "truths" have been challenged and reconstructed in light of feminist and womanist studies of gender.

Contemporary pastoral theology oriented around liberation perspectives generally begins in the lived reality of human experience. So, finding appropriate and liberating ways to look at the human situation is important. It is also crucial to be able to generate and critique personality theory and clinical theory when we come to building effective pastoral counseling practice. Contemporary gender studies has been able to pinpoint a number of dangers and problems in our primary personality and psychological theories. Those flaws range from ignoring the cultural realities in favor of an exclusively intrapsychic perspective to being primarily focused on psychopathology to being unable to be self-consciously critical of assumptions, social locations, and philosophies because the theories are seen as truths. Hannah Lerman has suggested eight criteria for whether a personality theory can be seen as useful for women. They are:

- whether a particular theoretical viewpoint has clinical usefulness for women's issues
- whether the theory in question encompasses the diversity and complexity of women and their lives

- whether the theory views women positively and centrally
- whether it arises from women's experience
- whether the theory remains close to the data of experience
- whether the theory recognizes that the internal world is inextricably intertwined with the external world
- whether concepts are confounded by particularistic terminology or the terminology of other theories
- whether the theory supports feminist or at least nonsexist modes of psychotherapy.[10]

Gender and liberationist studies in psychology and psychotherapy—two of the cognate disciplines that have significantly informed pastoral counseling—have radically reshaped our knowledge base and thus have deeply affected pastoral counseling.

Similarly, systematic theology—another primary cognate field for pastoral counseling—has been deeply affected and challenged as well. In pastoral counseling, theology is used in at least two ways (please note that I am writing out of my particular standpoint of Christian theology). First, it is used as a focus of commitment. Pastoral counselors have a working theology and sometimes doctrinal and ecclesial theologies to which they have a commitment. The proposals that are made for any theory and set of practices are grounded in normative theological commitments that guide the entire pastoral counseling task. These commitments might be to certain strands of theological tradition, to doctrinal or tradition faithfulness, to certain aspects of Jesus' models of ministry, to ecclesial teachings, to what people's parents taught them as children. These may or may not be conceptually or consciously available to the practitioner, although I think that it is the pastoral counselor's responsibility to be able to articulate his or her theological commitments. Obviously, our theological groundings are affected by other normative commitments we carry, although the theological and faith commitments tend to shape those other commitments.

The second way we use theology as pastoral counselors is as a lens of assessment. We listen to the counselee's story, in part, through theological categories and we use those categories to explore, evaluate, and pursue important life issues. Through varieties of theological norms held by counselor, counselees, and their communities of nurture and accountability, the life experiences and hopes of the counselees are tested and challenged and new directions are envisioned. We might ask how people perceive God in their lives, how they imagine God perceives them, how they manifest the *imago dei* within. We might wonder what is at stake for them, theologically, in the life directions they are pursuing. We might explore how the counselees experience God's grace in their lives and God's judgment. Are these consistent with the theological meanings held in their communities of nurture and accountability? Are they consistent with a liberating and empowered view of God and God's intention for them and for creation? We might wonder about how they understand the crisis or pain they are currently experiencing—how do they make sense of this within their faith perspective? How might it be related to a view of atonement, for example? Is this suffering seen, possibly, as a participation in the divine, as a cross to bear, perhaps? As for or against God's will or hope for them, or even, maybe, as separated from any religious meaning? And how do they see their current crisis fitting in with their larger life experience? Issues of God's providence might be raised here and issues of God's imminence may also be relevant—how is God immediately and ultimately involved in their lives? We might also ask how our counselees see themselves in relation to the community—how are they a part of the larger whole of creation? These are a few examples of how we might use theology as one lens through which we and our counselees make meaning out of their lived experience in the world. Every pastor and pastoral counselor, by virtue of their vocation and training, has a set (either implicit or explicit) of theological pathways for interpretation and meaning making. These compose a lens within which other lenses on the counseling process sit.

Now, obviously, these categories are not neutral. They have tremendous power over the way life events and future directions are interpreted and chosen. We are responsible for having theological lenses that contribute to the life-giving, just, empowering, and compassionate processes called pastoral counseling. Because theology is such a crucial lens, one of ultimacy in the work of pastoral counseling, if our theology is unclear, ambivalent, or, even worse, contradictory in relation to the other lenses we use in pastoral counseling, we will be at risk to do harm in our work.

Feminist and profeminist approaches to theology, along with other liberationist and postmodern perspectives, have revolutionized the way we formulate the kinds of questions I just named and, thus, the way we understand the meanings of health and wholeness for the people who come for pastoral counseling. Many volumes have been written about feminist, womanist, and other liberationist perspectives on theology, so I will only be suggestive here as I name three theological themes that have been challenged and reshaped by studies in gender from feminist perspectives.

For virtually all feminist theologians, language and imagery for God have been of central importance. This focus reflects the philosophical understanding that language does not just describe cultural reality, but also informs, influences, and to a certain extent determines that reality. How God is named, imagined, and conceptualized significantly affects how we understand ourselves, how we understand our purpose, how we order our social and familial relationships, and how we structure our culture. If we believe, for example, that there is a natural order or hierarchy of value that God has ordained and that God represents, then we create cultural structures that keep that order in place. If we believe that God is male, and thus, that the male is closer to the image of God than the female, then we value males more highly than females and we claim that males are naturally created to do more "godlike" things than are females. We would use that rationale to develop theories of gender complementarity or theories stating that heterosexuality is the only appropriate sexual orientation. We would then use these theories to create separate characteristics and even separate worlds for women and men that reflect this similarity and dissimilarity with God. We would also make the maintenance of these characteristics and worlds a divine obligation. We find this today in many dimensions of our society.

It's not just that this image of God is destructive for women and the social ordering of women's place in the culture. The core critiques of idolatry and irrelevance proposed by many feminist theologians have more recently been joined by those of male theologians looking at the religious concerns of men. Images of God that combine authority, power, rationality, protectiveness of others, kingship, dependability, righteous anger, maleness, and fatherhood have a formative and normative effect on dominant definitions of manhood and masculinity. Philip Sheldrake suggests that

> images of God as self-possessed, invulnerable, and perfect tend to reinforce [for men] this [overvaluing of objectivity and emotional control]. It [is] difficult to accept vulnerability and incompleteness and easy to be guiltily preoccupied with the lack of perfection and sin. To become an "adult" male, you [have to free] yourself from natural weaknesses, gain

certain desirable powers, and take up specific roles. The greatest anxiety is about loss of self-possession. This is especially threatened by sexuality and the vulnerability inherent in intimacy with people and God.[11]

It's not just that women and men are damaged by this dominant, often exclusive, male image of God. Liberationist and postmodern perspectives have shown the theological danger of limiting God's image to a single form. It distorts the richness of God revealed in the scriptures and traditions of the church and it distorts the ways we understand God's intentions for creation. In addition, it supports the dualistic system discussed earlier that has been shown to be so damaging to people, culture, and world. Building the reimagining of God into our ministry practices is important for the health of individuals, relationships, and cultures.

A second theological theme that has been deeply affected by the study of gender is Christology and theologies of atonement. As Rosemary Radford Ruether says, "The doctrine of Christ should be the most comprehensive way that Christians express their belief in redemption from all sin and evil in human life, the doctrine that embraces the authentic humanity and fulfilled hopes of all persons." And yet this once fully inclusive approach for all persons has become "the doctrine . . . that has been most frequently used to exclude women from full participation in the Christian church."[12] Who theology understands Jesus to have been and the Christ to be is of primary concern in feminist and profeminist theology precisely because this doctrine has been so influential in excluding and devaluing women throughout Christian history.

There are many debates within feminism and womanism about these issues. Certainly, some of the major debate has been between the way Christology has been understood in African American traditions and the way it tends to be understood in white feminism. As Jacquelyn Grant writes, "The condition of Black people today reflects the cross of Jesus. Yet, the resurrection brings the hope that liberation from oppression is immanent. The resurrected Black Christ signifies this hope."[13] As Grant suggests, white feminist theologizing about Christology cannot assume black women's agreement because of the gulf that both slavery and segregation have caused between the two sets of experience. For African American women and others, Jesus offers evidence that God both suffers with and liberates those who are oppressed. White feminism has tended to look at Christology through either the lens of the nonessential maleness of Jesus—the lens of Jesus' liberating and inclusive practices of ministry—or the lens of orthopraxis—continuing Jesus' ministry of liberation and empowerment.

In addition, feminist theology has been deeply invested in looking at atonement theory in terms of its relationship to the normalization and even glorification of women's suffering. As we will explore in chapter 4, which is on intimate violence, these issues around Christology and the way suffering and redemption are understood are of major importance in our pastoral counseling work with women.

A third theological theme that has been strongly influenced by feminist studies is the meaning of sin and evil.[14] We have frequently defined sin and evil as personal or superpersonal experiences and forces and we have looked at individual life experiences as the locations for sin and evil. Contemporary theology is moving toward understanding evil in systemic ways. As Mary Potter Engel suggests, sin and evil together can be thought of as wrongdoing:

> Evil is systemic. It is not superpersonal forces but structures of oppression; patterns larger than individuals and groups with a life of their own that tempt us toward injustice and impiety—social, political, economic arrangements that distort our perceptions or restrain our abilities to such an extent that we find it difficult to choose to do good. By contrast, sin refers to those discrete acts of responsible individuals that create or reinforce these structures of oppression. Neither causes the other; sin and evil are mutually reinforcing.[15]

Engel suggests that this understanding of sin "highlights the personal side of wickedness and in so doing fights against the common tendency to externalize evil to such an extent that each individual is exempt from all responsibility and accountability for it."[16] She also suggests that sin and evil ought to be stressed differently in particular contexts while never breaking their inseparability. Thus, when speaking of perpetrators of violence, the emphasis should be on sin—and on structures of accountability. When speaking of victims, the emphasis should be on evil. In neither case, however, should the companion concept be forgotten, it should just not be primary.[17]

When evil and sin are understood as systemic wickedness in terms of structures of oppression and acts that sustain those structures, we are able to understand violence in such a way that we see our task not just as stopping one perpetrator, but also as working to dismantle systems of oppression that make intimate violence (and, indeed, other kinds of violence) more likely to occur.

These new proposals in theology, which have resulted from feminist methods of deconstruction, reclaiming, and reconstruction, are illustrative of the revolution in knowledge and knowing that has happened (and is happening) in the context of feminist, womanist, liberationist, and postmodern perspectives. All of these proposals have a significant effect on the theory and practice of pastoral counseling. The larger shifts in theoretical and theological knowledge, however, always have to be seen and interpreted within the particularities of people's lives and circumstances. This means that the particular stories that people bring to pastoral counselors are central lenses through which theories and practices are evaluated. This has always been true in modern pastoral counseling. It also means that those stories must always be evaluated within the larger cultural realities in which they take place.

It is the responsibility of counselors to have a complex enough understanding of the cultural dynamics around sexism, racism, classism, and heterosexism that they can place the particular stories of counselees in the context of those dynamics. In doing pastoral counseling, the pastoral counselor must know about the cultural realities for women and men, of all races and classes, that, if unknown, distort the counselees' stories in harmful ways. In other words, if the counselor doesn't know that approximately 4 million women in the United States are severely assaulted by their boyfriends or husbands each year and that battering is a frequent cause of depression in women, then he or she might not think to look for violence in the relationship of a woman who has come for pastoral care.

The Realities of Patriarchy

This leads us to the second important reason for a book like this: the reality that sexism in our culture—along with racism, heterosexism, and classism—is alive and well. The pastoral counselor needs to be informed about, sensitive to, and resistant to the overwhelming realities of patriarchy and how they affect women (and men) at every level of their lives. Too much of our pastoral theology and our pastoral counseling operates as if this reality were not so.

The following statistics will help readers to see some of the ways that sexism, racism, and classism work together to make the culture a dangerous and debilitating place for many people. The purpose of putting them together is to help offset tendencies toward denial or minimization of these realities. The circumstances that these statistics represent can't help but point out the significant effect our culture has on the lives of women who come to pastors for counseling.

It is important to note that the world in which women are embedded can be painted only in broad strokes. The complexities of race, class, and gender will be represented but can't be fully depicted by these statistics. Pastoral counselors cannot assume that the oppression of each woman, or her responses to life circumstances, will be identical. Nonetheless, every woman lives in a world that devalues her because of her sex. The purpose of this picture of the world of women in patriarchy is to look at the world in terms of being women, while trying to pay attention to the particularities of different women's, and groups of women's, experience. That is, we need to pay attention to commonalities without losing sight of the significant differences.

Women's Employment, Economics, and Labor

Women have been increasingly entering the paid workforce over the past several decades, although their participation rate has not grown in recent years.[18] This has been especially true for European American women because, "for women of color, immigrant women, and female heads of single parent families, paid employment outside the home has historically been an integral, normative component of their roles as daughters, wives, and mothers."[19] Between 1960 and 1992, female labor-force participation rose from 38 percent to 58 percent.[20] During that same time, women's reported earnings have been increasing while men's real earnings have been dropping, thus somewhat narrowing the wage gap between women and men. These increasing wages for women have been steady for European American and African American women but not for Hispanic women. Real earnings for female, full-time, year-round employees grew 11 percent between 1976 and 1991, but only 1 percent for Hispanic women.[21] In 1995, women in the United States earned almost seventy-six cents for every dollar earned by men.[22] The wage gap is widest, however, between European American women and European

American men. African American women make approximately 81 percent of what African American men make and Asian American women make about 81 percent of what Asian American men make. Hispanic women make about 77 percent of what Hispanic men make.[23] What this means is that the median income for female high school graduates, age twenty-five and older, with no college, working year-round full-time is less than that of fully employed men who were high school dropouts. Men with associate degrees working full-time, year-round had incomes comparable to similarly employed women with a bachelor's degree.[24]

Job segregation by gender is still significant. Twenty percent of all working women hold secretarial or clerical jobs (98 percent of all secretaries are female).[25] This proportion of women in secretarial/clerical jobs has remained unchanged since 1950. Ninety percent of nurses, bookkeepers, bank tellers, and housekeepers are female and 80 percent of all waiters, librarians, cashiers, and telephone operators are female. Fewer than 2 percent of carpenters or auto mechanics are female, although there are significantly increasing percentages of women among lawyers, physicians, and mail carriers. Seventy-five percent of working women still earn less than $25,000 per year. As a recent *New York Times* article stated, "Even within those job categories in which women now outnumber men, they generally still lag in wages.[26] And there are only two women who are the chief executives of the one thousand largest companies in the United States—the same number as there were twenty years ago.[27] White men are 43 percent of the workforce but 95 percent of senior management.[28] One has to ask why these numbers are so little changed in the past thirty years, and the usual answer is the relatively short length of time women have been attempting to work their way up through corporate systems. In 1985, however, the United States Census Bureau reported that the differences in education, labor-force experience, and commitment accounted for only 15 percent of the wage gap between women and men. Fifteen years of additional education and experience in women's lives have reduced even that number. The only plausible answer is that women's perceived worth is less than that of men's, which is supported by studies in occupational prestige.

Occupational prestige studies explore the status position that a job has in our culture. Wu Xu and Ann Leffler report that "the significant positive correlation for white males indicates that the more exclusively an occupation is composed of white men, the higher its prestige. . . . White and

Asian men are most likely to be concentrated within the highest prestige jobs" (followed by white women and black women). The lowest concentrations in prestigious jobs are African American men, Hispanic men, and Hispanic women.[29] The report goes on to say that "race influences the occupational prestige level a worker is likely to occupy more than gender does. Black men and Hispanic men have the lowest mean score of all gender/race groups. White women have the highest mean occupational prestige (after white men) followed by Asian American men, black men, and Hispanic women.[30] They also state that, in terms of earnings, gender effects are more discernible than race effects.[31]

The consequences of these numbers in the lives of women include poverty, low self-esteem, and frustration. In a recent Roper study, 84 percent of three thousand women surveyed said that "regardless of changes that may have occurred . . . [women] still face more restrictions in life than men do." The report also said that "women are less satisfied with their careers than they were five and ten years ago [compared to the survey results done at that time] whereas men are more satisfied now than they were then."[32] This frustration and anxiety are important, but even more significant are the levels of poverty that women today face.

In 1993, women represented 62 percent of all persons eighteen years and older who were living below the poverty level.[33] When a family is singly headed by a woman, the odds that it is in poverty are extremely high. Almost 40 percent of families singly headed by white women are in poverty, as are 61 percent of families singly headed by African American women and 60 percent of families singly headed by Hispanic women. These numbers compare to single male-headed families in startling ways: 16 percent of European American single male-headed families are in poverty, 32 percent of African American male singly-headed families, and 29 percent of Hispanic male singly-headed families.[34] Also, approximately twelve million (18 percent) of American families are singly headed by women (14 percent of European American families, 48 percent of African American families, and 24 percent of Hispanic families).[35] By the time a woman is sixty-five years old, she is almost twice as likely as her male counterpart to be living in poverty.[36]

These statistics have many important implications for the pastoral counselor of women. The often oppressive and frightening economic realities are crucial for the counselor to consider when working with a woman client. What risks is she facing economically? How have her eco-

nomic and employment conditions affected her self-worth and sense of
the future? What are the live options available to her? In addition, in
evaluating these statistics it is very important to note what they suggest
about women's value in the culture. In a society that measures worth by
salary and economic success, for better or worse, women are told very
clearly that they are not valuable members of the public sphere. We will
see that they are given a similar message in the private sphere, too.

The work hours of women are also significant. In large numbers,
women have entered the male workforce, but the reverse has not been
true. One book suggests that what has changed in the past twenty years
is that more women work at what the authors call "double days" (one
shift at home and one at work).[37] Of course, this has been true in many
women's households historically. As Esther Ngang-Ling Chow says,

> At the same time [as they have been engaged in paid employment] such
> women [women of color, immigrant women, and female heads of single-
> parent families] have engaged in unpaid domestic labor, child care, and
> maintenance in the home, creating double or even triple shifts for many of
> them. These women are overburdened but undervalued both as produc-
> ers in the public sphere as well as social reproducers in the private
> sphere.[38]

In 1988, researchers at the University of Florida found that wives average about thirty hours per week on household tasks and husbands average
about six hours. Wives who do not work outside the home do about 83
percent of the housework while full-time employed wives do about 70
percent of the housework.[39] The tasks that men do take over in the home
are usually the easier tasks that have a clear completion, such as grocery
shopping and running errands. Women tend to accept this status quo in
families primarily because of their strong gender training, which causes
significant guilt feelings if they do not live up to their traditional sex role
expectations—and yet they experience frustration at the lack of fairness.[40]
For example, a Roper survey found that (next to money) the biggest
source of resentment in the lives of women is the inadequate amount
their partner "helps around the house."[41] This has significant implications for pastoral counseling because the church has traditionally played
an important role in defining family norms.

Abuse and Intimate Violence

In 1985 the United States Justice Department released a comprehensive study on the price of violence in our society. It attempted to include the costs of domestic violence and child abuse in addition to the kinds of violence more typically studied. The report found that "child abuse and domestic violence account for one-third of the total cost of crime."[42]

According to Margi Laird McCue,

[Domestic] abuse may be the single most common etiology for injury presented by women, accounting for more injury episodes than auto accidents, muggings, and rapes combined. A review of 3,676 records randomly selected from among female patients presenting with injury during one year, revealed that forty percent of the women's injury episodes were identified as resulting from a deliberate assault by an intimate. Nineteen percent of the women had a previous history of abusive injury.[43]

The American Medical Association estimates that four million women suffer severe assaults by boyfriends and husbands each year and that one in four women will be abused in her life. Estimates in a variety of studies range from two million to eight million women assaulted every year by partners and up to one in two women being abused sometime in her life. The American Psychological Association Task Force on Depression suggests that almost 40 percent of women in the United States are physically or sexually abused before the age of twenty-one and McCue reports that medical personnel in emergency rooms feel the number is more likely to be 50 percent or higher.[44]

According to the Bureau of Justice, intimates commit 13 percent of all rapes, robberies, and assaults where most of the violence is assault. Men are more likely to be the victims of violent crime in general (by a ratio of 26 men: 19 women) but women are more than ten times more likely (92 women: 8 men) to be the victim of violence by an intimate. It is important for the pastoral counselor to recognize the effect this reality has on women, whether they are directly victimized or only victimized by knowing their risk of being abused by someone they love or have loved. A Bureau of Justice report suggests that, "Based on evidence collected in the National Crime Survey, as many as half of the domestic 'simple assaults' actually involved bodily injury as serious as or more serious than 90 percent of all rapes, robberies, and aggravated assaults."[45] And yet only somewhere between 40 and 90 percent of domestic violence incidents are reported to the police.[46] (Most studies suggest that between 40 percent and 50 percent of domestic violence goes unreported.) The reasons given for not reporting violence were (1) a fear of reprisal, (2) the sense that it was a private matter (the woman often felt that she must be somehow to blame), and (3) the feeling that the crime was just not important enough.

According to the Bureau of Justice, African American, European American, and Hispanic women had equivalent rates of intimate violence in 1992. Women who were between the ages of twenty-two and thirty-four had the highest rates of victimization and women who were college graduates had lower rates than noncollege graduates. Women in center cities had about the same rates of domestic/intimate violence as those in suburbs and rural environments. Somewhere between 30 and 50 percent[47] of all female murder victims over the age of fourteen are killed by a current or former spouse, or a partner (compared to 4 percent of men).[48] Obviously many more women need shelter from domestic assault situations than are able to find it. According to McCue, "Shelters for battered women are only able to admit between ten and forty percent of women who apply. Shelter personnel believe that for each woman who calls a hotline or enters a shelter, there are at least ten battered women without a safe place to stay."[49]

Police response has been consistent with an acceptance of violence against women. Generally, police officers have long been confused as to their role in domestic abuse situations. Because traditionally women were understood to "belong" to their husbands, the right to "discipline" one's wife was thought to be part of each husband's prerogative. It was a "private" matter. There were occasional laws limiting the severity of the "discipline." For example, the "rule of thumb," which we use so freely in everyday speech, refers to a law enacted in England describing how thick a stick could be when used by a husband for beating his wife: the diameter of the stick could be no greater than the diameter of the man's thumb. For the most part, issues of "discipline" in a family were not for the public realm. Recently, police have been trained to take a more active role when called into a home, and in fourteen states and Washington, D.C., police are mandated to make an arrest in a domestic abuse call.[50] Until quite recently, however, women who were murdered by their spouses in domestic battering incidents had called the police an average of five times before the homicide took place.

Despite the prevalence of this crime, many women feel that they are the only ones who are experiencing this abuse. Further, they often feel they either deserve this violence or that they should somehow figure out how to prevent it. This sense of isolation and self-blame contributes to the difficulty women have in trying to get out of these violent situations. Battering is a demoralizing, humiliating, dangerous experience that is perpetrated by one with whom there has generally been an intimate and loving relationship. It frequently embodies a deep betrayal of trust along with the sense of isolation. It is important for clergy to understand all of these dynamics as they work with victims of domestic violence.

Domestic violence is only one form of abuse perpetrated against women on a regular basis. Rape is extremely common in the United States and has been on the rise since the 1960s. Some data suggests that rape occurrences are beginning to level off, but between 1960 and 1970 the number of reported rapes doubled in the United States and between 1970 and 1980 the number doubled again.[51] In 1994 there were 430,000 rapes. Almost two-thirds of the victims of rapes did not report the crime to the police and two-thirds of the victims knew their assailants.[52] It has been estimated that between 20 and 30 percent of women over twelve years old will be victims of attempted or completed rape in their lifetimes.[53] It is important not to be numb to these numbers: between one out of five and one out of three women may well be raped in her lifetime. No wonder that women, even though often deeply damaged by rape, are rarely surprised.

Equally disturbing, most rapists walk away from the crime without consequences. According to Camille LeGrand, "A man who rapes a woman who reports to the police has seven chances out of eight of walking away without any conviction. Assuming only one in five women reports her rape, his chances increase to thirty-nine out of forty."[54] These statistics reflect what many feminists have labeled "a rape culture." We, in the United States, live in a society that generally assumes that men are sexually aggressive and women are sexually passive and, consequently, tacitly considers rape to be normal. There is increasing consensus that the personality traits of rapists do not differ from the general personalities of men who have not raped. Analysts are finding that men who rape are acting out of a cultural milieu that normalizes this kind of violence against women. In one study of college men, 51 percent said that they would rape if they didn't have to fear getting caught and in a study of teenagers, 51 percent of the boys (and 42 percent of the girls) felt that it was all right for the boy to force sex if the girl "got him excited."[55] The fear of rape and of other forms of abuse helps keep women "in their place" and perpetuate stereotypically "feminine" behaviors that damage women's self-esteem and isolate women from each other. Living in fear of rape is a significant dimension to the world in which women are embedded and must be taken as primary information when working with all women in pastoral counseling.

Other forms of abuse also exist on the spectrum from street harassment of catcalls, whistles, and unwanted touch through rape and incest. For example, in a study by the Merit Systems Protection Board, it was discovered that 42 percent of the federal government's female employees between May 1985 and May 1987 experienced some form of sexual harassment. In the State Department, more than 50 percent of female employees had been sexually harassed at work.[56] In a Cornell study of 155 women employees, 92 percent felt that sexual harassment was a serious problem for women and half of these women reported that they had been the victims of harassment. Seventy percent felt that they had been the victims of unwanted sexual comments, suggestions, and physical contact.[57] Other studies report similar numbers. Sexual harassment, frequently trivialized and dismissed as unimportant by perpetrators, victims, and the legal system alike, is another part of the world of violence in which women live. It is important to say explicitly that pastoral counselors must never fall into the trap of trivializing any of these forms of abuse. Each form is damaging in its own way.

Women learn at a very early age that it is unsafe to be a woman/girl in this culture. According to reliable studies approximately 40 percent of all girls are sexually abused by the age of eighteen—either inside or outside of their families.[58] A conservative estimate suggests that one out of two hundred girls is sexually molested as a child by her father. When one considers abuse by other male members of a family, including stepfathers, uncles, and close family friends, studies suggest that close to two out of five girls experience sexual abuse.[59] According to E. Sue Blume, 35 percent of all reported child sex abuse cases in 1988 were girls under six, while most rape victims are between the ages of ten and nineteen, with 25 percent under the age of twelve.[60] Young girls learn that the world is not a safe place. Women find out either by experiencing victimization, by knowing others who are being hurt, or by being exposed to a variety of media—

all of which communicate the message of danger to women. Pastoral counselors must keep in mind that the vast quantity of violence against women happens in relationships that are supposed to be trustworthy. Looking at a culture that normalizes, colludes with, and denies this kind of intimate violence is much more productive than it is to study what it is about women that makes them victims. As Gerald Hotaling and David Sugarman write, "It is sometimes forgotten that men's violence is men's behavior. What is surprising is the enormous effort to explain male behavior by examining characteristics of women. It is hoped that future research will show more about the factors that promote violent male behavior and that stronger theory will be developed to explain it."[61] One way that we can continue to explore the issues of violence and the devaluing of women is to look at how our media, especially television, portray women and men and their relationships with each other.

Media and Self-Image

Although not exclusively, it is in great part through the media that threats of abuse to women are communicated, that unhealthy images of women are taught, and that the limits of women's world are delineated. It is helpful to look closely at some of the oppressive ways media functions for women.

There has been an increase of violence in the film industry over recent years, especially in terms of explicit violence. It is becoming more evident that violence against women, even when that violence is not explicitly sexual in nature, causes people to become desensitized to violence in general and to the violence of rape against women in particular. A set of studies by Daniel Linz, Edward Donnerstein, and Steven Penrod concluded that

> when subjects are continually exposed to graphically depicted film violence against women, individual feelings of anxiety and depression begin to dissipate. Material that was anxiety provoking became less so with prolonged exposure. Perceptual changes found in the study also proved to be reliable in later studies. Subjects reported seeing less violence with continued exposure. They also rated the material differently with continued exposure. Material once found somewhat degrading to women was judged to be less so after prolonged exposure.[62]

Along this same line, exposure to aggressive pornography alters perceptions about women who are victims of rape. They are seen to have been more at fault and secretly wanting the rape to occur.[63] Even subjects exposed to R-rated levels of nonsexual violence against women were less sympathetic to victims of rape after the exposure than they had been before.[64] In another study about long-term effects of exposure to sexually explicit material that showed women as sex objects, Dolf Zillman and Jennings Bryant found that both males and females became more tolerant of bizarre forms of pornography, became less supportive of sexual equality, and became more lenient in assessing punishment for a convicted rapist.[65]

When we consider both the quantity and quality of violence in today's "entertainment" industry, these conclusions become very disturbing. In addition to film viewers, there are large numbers of pornography readers (pornography defined here as sex being used to reinforce or create domination, pain, and humiliation—violence, dominance, and conquest are the essential ingredients). There are approximately two hundred pornographic magazines in the United States and around fourteen million readers of pornography, while there are fewer than one million readers of feminist magazines.

Pornography itself became more violent in the 1990s. In addition, music videos have joined the violence movement. According to some studies, more than half of the music videos on MTV feature or suggest violence, present hostile sexual situations as acceptable, or show male heroes abusing women for fun.[66] There are more peep shows and adult bookstores in the United States than there are McDonald's.[67] One out of eight Hollywood movies depicts a rape theme. By the age of eighteen, the average youth has watched 250,000 acts of violence and 40,000 attempted murders on television.[68]

Another trend attempts to return women to the home and reemphasize the centrality of culturally defined femininity in advertisements, women's traditional magazines, and television. For example, Nijole V. Benokraitis and Joe R. Feagin suggest that since the mid-1970s there has been a new intensity of interest in women looking beautiful. They state that "we still live in a society where more money is spent on women's looks than on social service programs."[69] In 1991 nearly 70,000 women had face-lifts, 159,300 had cosmetic breast operations, and 30,000 women had liposuction of over 200,000 pounds of fat. In the same year there were only about 5,000 hair transplants for men, which is the largest male cosmetic surgery market.[70] According to Jean Kilbourne, a study in California showed that nearly 80 percent of Bay Area fourth grade girls are "watching their weight" and a comprehensive survey in Chicago found that 50 percent of fourth grade girls were dieting and 75 percent of the girls felt they were overweight.[71]

The average American is exposed to over 2,000 ads per day. This sweeping form of education teaches us a great deal about who we are to be. Kilbourne, an expert in the analysis of advertising, says that

> the aspect of advertising most in need of analysis and change is the portrayal of women. Scientific studies and the most casual viewing yield the same conclusion: Women are shown almost exclusively as housewives or sex objects.
>
> The sex object is a mannequin, a shell. Conventional beauty is her only attribute. She has no lines or wrinkles, no scars or blemishes— indeed, she has no pores. She is thin, generally tall and long-legged, and, above all, she is young. All "beautiful" women in advertisements (including minority women), regardless of product or audience, conform to this norm. Women are constantly exhorted to emulate this ideal, to feel ashamed and guilty if they fail, and to feel that their desirability and lovability are contingent upon physical perfection.[72]

Gray Advertising recently reported on a study of women and advertising where the researchers discovered that women thought advertising was even more unrealistic and alienating than it was two years ago. "They specifically despaired of the images that advertising agencies presented of women."[73]

Along with the various forms of advertising, television images in general are problematic for girls and women. A study by the nonprofit organization called Girls, Inc. (an association that has been operating for the past fifty years to improve the self-image of school age girls) found that girls get their ideas about who they are or who they should be from television. Children in this survey of girls and boys in third through twelfth grades were found to watch more than twenty hours per week of television and African American girls watched about twenty-eight hours per week. African American girls, however, were much more critical of the material they were seeing.

The findings from this study are disturbing. Girls, Inc. discovered that the more television a girl watches, the more likely she is to think that household chores are women's work and the more boys watched television, the more they agreed with this assessment. The less television a girl watched, "the more likely she was to focus on career goals." They also found that, except on Public Television, most children's shows are aimed at boys. In addition, television programs distorted the realities of women's and men's lives. For example, they said, "in the real world, eighty percent of single households are headed by women, but on television, half of the single parents are men." In addition, they found that for every female character there are three male characters in the average television series and on children's shows more than three-fourths of the adults are men. Finally, they revealed (to no one's surprise) that most of the victims in television shows are women.[74]

The implications of these findings are very serious. Television is one of the most significant influencers of self-image and relational expectations. We need to be able to teach our children (and ourselves) to be more observant, critical, and questioning of the images and stories we are fed through our entertainment as well as work to change the kinds of programming available. We also need to know how significantly these primarily negative messages influence the development of girls' and women's self-images and expectations in the world.

Implications

For the most part, the reality of the world of women, illustrated by these statistics, is minimized and hidden. As a society, we have had our consciousness raised about some forms of sexism but not about the pervasiveness and normativity of violence, oppression, and repression. Most men and women, when asked, will agree that women have experienced discrimination in their work lives. Most people, however, will add to their answer that things have improved considerably for women and that sexism is no longer a major problem in the United States today. They see the women who have moved into positions of influence in the public world and assume that such access is available to all women. They fail to recognize the profound role that this hidden world of violence and oppressive media messages plays in women's private and public lives. Paula Rothenberg, in her book *Race, Class, and Gender in the United States,* says that

> Plato was correct that the most effective way for rulers to maintain power is to persuade those they rule that the situation is natural, inevitable, and desirable. It is here that stereotypes, ideology, and language have their role to play. . . . For example, stories in the media as well as all forms of advertising create the impression that particular groups—say women or African Americans—have made enormous strides in all areas of society, implying that they are now the recipients of special treatment that give them an advantage over white men and other groups. Never mind that statistics paint a very different picture.[75]

I have explored the first two reasons for writing this book: the revolution of knowledge grounded in contemporary gender studies, and the oppressive realities of patriarchy in women's lives. But there is also a third reason, and that is the specific crises and challenges that women face because of the culture that has been partially described thus far.

Pastoral Issues in Counseling with Women

The three pastoral care contexts that I will use for this book are certainly not limited to women. Obviously, depression, for example, can occur in anyone's life. But depression occurs much more often in women's lives, and much more often in married women compared to single women. This makes it an important issue to study because it is probably the most common problem that presents itself to pastoral counselors. Although certainly issues like depression are addressed in a variety of places, the intent of this book is to explore them from the perspective of women's experience and from the clear starting place of a culture that is problematic for women at many levels. Women's susceptibility to a particular distress is not the central issue; rather, women are understood to be living and making decisions in some very complex and oppressive situations. The focus will be on how to help women see their circumstances and symptoms from the perspective of the larger culture and how to make choices that resist harmful forces, rather than on developing a model to treat women's problems as individual and idiosyncratic to a particular person.

This book will be set up in such a way that each of these pastoral contexts will be used to illustrate a particular aspect of the pastoral counseling theory being developed. After discussing the theological and theoretical dimensions of the first aspect of counseling, *coming to voice,* I will present the issue of recovery from various forms of intimate violence. After the second counseling phase, *gaining clarity,* we will explore issues of depression in women's lives. To illustrate the third phase, *making choices,* we will talk about the complexities of women's lives as they age. The final phase, *staying connected,* will serve as the conclusion for the book. Let me briefly discuss each of these pastoral contexts.

Recovery from Physical and Sexual Abuse

The problem of violence toward women is immense. Obviously, this whole book could be written on pastoral counseling with women survivors of violence. As we have seen, the statistics show a picture of women's lives in which violence against them—especially by intimates in their lives—is essentially normalized and tolerated by society, including the church. Whether it is seen in the enormous amounts of incest, the epidemic rates of battering, or the preponderance of women victims of violence in our "entertainment" industry, our society seems to expect these kinds of violent acts directed toward women. The reality is that there are numerous survivors of intimate violence in our congregations and communities.

Obviously we, as pastoral caregivers, must be prepared to help women who come to us for care who have been hurt by people who were supposed to care for them, and we must understand that those experiences will be at the core of their psychological and spiritual distress. Some who are caregivers themselves may also share those deep hurts from intimate violence. Healing is vital and often difficult when harm has been done in the context of families and friends.

One of the particular problems with having experienced intimate violence—especially in one's own life—is the tendency of women to feel personal guilt and shame at being victims. Thus, often there is a great deal of secrecy. Many women will come to counseling, and even go through the whole counseling process, without ever having mentioned that they are survivors or current victims of violence. Women often fear, as we saw in their reluctance to report crimes of intimate violence, that their experience "isn't worth talking about" or that it will be trivialized or they will be held as responsible ("what are you doing to provoke the battering?" for example). Discussing issues of violence—especially violence done by intimates—is particularly appropriate for illustrating some of the difficulties of women coming to voice.

Depression

Depression is much more common in women than in men. Nearly 5 percent of women compared to 2 percent of men suffer from major depression.[76] Various studies confirm that depression is between two and six times more prevalent in women than men. Although all women—despite their racial or ethnic group membership—have higher rates of depression than men, European American women have the highest rates.[77] There has been an enormous surge of both research and interest (much of it stimulated by pharmaceutical companies) in biological explanations for depression in women. Yet numerous studies, many of which have difficulty being published, find significant evidence that women's depression is clearly linked to the particular stresses in their lives. As Wu and Leffler conclude after an extensive study, "At this point we postulate that the reason that more women than men feel depressed is, to some degree, due to the fact that women's low economic status position and their family roles as homemakers are more frustrating and less rewarding than men's day to day activities and this produces higher stress in women."[78]

In a 1990 study done by the American Psychological Association that is not widely published, Ellen McGrath, the chair of the research group, reported that "the task force found that women are truly more depressed than men, primarily due to their experience of being female in our contemporary culture."[79]

Tavris suggests that there is a major shift toward searching out biological explanations for women's problems and illustrates her point by exploring the current philosophies about premenstrual syndrome and about depression:

> Researchers in the fields of science, medicine and psychology all celebrate
> a renewed emphasis on biological explanations of women's behavior and
> a medical approach to women's problems and their cures. They enthusi-
> astically seek physiological differences in brain structure and function,

biochemical reasons that more women than men suffer from depression, and hormonal changes that supposedly account for women's (but not men's) moods and abilities. Their assertions are more likely to make the news than is the evidence that contradicts them. Similarly, women hear much less these days about the psychological benefits of having many roles and sources of esteem, let alone the benefits of having a personal income.[80]

Since depression is a major source of distress in women's lives and one of the most common problems that women will bring to the pastor, it is crucial to explore it in a book like this.

Aging

Obviously, aging is not a pastoral crisis in the same way that recovering from violence and depression is, but it is a context within which one can see the dynamics of a sexist culture at work. Exploring aging in the context of making choices helps pastors to understand some of the unique dynamics for women as they move through the life cycle. Some of these include the following: on average, women live considerably longer than men and often are without family caregivers when they themselves may need them; women's pensions and economic support systems may be inadequate due to the unequal employment opportunities for women and men today; retirement needs of women may be very different from those of men, even though we have consistently looked at men's experience as revealing normative retirement dynamics.

Another significant factor is the lack of positive images of the elderly, especially elderly women. While working with students in pastoral care classes, I have been surprised at how negative their dominant imagery is about the elderly. When asked how they would feel about going to a new call that has been described as having a large percentage of elderly women, almost 60 percent of my classes in pastoral care gave exclusively negative emotional responses and images. Ministry images in all of the responses were overwhelmingly perceived as giving needed or demanded care to these women without any sense of what they might be offering back to the church.

Exploring the issues of women and aging will include examining the processes of making choices in a culture that adds ageism to its other perspectives on women. It will also include looking at the freedoms and wisdoms that often emerge later in life when the demands of a patriarchal culture seem less important for women.

This book explores ways to care for women through individual and communal pastoral counseling in their various life situations. At the same time, it pursues ways that the church can resist oppressive and destructive forces as congregations of liberation. The next chapter sets some of the theological and psychological frameworks for the pastoral counseling processes described in the balance of the book.

two

Building the Frame

In the first chapter we alluded to the foundational methods of pastoral theology when we talked about the correlational spiral that starts in lived human experience, which is analyzed and understood in its particular contexts. The process continues by bringing that behavior, experience, and contextual analysis into conversation with resources from the social sciences and from theology, using these disciplines to better understand the experience of individuals and communities seeking care and to use their experience to critique and hold accountable the disciplines and resources of pastoral theology. These conversations help to generate effective and relevant practices that can be taken into the lived experience of people as we attempt to provide ministries of care. That care might consist of one-to-one counseling, building communities of nurture and support, creating better structures of accountability, generating new educational processes and goals, finding ways to resist forces of oppression and evil, and empowering justice and liberation in the lives of people and communities. All of these kinds of care are tested in their engagement with people's lives and the methodological spiral begins again.

This process happens on a daily basis in every minister's regular work and it happens in a larger, sometimes more intentional, arena in the scholarly discipline of pastoral theology. When the spiral process stops and the practices exist without these dynamics of correlation, pastoral ministry becomes stale, irrelevant, and often dangerous. This is a more common problem than we like to think. We develop creative and transformative ministry practices and then forget that, over time, they must be continually engaged in critique and reconstruction in order for them to stay creative and transformative.

As discussed in chapter 1, each of these dialogue partners has been radically challenged and reconstructed by feminist, womanist, other liberationist and postmodern perspectives. This means that it is necessary to take a closer look at some of the foundations for a new proposal in pastoral counseling. It is the goal of this chapter to take a "snapshot" of the dynamic methodological spiral as I use it and explore the psychological, clinical, and theological groundings as they relate to women and as they inform the pastoral practices to be proposed throughout the rest of this book.

One who is attempting to develop a constructive position in pastoral theology must ask three basic questions when conceptualizing this process. The first is, How might we think about the way people form a sense of self, a sense of self-in-community, and a sense of how they are to engage and respond to the world? This question helps to incorporate the study of personality theory into an evaluation of this constructive position. The second is, When the sense of self and world isn't accurate or causes significant problems for people, how do they go about changing their self-perceptions, among others, and their ways of being in the world? This question leads into the development of counseling (psychotherapeutic) theory, which studies the process of change in people and their behaviors. And the third is, Why does it matter? or Who are people and communities called to be? This question explores this position in the context of theology. Consequently, this chapter will look at the assumptions and theories of personality, counseling, and theology as they apply to the ministry proposals to be made in the following pages.

Personality Theory

There are a lot of ways we could go about discussing personality theory. Since there are over 250 schools of psychotherapy—each of them built on somewhat different assumptions about both the nature of personality and theories of change—we could spend a great deal of time looking at the possible options for an appropriate theory of personality. Or, we could go to the other extreme and suggest that, since there are so many proposed approaches to personality, there must be no reliable way to talk about this mythological entity and, thus, it must not be an important focus. Neither of these perspectives is very helpful. Instead, we need to acknowledge that obviously no one lens could ever be adequate to fully understand something as complex as human personality and its relationship to families, institutions, and culture. Several lenses must be used even to begin to make sense of how people form a concept of self and relationship. In contemporary theory building it is important to walk the fine line between using the modern concept of self-in-isolation—a core of personality that is formed and is idiosyncratic and autonomous in each individual—and the postmodern concept that there is no self, but only expressions of different contexts and social arrangements.

It is helpful to look at what kinds of major critiques apply to current approaches when building a new one. I will present eight critiques of the psychological theories (both the personality components and the counseling implications that emerge from them) that have informed pastoral counseling over the past thirty or so years. These critiques are a summary or compilation of a great deal of work by feminist psychologists.

The first critique has to do with a problem named in chapter 1, and that is that women's experience has largely been left out of the culture's stories and that men's experiences and interpretations, the dominant culture, have been used as normative in creating theories (and theologies). Women's personality structures, needs, and realities have been derived from comparing them with those of males and naming any difference a deviance. Women have been put into the theoretical double bind of being defined socioculturally as different from men, complementary to them as part of the "natural" order, and yet held accountable for the "deviance" of those differences. As Carol Tavris has said, "We are used to seeing women as the problem, to thinking of women as being different from men, and to regarding women's differences from men as deficiencies and weakness."[1] And Laura Shapiro, in an article about studies of sex differences in children, says that "whether the question is brain size, activity levels or modes of punishing children, the traditional implication is that the standard of life is male, while the entity that needs explaining is female."[2]

An example of this might be the sociocultural expectation that women are to be the ones who are in touch with their emotions and who are to help men and children gain access to their emotions, while many forms of psychodynamic theory have focused on the problem of women's emotion-alism/hysteria as primary pathology; family systems theory still tends to blame women for being overinvolved with their families, even though they have been assigned primary responsibility for family life by the culture. These are two small examples of the numerous theoretical binds that women are caught in when psychological theory derived from male norms is used uncritically.

The second generalized flaw of most personality theories is that there has been no adequate definition of mental *health* for women. In a study done in the 1970s but replicated several times since then, it became clear that counselors of all types who worked with men and women had different expectations for them in terms of mental health. In that study, seventy-nine clinicians were sent questionnaires concerning how they defined mental health. The clinicians were to indicate which pole of numerous paired personality traits and behaviors would be closer to their understanding of a mature, healthy, socially competent adult. One-third of the clinicians had the term *socially competent adult* on their questionnaire, one-third had the word *male* substituted for adult, and one-third had the word *female* substituted for adult. The study found that both male and female clinicians described healthy men and healthy adults in the same ways. Healthy women, however, were described much differently, with a heavier emphasis on qualities such as submissive, less independent, less adventurous, less aggressive, less competitive, more easily influenced, and so on. Consequently, therapists treated female counselees differently and developed different counseling goals and standards of normality with them than they did with males.[3] Several other studies since then have found, for the most part, that both male and female therapists, but especially males, are still more likely to treat women counselees differently from men counselees.[4] These counseling behaviors are generally more subtle than they used to be before we became somewhat more conscious of our gender biases, but they still operate.

The third problem with most current theories is that they locate the source of the problem consistently inside the counselee or the counselee's relationships and don't do adequate sociocultural analysis. Miriam Greenspan has said that most psychotherapeutic theories operate out of the assumption that "it's all in your head" (psychoanalytic and humanistic theories) or "it's all in your hands" (behavioral theories) or, I would add, "it's all in your interactions" (family systems theory).[5] These ignore the cultural contexts of sexism, racism, classism, and heterosexism. Any theory that assumes that by helping a woman adjust better to her environment, which is unhealthy in the first place, it is adequately helping her, is misguided. As implied in chapter 1, it doesn't help a woman who is struggling with depression, for example, to focus on her depression, her self-care, or her relationship with her husband without helping her to recognize how deeply she has internalized negative messages about who she is at her very core. She needs to know that her experience isn't only personal but may well also be a part of the larger experience of women in her culture. The traditional psychological theories do not have this built into their principles.

A fourth flaw in most personality theories is that they are primarily pathology-oriented. I believe that we find what we look for in counseling. If we look for problems, for inconsistencies, and for deviance, then that's where we will focus in the counseling work. Most women have been taught to see their inadequacies much more clearly than their strengths. They will collude with a counseling approach that focuses on pathology (or deep personal problems) because it is familiar to find problems within the self—sometimes it even feels like a relief to name what has been only an amorphous feeling of anxiety and dread. As we will be exploring later, it is helpful to understand many of the problems that women bring to counseling as adaptive rather than pathological. In other words, many women demonstrate distressing or problematic behaviors or feelings that are the result of adaptive/survival responses to untenable double binds. This is a key assumption in feminist counseling theory. We currently have very few resources that help counselors to understand counseling problems in this way.

A fifth related problem in personality theory is demonstrated through our diagnostic systems. I would propose that counselors should stay very suspicious of the kinds of diagnoses that have become common parlance in counseling circles. I hear the term *borderline personality* applied to women counselees with such regularity that it has become an almost empty category in my opinion. As many feminist theorists point out, it is interesting that borderline personality disorder surfaced about the same time that the women's movement gained power. The kinds of dynamics that occur when women become aware of the process of harmful adaptation to the culture and their attempts to move out of that frame are similar to many of the diagnostic criteria for borderline personality—

rage; confusion; low self-esteem; swings in emotion; uncertainty and ambivalence about things like careers; self-image; long-term goals, values, and relationships; chronic feelings of emptiness; the paradox of intense efforts to avoid abandonment and at the same time desiring to leave relationships that are harmful. To make this set of symptoms a case of personality disorder rather than what happens to many women who are becoming aware of their destructive gender socialization seems to me to be a form of punitive backlash.

Another example of diagnostic sexism is the category of co-dependency. This diagnosis is a classic example of a psychopathological category designed (when separated from the process of chemical addiction) to help women blame themselves for the consequences of life in patriarchy. Its focus is on internal and relational dynamics rather than on the cultural milieu that teaches and expects women to behave in self-defeating ways. As Carol Plummer points out, "Co-dependency is not gender neutral. Women get it more than men. In fact, if women don't have the 'disease' it is only because they have worked very hard against their gender socialization." She goes on to say that

> co-dependency is, in fact, a smorgasbord of behaviors used by all types of oppressed people when with their oppressors. It is a set of survival skills when one is in a subservient position economically, emotionally, politically, or spiritually. The list of co-dependent characteristics is true not only of women, but of workers with their bosses, or the poor with those in power. Telling women to "heal themselves" in a culture which trains them in co-dependency cannot work without transforming the context of their behaviors.[6]

Also, after listing the familiar qualities of the co-dependent person, Tavris says that

> the person who has these problems is familiar, all right; she is . . . the stereotypic woman. The qualities of the co-dependent person are most of the hallmarks of the female role, writ large. . . . A recovering co-dependent becomes independent, becomes selfish without feeling guilty, becomes self-reliant, lives serenely without being hooked by the problems of others, develops more of a self, says no to the demands of others, and wants to be loved without being needed. Are these qualities familiar? The

"co-dependent no more" person is . . . the stereotypic male! . . . It is based on the model of the normalcy of men.[7]

And yet, many women have gladly accepted the label of co-dependent, often clinging to it. I think that it is important for pastoral counselors to pay attention to this phenomenon and attempt to understand the needs that are met for women who find their home in co-dependency definitions and support groups. These definitional and supportive experiences provide access to three main resources that women are generally denied:

1. Someone pays attention to and records the women's experiences of feeling overresponsible in relationships, of using indirect power to achieve goals, and of feeling not in control of creating the kind of family life they are supposed to. Their stories are told and their experiences are named, thus creating meaningful community.

2. Co-dependency provides a place to belong, both in terms of not being alone with feelings of helplessness and frustration and in terms of the thousands of self-help co-dependency groups that have sprung up where women can come together to counter the feelings of isolation that patriarchy engenders.

3. Co-dependency gives a sense of control to women who have felt trapped. It offers a conceptual way out, even though that way out is one of taking the blame for behaviors that, in reality, are expected from and taught to girls and women. We can learn a lot from what women find helpful in co-dependency groups while still working against needing to label women's experience deviant and pathological.

The sixth critique of psychological theory is that much of it sets up counseling practices that demand too much time and involvement between the counselee and counselor. Most women can't afford the time or cost of years of counseling. Beyond that, the theoretical perspectives have been developed with the middle- or upper-class, generally white heterosexual in mind and thus have considerable class, race, and sexual orientation biases. These theories make assumptions about the ability, desire, or need to be introspective, the leisure to engage in long-term counseling, the financial resources to pay for long-term counseling, and the luxury and interest to address intrapsychic dynamics. Also, for many of the people who need counseling services, day-to-day life problems are much more demanding and have greater priority than focused self-understanding and introspection do. For many people, time and money cannot be spent on long-term counseling and assumptions of high levels of literacy and "psychological sophistication" cannot be considered valid. These issues are of concern for counseling with all people and apply especially to many women's lives. Women tend to feel responsible for relationship failures and thus will invest time and money in long-term counseling that they don't really need. We need theories that will help us empower people to live more satisfying lives and to address their real-life dilemmas in a reasonable period of time. Short-term, problem- and solution-focused methods and narrative are, I believe, the primary therapies of the very near future and the approach of choice for most pastors.

The seventh critique is that most counseling theory has been adjustment-oriented. We have been taught how to use the primary metaphor of adjustment (helping people to adapt to their contexts better) as a primary goal in counseling work, although this is not universally true. Certainly other therapies, Rogerian and Gestalt for example, have worked against simple adjustment. Yet the adjustment bias appears in a majority of traditional approaches. The adjustment goal seemed to bring people comfort and even satisfaction with their lives, so it wasn't often challenged. As we noted earlier, however, helping people to adjust to an unhealthy culture is not ethical. We need theories that allow us to help women "mal-adjust" to their destructive cultural contexts, with the appropriate support that will empower them to thrive.

Finally, most psychological theories have not been self-consciously critical of their own assumptions, social locations, and philosophies. They have assumed reality rather than identifying the perspective they bring to defining reality. This sense of self-conscious identification of assumptions, starting places, and self-interests is crucial in theory building for pastoral counseling with women.

So where do these critiques leave us in the development of a personality theory for pastoral counseling with women? How do we go about building a theory of personality that will avoid the problems that have just been noted? We must make sure that women's life experiences are at the core of this theory building and that we take seriously the sexist, racist, classist, and heterosexist contexts in which women live. We must also have ways to understand women from an individual perspective and from a perspective of relationships and systems. A counseling theory must have the ability to engage both of these positions.

As we have noted, each personality theory is an attempt to give some insight into the complex process of identity formation, meaning making, and interaction with others and the society. Each attempt is like standing in a different place on the Grand Canyon and describing its character and its formation. Each tries to give the most accurate and complete description and an explanation for the description. There is a significant danger, however, in forgetting that there are other places on the rim that can describe the phenomenon differently, possibly with more completeness, and certainly as well. Also, standing on the bottom of the canyon and describing it from that perspective would produce a completely different result. Whenever someone chooses one dominant theory of personality, she or he has said that this is the perspective that fits her or his experience, observations, goals, needs, and standpoint best. This starting place must always be taken into consideration when the theory is under discussion.

I define personality, then, for the purpose of this work, as the means by which one takes in information about the self, others, and the world, assesses that information so that it has meaning, and then makes decisions, builds relationships, predicts future possibilities, and takes action out of it. Personality, therefore, is an integrative yet dynamic structure that gains complexity over time as physiological structures mature, as perceptions are confirmed and disconfirmed, and as experience deepens.

My understanding of personality has been most deeply informed by the work of Alfred Adler, a contemporary of Freud, and by narrative therapy theory. This is not the place for an elaborate explanation of Adler's theory as it is the assumptions that are most important for understanding the following proposals of pastoral counseling practice. Suffice it to say that Adler had certain foundational assumptions about human nature and about individuals' relationships to one another and to society, and about women, that were quite optimistic and pragmatic. The primary assumptions, for our purposes, are that human personality is a complex interweaving of biology, of meaning making, of striving for perfection, problem solving, and of what he called "social interest"— *Gemeinschaftsgefühl*. He was adamant that the personality must be seen in this fundamental wholeness and that elements of the personality arise from challenges to, and the maturing of, each of these aspects. As information about the self and world are taken in (and the personality always forms in dynamic interaction with people and groups), a set of beliefs forms, which Adler called the "life style" of the person. This life style, which begins forming early, is the personality process that makes sense out of self and world and that allows for "successful" choices to be made in interpretation and action. The life style is a self-narrative that begins simply and gathers data out of life experiences and cultural rules in order to become more complex and more fully explanatory. As the personality develops, a person tends to gather in information that fits better with the life style and to discard information and interpretations that contradict it (except in crises where it is demonstrated that the life style is inadequate for making sense out of the experience and taking successful action). Often interpretations or actions that seem incomprehensible or dysfunctional to the outsider can be shown to make perfect sense when seen in light of the revealed life style of the person. Adler's belief was that people wanted to "belong" and be valued by the society of others and that they were continually striving to overcome a perceived sense of inferiority. Their striving for power was always for the sake of being found worthy of acceptance. When they experienced this sense of belonging, they were best able to express an innate drive toward social interest.

Adler's concept of social interest is of considerable value. Adler believed that people have within them a given potentiality that motivates them toward acting on behalf of the best interests of humanity as well as on their own behalf. He states that this is not seen in its ideal form but that the potential is a strong force in the human personality. He writes that

> social interest means much more [than an interest in private community].
> Particularly it means feeling with the whole, *sub specie aeterneitatis,* under
> the aspect of eternity. It means a striving for a form of community which
> must be thought of as everlasting, as it could be thought of if [humanity]
> ever reached the goal of perfection. It is never a present day community or
> society, nor a political or religious form. Rather the goal which is best
> suited for perfection would have to be a goal which signifies the ideal
> community of all [humanity], the ultimate fulfillment of evolution.[8]

Adler was not a traditionally religious person, but this concept of social interest is not dissimilar from many interpretations of being created in the image of God—always understood as potentiality in its manifestation.

It is also useful in a text on pastoral counseling with women to recognize Adler's commitment to the equality of women and men. Adler wrote, in his work *Cooperation between the Sexes*, that "women often are presented as the cause of all evil in the world, as in the Bible story of original sin, or in Homer's *Iliad,* in which one woman was sufficient to plunge an entire people into misery. . . . The low esteem of women is also expressed in far lower pay for women than for men, even when their work is equal in value to men's work."[9] He also wrote that "we have no reason to oppose the present goals of the women's movement of freedom and equal rights. Rather, we must actively support them. . . ."[10] These statements were written at about the same time as Freud was writing about the inevitability of women's inferiority. Adler's commitments to equality, his focus on the importance of relationship and connection, and his foundation of beliefs, life goals, and narrative all make his theory a useful adjunct to both narrative and feminist theories.

Narrative theory as created and discussed by Michael White and David Epston will provide the primary counseling framework for this book. Like Adler's approach, it also starts with the assumption that people live their lives in keeping with the story/narrative that they create early and then "thicken" throughout life. This narrative has many strands within it, even potentially contradictory strands, that are held together by foundational interpretive assumptions. These assumptions, story lines, and plots are generated through personal experiences, familial roles and stories, institutional influences, and larger cultural themes. They are woven by an individual into a personal history that makes meaning out of the past, sense out of the present, and direction out of the future. When a person encounters experience that contradicts the stories by which she or he lives, that experience is either ignored, reshaped to fit with the guiding elements of the story, or, in certain circumstances, taken in and made meaning of in ways that transform the interpretive lenses by which she or he lives. The more deeply ingrained an interpretive lens of a narrative is, the more difficult it is to challenge.

Narrative therapy theory is based in postmodern/poststructuralist philosophies that include the assumption that our interpretation of reality *is* reality and that this reality is socially constructed. Realities, according to this theory, are organized and maintained by stories that are personal, familial, and cultural. Thus, a major part of the work of narrative counseling is to help people generate new language and new interpretive lenses and thus create new realities. How people engage the experiences they have and the contexts in which those experiences occur is fundamental to the way they move forward in life and build their future stories.

Narrative theory acknowledges that not only do people create stories and plots in which they live and make meaning, but they are also characters in the stories and plots of other people, systems, and cultures. Changes in the plotline or interpretive lenses of any of these (individuals, systems, and culture) mean the potential for the transformation of all. The personal is political and the political is personal in narrative counseling.

When a counselor uses narrative theory, she or he seeks to help a person identify the story content that is causing the distress. The assumption in counseling, as Gerald Monk states, is that people are people and problems are problems and that people are never problems in and of themselves.[11] So the counselor begins deconstructing the problem-filled narrative by externalizing the problem or separating the person from the problem. In a process called deconstructive listening, the counselor changes the typical problematic adjective into a problem noun. Instead of being a depressed person, for example, the counselee is now a person who struggles with depression. This seemingly small "grammatical" change does several things. It makes the problem one aspect of the person's life rather than the definition of the person. It aligns the counselor and the counselee on the same side against the problem, avoiding the often found dynamic of pitting the "healthy" counselor against the "unhealthy" counselee. And it brings the problem into the foreground in a more tangible way: the problem becomes an enemy to resist rather than a vague part of the self. In doing this, reality shifts almost immediately.

The counselor and counselee then work together to discover when the problem has more or less power. There is a deliberate effort not to further thicken the negative story line but to weaken its hold by looking for exceptions to the plot. Since problem stories serve as interpretive lenses on reality (as do helpful stories), the counselee has often had experiences that challenge the problem story that have been discarded or reshaped in order to not dislodge this meaning-making plot. Those experiences become the focus of the therapeutic conversation. In finding the exceptions and exploring the meaning of those for the problematic story, counselees are able to discover their own existing strengths and resources and recognize that this problem story had a beginning and presumably can also have an end. The counselee recognizes that what has seemed global and eternal is boundaried and time limited. It does not define the person.

Throughout the counseling process, the counselee has full choice about what problem to explore, whether the conversation is helpful or should move in a new direction, and what she wishes to work on. Narrative counseling consists of deconstructive and reconstructive conversations where the counselor's comments, questions, and attempts to positively reframe problems may serve to disrupt the problem narrative and engage previously ignored but helpful resources. These recovered strengths and resources can work to reshape the interpretive lenses for the present and future. The counselor always does this from a position of "not-knowing." The counselor does not know the counselee's problem, nor where the counselee "should" be headed. Only the counselee knows that. The counselor only works to lessen the grip of the problem narrative so that preferred narratives and resources may emerge.

This theory thus serves as a bridge between individual and systems' orientations, between problem-focused and solution-focused approaches, and between directive- and nondirective-type counseling. It is a relatively brief counseling method. It is also amenable to normal pastoral care strategies in that its primary intervention is conversational, which lets the counselee lead the process. It helps counselees to find their strengths instead of focusing on "pathology," or opening wounds that can't be healed. This counseling method does not, when done well, create role confusion or conflicts between parishioner and pastor because it allows the counselee to be in charge and it is relatively brief and well boundaried. Finally, it is particularly compatible with a feminist orientation because it includes the deconstruction of stories generated by cultural and familial patriarchy.

It's worth saying a few words here about the kinds of dysfunctional beliefs that the culture teaches to women about who they are and what they are to be. We have seen some of the images that the media gives to us about women and we have seen how influential those messages are for all of us. What is even more difficult is how many double-binding or paradoxical messages are offered to women—double-binding in that at least two contradictory messages are inescapably linked together, and, in their linkage, are terribly damaging. I have listed some of these double-binding messages elsewhere but they are useful to see in this context.

- You are valuable as a woman because of your nurturing and relational capacities. As a culture, we value independence and autonomy.
- You are created in the image and likeness of God. God is male.
- You are small, weak, dependent, and in need of male protection. You have the power to destroy the lives of men and children.

- You represent moral and spiritual purity. You are the sexual object to more than fourteen million readers of pornography and to the advertising world in general.[12]
- You represent moral and spiritual purity in your endurance, steadfastness, and lack of self-interest as woman and mother. You are responsible for sin (especially sexual sin) in the world.
- You need to be submissive, patient, and supportive in your family life. Why didn't you leave your battering husband? You must, at some level, like the violence.
- You must keep your body pure and your sexuality contained. You must use your body and keep it accessible to sell products, gain power, and make men feel good.
- You are a welcome, valuable, and full member of the church. Your vocation is to support the work of the church from behind the scenes—not from the pulpit.
- You need to be protected by an intimate male partner. One-third (to one-half) of all female murder victims are killed by their husband or "lover."[13]
- You, as woman, are to be respected, cared for, and protected. A woman is raped in the United States every 1.3 minutes.[14]
- You are weak and vulnerable. You are so dangerous as tempter that you must be dominated and controlled.[15]
- The church supports and empowers justice. The church says for women to be silent and submissive and disbelieves women who report abuse.[16]

Although all narratives are formed out of a complex interaction of family life, body experience, social location, crises, networks of support, and so on, these kinds of double-binding messages make it difficult to develop narratives that are healthy and empowering. This is why the balance between individual experience, family system dynamics, and cultural location must all be held together in doing pastoral counseling with women.

It is important to discuss one last component to this construction on personality theory in women before moving on to discuss counseling theory, and that is the paradigm provided by Mary Ballou and Nancy W. Gabalac called *harmful adaptation*. Ballou and Gabalac suggest that women are born into a sexist culture that helps them to "adapt" in ways that are useful as far as the distorted cultural narrative about women and men goes, but are harmful and disempowering for women themselves. This is a developmental process that begins at birth and continues through life in an ongoing spiral unless significant intervention into it occurs. It is a five-stage paradigm, although it operates more like an ongoing spiral.

The first element of this spiral is called *humiliation,* which is the experience of being demeaned and devalued in one's own and others' eyes. It is a chronic process and can also happen in acute ways. For example, many of the media images discussed in chapter 1 participate in girls' and women's chronic humiliation. Experiences of incest would be an example of acute humiliation. Incest deeply affects girls' and women's sense of themselves and their potentialities.

The second phase is called *inculcation.* It is in this phase that girls and women are taught what it means to be female. Since their sense of self has already been lowered in the first phase, girls and women are more ready to learn the "rules" about being female, even when they don't seem appealing or fair. The rules about being female include what one should do and be as well as prohibitions (e.g., don't be more successful than a man you wish to attract). These rules are learned "by heart." When asked, women tend to be able to name them quite thoroughly and spontaneously.

The third movement is called *retribution.* This is the punishment for breaking the rules of being female. These punishments can be subtle or very obvious. They can range from name-calling (the strong, aggressive woman boss is "the bitch," for example) to being placed in the control of the psychiatric system (major depression, borderline personality, co-dependent) to being battered (many women claim responsibility for their own battering because they know they broke the [unfair] rules about being a good wife). The purpose of this phase is to extinguish the desire to break the rules.

The fourth phase of Ballou and Gabalac's paradigm is called *conversion.* In this phase women learn to believe that who they have been named to be and the rules they have been taught to follow are actually true and natural. Women become converted to beliefs like, for example, they are really created to unselfishly serve others (differently than are men) or have unique and innate capacities to nurture and relate. Women may even find it "salvific" to believe the rules of inculcation.

This fourth phase, however, isn't enough because there are still the voices of other women who point out the injustices and the double-binding rules of gender development. These women cause discomfort and conflict in converted women and so the fifth phase, *conscription,* arises. This is the process of women attempting to persuade and convert other women to patriarchy's point of view about gender. As Ballou and Gabalac point out, conscription is a betrayal of women by women.[17]

This five-phase proposal seems to me to be a frighteningly accurate account of cultural gender training in women's lives and serves as a core element of women's personality theory. It is important to remember that the shape of harmful adaptation shifts depending on varieties of particularities like race and class. The rules, the punishments, and the rewards are all different, based on social location. In addition, the amount of damage done by harmful adaptation and the forms in which it finds its way into individual women's narratives depends on all sorts of factors. Many of these factors have to do with the quality of empowering support in girls' and women's lives, the number of contradictory messages to those of patriarchy, and other sources of power and self-esteem available.

These assumptions about personality formation and maintenance create the context for the next section, which explores what it means to offer effective help in the pastoral counseling process. This will be discussed under the rubric of counseling theory.

Counseling Theory

The purpose of counseling theory is to describe the process by which intentional change can occur in a person or group seeking that change in relationship with one or more helping persons. When the dynamics of the change process are understood, then effective practices can be generated that facilitate the changes desired by those in the counseling relationship.

One can talk about both the *conditions* of change and the *processes* by which change most effectively happens. The conditions for change have both pragmatic components (under what circumstances is the desired change most likely to happen) and ethical components (what guarantees that this change is both desired and helpful for the person seeking it). It will be helpful to explore conditions for change before we move to the dynamic process of change.

Conditions for Positive Change

Certain characteristics of counselors are most helpful to the counseling process. Those characteristics, most clearly articulated by Carl Rogers, include warmth, acceptance, and positive regard, all directed toward the counselee. Rogers also suggested that congruence between the counselor's body language, tone of voice, and verbalizations are important. Finally, a general consistency over time is a helpful part of the counselor's approach. All of these counselor traits contribute to a constructive condition for change in the counseling process—the condition of safety.

Safety is a fundamental component of counseling work. When the counselee feels threatened or unsure, she is unlikely to be willing to give up familiar coping strategies and attempt new and vulnerable behaviors. She will, in conditions of danger, generally feel the need to create or maintain defensive strategies that demonstrate her invulnerability. This posture will get in the way of the kind of mutual exploration that is necessary to produce positive change. Obviously, certain circumstances make it more difficult to create a safe and trustworthy environment for the counseling process—court-mandated counseling would be an example of circumstances that make it difficult for a counselee to assume safety. There are, however, a number of ways to help create a safe counseling context beyond the consistent counselor traits named above. Those might include a setting that is private and protected; a verbal contract with the counselor that gives maximum control to the counselee; appropriate self-disclosure on the part of the counselor to reveal credentials, style, and values; and respectful and careful listening to the counselee's concerns and worries. The condition of safety and trustworthiness, I believe, cannot be overvalued.

There are several other conditions that make it most likely that positive change can occur when working with the kinds of assumptions about personality named above. First, a counselee generally needs to be experiencing a sense that something isn't working well and that it needs to change. That may be a concern about behavior, about disturbing feelings, about relationships, about beliefs, or about something in her life that is no longer acceptable. In some cases, those concerns are "borrowed" from someone else, like an unhappy spouse or a disciplinary body, but generally it is something that counselees bring to counseling themselves. In addition, the counselee needs to have (or be given) the hope that something better can be gained that will make the counseling process worthwhile—that something will be achieved that will be better than the current circumstance. This assurance, or at least possibility, that things can be better is often difficult for counselees, especially in the case of depression. Yet, without at least a small amount of this hope, people won't usually come for counseling or continue in it. A counselor can assume that there is a certain level of hope in a counselee when the counseling begins, but that hope must be given substance and confidence early in the counseling work. This has several facets. First, it means that the counselor must appear (and hopefully be) competent and reliable in facilitating change. Second, it means that the counselee must be helped to envision, at least partially, what her life would look like if counseling were successful. And third, it means that achieving some small part of the change (for example, a small behavioral success or a reorienting perspective) must be an early part of the counseling process.

Related to this condition of hope must be a fairly clear image of what positive changes might look like. Not only does this help provide the energy for the change process, but it also allows the counselee to make early choices about the direction of the counseling. The counselee needs to be able to know that the changes will not conflict with deeply held values and positive self-images. Although values may change over the process, and consequently bring unexpected changes in behavior, the initial conditions for change need to confirm values that are important to the counselee. This is especially important in working with women whose self-image and value systems have been established in conditions of harmful adaptation. If a counselor indicates to a woman that, at the end of counseling, she will not worry so much about her family or be as selfless, this may well close down the change process because the value systems of counselee and counselor are too different.

Many feminist counselors suggest that the most important first step in counseling is to help women counselees to see some of the value conflicts or injustices in their lives. This is in part an educative process, but it is also, more importantly, a tapping into the latent self-story within most women. In other words, at some level women know that they are frustrated with sexist expectations and demands in their lives and they know that something different and better must exist. To voice those hopes early in counseling, however, may well be impossible because voicing those kinds of judgments may feel to the counselee like she is "breaking the rules" and being self-centered or selfish. Therefore, it is helpful, not just for the counselor to do educational work, but to help this alternative narrative (with its strong ambivalences) to be voiced, which will be discussed further in chapter 3.

Along with maintaining congruence with current value systems, the counselee generally needs to be reassured that the counseling process will not destroy or damage those things she holds dear, such as her friendships, family, job, or reputation. One of the most poignant counseling situations I worked with occurred when a woman said to me after two or three weeks of work, "If I get healthy, I'll lose my family and I can't let that happen." The challenge of facilitating women's health in a world that has been built around roles and structures that are unhealthy for women is a profound one. Nonetheless, it is important in creating conditions for change that women are reassured that those things they hold dear won't be lost to them. The best way to do that is to put the counseling goals and speed in the hands of the counselee. My response to the counselee who feared the loss of her family was to say that we should probably go very slowly, then, so that she would know if anything she valued began to be put at risk.

Another condition for positive change is the creation or knowledge of a safe place to practice new behaviors, test out new self-images, and experiment with expressing new feelings. Sometimes a person has this kind of community or support already existing when coming for counseling, but for most women, creating or joining a women's group is a fundamental and necessary part of the counseling process. Some of the values and behaviors gained in the counseling process challenge and break the rules taught in the inculcation phase of harmful adaptation and these changes carry with them a deep and frightening threat of retribution. This is not just a paranoid fear. One young woman counselee's alcoholic mother called me after a few weeks of counseling to tell me that she no longer liked her (adult) daughter and her daughter would soon be disliked by all if she continued in the counseling. She had, of course, already told her twenty-five-year-old daughter the same thing. Retribution can be expected when women attempt to change some of their harmful adaptation. Consequently, there must be a supportive environment that is larger than the one-on-one counseling process where encouragement and reality testing can be offered to someone who is trying on new—and sometimes frightening—behaviors.

Finally, in order for change to occur best in counseling it is necessary that the counselor communicate to the counselee that she or he understands the complexity of the person and her story. In communicating one's self in the counseling process it is necessary that a person talk about elements of her story in bits and pieces that, only when seen as whole fabric, come close to approximating her life experience. It is my firm conviction that unless a counselee believes that a counselor can keep from reducing her to one or a few elements of her story and that the counselor will hold all the story themes—even the contradictory ones—in safekeeping as the whole story is gathered, it will be hard for her to trust the counselor or the counseling enough to engage in the process of change. Also, the story heard has to be the counselee's story, not the counselor's projections or assumptions about the story. It is easy for the counselor to mis-hear a story because of being influenced by her or his own class, race, sexual orientation, and ethnicity and the stereotypes she or he has about those particularities of the counselee. Pastoral counselors must listen very carefully to what the counselee is saying in both its wholeness and its particularities and regularly check for accuracy in the understanding. This listening process is a challenge for the counselor, who tries to walk the fine line between accurately hearing enough of the story to discover with the counselee where the changes should best occur and not taking more time in counseling than is fundamentally needed to accomplish the goals.

Finally, the purpose of these conditions is to generate adequate security, hope, energy, and vision to move through the processes of change in ways that will nurture, heal, and empower the counselee in her own life and relationships and in the culture in which she lives.

Processes of Change

Every theory of counseling (and there are many of them) has a different conceptual frame about how and why change occurs in people who seek counseling. Counseling that is based on a narrative theory of personality has its own idiosyncrasies. Nonetheless, virtually every theory of counseling begins with some form of storytelling. The counselee begins by talking about her distress or problem in the context of her life and its history. As noted earlier, the counselor listens to this carefully. In narrative counseling theory, the story is listened to with an ear toward the counselee's internalized problem so that it can be externalized, toward exceptions to the problematic story in order to deconstruct the problem, and toward new, more preferred, stories that can be integrated and strengthened.

Narrative theory assumes that people's problems don't have to be solved by their undergoing deep personality change—if indeed deep personality change is ever a real option. It assumes, as White and Epston do, that "in striving to make sense of life, persons face the task of arranging their experiences of events in sequences across time in such a way as to arrive at a coherent account of themselves and the world around them. Specific experiences of events of the past and present, and those that are predicted to occur in the future, must be connected in a lineal sequence to develop this account. This account can be referred to as a story or self-narrative."[18] People develop this narrative with a variety of subnarratives over time and the thicker it gets, the less likely people are to notice exceptions to it or to deconstruct it. Yet, with the motivation of pain from problems, people can be helped to notice exceptions to the strands of narrative that generate or maintain problems in their lives and to create a new narrative strand that thickens the exceptions that make a preferred life possible.

Wendy Drewery and John Winslade say that

> the simple idea from which the narrative approach developed is that people make meaning, meaning is not made for us. This simple statement contains a wealth of implications. For one thing, it puts people in the driving seat of their lives: we produce the meanings of our lives. Certainly, the way we speak and the things we speak about are part of our cultural heritage; they are handed down to us, and they are our tools for making sense. The argument of this book is that these ways of making sense are susceptible to change. We can change the ways we speak. In doing so, we can also change much about the way we organize and understand our worlds. Language is not simply a representation of our thoughts, feelings, and lives. It is part of a multilayered interaction: the words we use influence the ways we think and feel about the world. In turn, the ways we think and feel influence what we speak about. How we speak is an important determinant of how we can be in the world.[19]

So this theory of personality suggests that people create meaning-making structures out of the cumulative meaning making that they do;

that the core narrative gets "thicker" over time and the disconfirming experiences are less likely to be built into that core narrative; and that when people have problems in their lives, they use their core narrative (by definition) to make sense of them and make decisions about what to do with them. This means that a problem-saturated narrative strand can be a source of ongoing problem behaviors, relationships, and feelings. A narrative strand constructed around experiences that serve as a counterstory to the problematic story but that has not previously been substantially built into the core narrative may well serve to create new options for the present and a new direction for the future.

Culture plays a major role in providing the interpretive lenses by which people make sense of their lives. Gerald Monk states that "from such a perspective, clients are viewed as being positioned by social and cultural factors that shape their desires, ambitions, and purposes. The counselor does not see the person as embodying the problem. Externalizing conversations help to locate the problem within the beliefs of the culture from which the problem emerged. An externalized description can serve as shorthand for a set of values or for cultural discourse."[20]

When one is working from a narrative perspective one has certain philosophical and psychological assumptions in mind. In fact, it is those assumptions in which the counselor is grounded that guide the questions and the intentions for listening. Pastoral counselors should always remember that narrative theory assumes that people construct their narratives, that there is no essential truth, but only interpretations of events that are real and that then guide responses to those events. The stories that we have made our own are informed by our relationships with families, with our culture, with our peers, with our own bodies, and, most important, the narratives are self-generating because of their selective focus. We assume in narrative theory that people have many experiences in their lives that would challenge or redirect the narrative toward new interpretations and meanings, but that don't get "storied" (that is, given significance and thus remembered in the person's core narrative) because they are in conflict with their dominant or core narrative. As Freedman and Combs suggest, "People who come to therapy can be viewed as living in stories where choice is restricted and available options are painful and unfulfilling. Counseling involves facilitating experience of new stories—life narratives that are more empowering, more satisfying, and give hope for better futures."[21] This is generally done by helping the counselee recover her unstoried life experiences that challenge, supplement, or even defeat the problem narrative.

The counselor needs to recognize that she or he carries this narrative lens and the deconstructive/constructive philosophy, but the counselee carries all knowledge and frameworks for meaning. Consequently, narrative counseling is truly collaborative—not just sort of liberally pseudo-collaborative where the counselee is consulted about what she wants out of counseling. It is truly that the counselor doesn't know where the counseling is supposed to go and operates from this sense of not-knowing. The counselor wonders a lot with the counselee and questions come out of this wondering. The wondering is, of course, guided by the belief that the current problem-filled narrative needs to be deconstructed in order to loosen its power and in order for room to be made for an alternative and preferred narrative. As Monk says, "the co-creative practices of narrative therapy require a particular ability on the part of the therapist to see the client as a partner with local expertise whose knowledge may, at the beginning of the counseling relationship, be as hidden as the artifacts of a civilization buried in the sod of centuries. And, because the narrative conversation is a process of unearthing dormant competencies, talents, abilities, and resources, it tends to produce numerous moments of excitement and vivacity."[22]

The counselor works to be a curious, compassionate, interested advocate on behalf of the counselee, who is figuring out how to resist the power of problematic ways of understanding her life and how to restory positive meaning-making elements of her life that will help her to live life more abundantly and less problematically. This does not mean that problems are "all in your head." If, for example, a woman has been shaped into a meaning-making framework that says that women are "the opposite sex" and don't have either the gifts or the right to make a meaningful contribution to the world, then finding the flaws in that story line and the exceptions to it won't change the fact that she lives in a sexist world with all of its dangers and problems, but it will make it more likely that she can resist some of those dangers and build a future that is less problematic and more satisfying. This is an example of narrative change. One of the main ways that this kind of restorying process works in counseling is through the process of deconstruction or deconstructive listening.

Bill O'Hanlon has written a good summary article about narrative counseling in *The Family Therapy Networker*. He ends his summary of narrative counseling with a profound and accurate warning. He writes, "If you don't believe that [a counselee's] difficulties are social and personal constructions, then you won't be seeing these transformations. Inevitably, many therapists will ignore the heart of narrative therapy, its fierce belief in people's possibilities for change and the profound effects of conversation, language and stories on both therapist and client."[23] This is the heart of the theory. It's not a set of techniques to use to change counselees. It's a set of beliefs about the strength and resiliency of people who have the possibility of re-authoring their lives in ways that make them more able to live full responses to their vocations. If we collapse what we are doing into techniques—and they are easy to learn, so this is a risk—we may do harm. This approach to counseling is deeply grounded in and compatible with the theology I carry of God's constant invitation to possibility, co-creation, and a closer approximation of God's "kindom." I think that every counseling theory used by a pastoral counselor needs to be in keeping with and informed by her or his foundational theology.

Theology

As was discussed in chapter 1, many of the foundational assumptions of pastoral counseling have been challenged by the various liberation movements of the past few decades. These challenges take a variety of shapes. Theology has been challenged by women who have experienced a dominant father God as exclusive and negative in a culture where dominant males have done a great deal of harm. African Americans have challenged the whiteness of Jesus and of God—images that do not mirror or reflect their experience or historical reality. African American women have challenged European American women about differing Christologies when European American women have assumed they were speaking for all women in challenging current understandings of Jesus. Hispanic women have lifted up the importance of Mary and some of the saints, while women incest survivors have critiqued the dominant model of female saints as sacrificial. These challenges by groups whose experiences have been assumed and subsumed have reshaped theological reflection in foundational and radical ways. Theology that is sensitive to and in dialogue with the lived experience of all people must hold a central place in the work of pastoral counseling.

Earlier, I suggested that theology plays two central roles in the work of pastoral counseling. It serves as a focus of commitment out of which interpretive norms and guiding images for ministry arise, and it serves as a lens of assessment when we accompany someone through the process of counseling. Each of those roles is vital.

Focus of Commitment

All people have an operational theology that guides the formation of their value systems and their sense of purpose in life. For some, these theological groundings are hidden and unavailable to them. For others, they are very conscious and dynamic. Pastoral counselors need to be conscious of the theological commitments that guide them in their ministries. Their faith commitments deeply shape the ways in which they listen to their counselees and the directions they take in trying to offer help. When theological commitments are out of counselors' consciousness, then they are unable to bring them into conscientious dialogue with the faith claims of the counselees. It is only in being clear with these theological claims that counselors can be in a truly mutual relationship with their counselees.

In my work, I find four theological themes to be most helpful. These theological themes help me to formulate the kinds of interpretive norms by which I evaluate the pastoral counseling process with women and through which I understand my role. The themes are not universal. Rather, they are idiosyncratic to my history, my sense of call, my social location, and my counseling experience. Each pastoral counselor has her or his own themes, and it is the task of each counselor to articulate those clearly and carefully.

The first theme I would name is that of prevenient grace. It seems to me that the sense that women have of needing confidence in their own belonging and in their own truths prior to exploring their realities is not dissimilar to the notion of prevenient grace. That tenet claims that God's love and assurance surround a person before she or he even knows that it exists. It is this sense of confidence in God's love and of our own place in the world that gives birth to the possibility of life in faith. Prevenient grace is the necessary condition for our ability to respond to God's care and acceptance and thus it may be a very helpful theological starting place in a pastoral theology for the care of women. It seems to offer a counterpoint to the strong message of not belonging and not being of value that the culture persistently transmits to women.

It is the pastoral counselor's responsibility to mediate this kind of grace that allows a marginalized person who has been told in many ways that her reality is not valid to feel accepted for who she is. This is not a suspended judgment, as is advocated in client-centered care, nor the kind of therapeutic neutrality prized by psychoanalytic perspectives. It is the kind of care that is consistent with the mediation of prevenient grace. It says to the counselee that her reality is the reality to be taken seriously, her experience is that which is to be valued, and her being is that which is beloved. Obviously, the pastoral counselor must attempt to place herself or himself in the stream of that sense of grace in order to participate in it and communicate it to the other.

A second theological theme that guides me in pastoral counseling is that of the power of community in the body of Christ. We are all formed in dynamic interaction with the people and groups in our lives. As a tenet of family systems theory states, "By the family we are broken and by the family we are healed." Women's views of themselves, their understandings of vocation, and their life conditions are formed in the crucibles of communities. Many times these communities are not expressions of love and justice for the women in them. As we have seen from the statistics on intimate violence, many girls and women are hurt, even crushed, in the very communities that are supposed to be primary sources of strength and nurture. Even in the church, women are often told that they are not as valuable to the community as its male members are. They are told this when they are seen as indispensable to the church as long as their work is behind the scenes. The dominant negative sense of self and future held by so many women in our culture (as demonstrated by the epidemic rates of depression in women) is so strong because it is reinforced by community. It is not the kind of community that can help women experience a fullness of self. It is the kind of community that stunts the spirit.

Yet there are other kinds of community—communities that truly serve as the body of Christ and that reflect God's power of love and justice. They are "communities of resistance and solidarity" as named by Sharon Welch. They are communities of people who are learning to test their sense of self and their beliefs about the world against a different measure—a measure that overturns the false dualisms and the hierarchies of power and worth and that encourages strength, justice, and the power of truth. In this community, women can hear parts of their own stories in the lives of others who are seeking wholeness in themselves and in the world. In hearing and telling those stories in communities of support and truthtelling, women can begin to believe in the validity and worth of their own experiences. It is in these communities where the evils of cultural oppression are overturned and the search for justice is valued that selves are healed and societies are changed.

The third theological theme that is meaningful in my understanding of pastoral counseling is the richness and complexity of the divine presence to be found in many images of God. It is primarily through the images of God we carry that we experience and interpret our relationship with God. When the possibilities for those images are limited, especially by what the culture values in terms of maleness, power, and whiteness, then we are limited in being able to experience God's unlimited abundance. This has been a particular problem for women. It is not necessary here to reiterate all of the insights feminist theology has provided regarding the problems with dominant imagery we have as a culture for God. It is enough to say that the images of God we carry are critical not only for experiencing the divine presence, but also for understanding ourselves, our place in creation, and God's ongoing intentions for our world. In research that I have done on women's images of God and the effect those images have on their lives, I have found that when one allows God to be experienced through a greater variety of relational images (not conceptualizations, but images), then one's willingness and ability to integrate spirituality with other aspects of life are enhanced. Self-esteem is also strengthened and women are more able to trust God's activity in their lives.[24] Unless a person can find herself reflected in some way in the divine image, it is very difficult to experience a sense of partnership in the ongoing work of creation. If God is only father, for example, then women are only children. They cannot be fathers in their own lives and thus reflect the divine role as can men. They can only remain in the submissive and passive relationship that father-child means.

If women can indeed claim that they are created in the image of God, then they too must find ways to understand that God-likeness in their own beings. And that God-likeness is much more helpfully understood as the way that we are invited into loving and just relationships with one another, as God loves us, than it is understood as any particular traits or characteristics of God. As Larry Kent Graham describes so beautifully, being created in the image of God means that human beings are able to engage in a quality of relationship that mirrors God's relationship with humanity. As women and men are both better able to define the meaning of the image of God as that of "relational justice," then God's image will be able to be lived out more fully.[25] This sense of the image of God shifting from who God is to who we can be because of God's love and grace is helpful for both persons and communities.

The fourth theological theme is the one that I find to be most fundamental in my pastoral counseling work with women. This is the biblical theme of the Exodus. This theme is not without its drawbacks. Certainly, an image of a God who can wipe out a whole race of people has mixed benefit in any theological formulation, especially a liberationist one. Nonetheless, as I work to define a starting place for pastoral theology and pastoral counseling, at least for this point in our history, in a culture that embodies a deep pathology, it can be helpful to understand our work as participation in the liberation and empowerment of the Exodus. This has several sections if we look to the story of the Exodus for our guidance. The primary narrative in Exodus is the movement from a community of bondage to a new community based on freedom and on a sense of solidarity under the leadership of a God who has brought forth this liberation. The chronology of the Exodus was such that the people experienced their oppression and, in the midst of that pain, called to God for deliverance. God, through the leadership of Moses, Aaron, and Miriam, worked to bring the people out of their situation of oppression and brokenheartedness into a process that called them to faithful and hopeful relationship to one another and to God. Once they had experienced this community of empowerment, they were called by God to a new kind of accountability—an accountability that was based on their ability to see the fullness of their lives and the choices that faced them. This new accountability allowed them to live lives that could sustain the freedom to which they had been empowered.

In each pastoral counseling relationship one might see an analogous process to the Exodus story. In the process of counseling with women, the counselee is helped to claim her knowledge that she lives in an oppressive world that has stifled her spirit and limited her choices. She most often experiences great pain in coming to this awareness. To know one's familiar world as a place of oppression that requires challenge and change as a way toward health is a frightening and anger-producing experience. As one well-known feminist song says, "How I wish my eyes had never been opened." The counseling experience, then, consists of an intense journey to find liberation and empowerment, not just as individuals but as community and culture. Once women find a sense of liberation and community with one another, they are also able to find a way to accountability that makes life in this new land one of integrity and congruence. It becomes a place from which women are free to be in relationship with all of creation as whole beings. From that new space, women frequently choose periodically to return to that land of oppression, hearing the stories of women who are there with care, understanding, and advocacy, in order to help them make the journey. It is from this place that a new accountability means, for women and men, that we do not take part in or allow oppression and injustice without resistance. This is the work of ongoing cultural transformation for women and for men.

Lenses of Assessment

The theological themes named above form the hermeneutical or interpretive norms through which I assess the process of pastoral counseling and within which I try to create pastoral counseling strategies that serve to live them out. This is the work of the pastoral counselor in assessing her or his own theological foundations and starting places. But these themes and commitments cannot operate in isolation. They exist in the communities of support and accountability within which counseling takes place.

It is also the pastoral counselor's responsibility to help the counselee identify the theological and religious foundations that guide her life and make it available for scrutiny and growth. Consequently, pastoral counselors use a variety of theological questions or categories as ways to help counselees explore their theological belief systems, spiritual feelings, and places of religious belonging.

I have five theological questions that I find helpful in the pastoral counseling process. Again, these are both idiosyncratic to my experience and, I believe, helpful in looking at a proposal for pastoral counseling with women. A variety of theological assessment theories have been proposed over the years of pastoral care, but most came during the period when psychology was unquestioningly seen as the primary source of definitive knowledge about people. Theological systems of assessment were at best seen as supplemental or "add-ons" to the real revelation of psychological concepts. It is important to see theological assessment and religious empowerment as central aspects of pastoral counseling rather than addenda. Our most serious problem working with theological categories is that we have not kept up in building relevant theological language for pastoral theology (whereas our psychological terminology is continually updated), so it is difficult to use theological language in looking at the complex problems people experience today.

It seems to me that there are several very productive questions we can use with people who come for care that help us to get at the deepest level of concern—levels that psychology cannot touch. The first question is the one that seems most powerful in this process of meaning: the "what's at stake" question. Asking what's at stake gets behind the behaviors and even behind the feelings and thoughts of the problem presented. It asks the deeper question of what is the person's image of the risks, the goals, the possibilities, and the horrors that drive the choices that she is making. It asks, at some level, the source of her deepest meaning and deepest fears. It cuts through the defenses and the rationalizations and helps get at the central images that hold together the psychological, spiritual, physical, relational, systemic, and cultural dimensions of the self. And at the core is the spiritual, the ultimate meaning that is at stake in this person's dilemma, crisis, decision, or transition.

The second question that I find central in attempting to understand the needs of counselees is that of how they imagine that God perceives them. This is a reversal question. We often ask what a person's image of God is, and that usually results in a revealing and helpful conversation. But the question of how God is perceiving her requires, usually, a spontaneity that taps the deeper nature of her relationship with God. She generally knows but hasn't thought about God's attitude and perception about her. Therefore, she will respond with the more significant image that is operative in her. This will help the caregiver better know the state of her connection with the divine presence. I remember asking a counselee this question and she very precisely said to me that God was turned away from her, waiting for her to meet God's expectations before again turning toward her in a warmth and connection that she had previously experienced. She was unable to meet those perceived expectations and so assumed that God would never be able to turn toward her again. Her experience was one of spiritual death and despair and it required our exploring her beliefs about what it meant to be in right relationship with God, with her community/family, and with herself (the part that had been completely left out). The images of how a person experiences God's eyes, God's energy, or God's hope help frame the core nature of the care seeker's faith relationship.

A third question for getting at the nature of the issues for care is the question of how this person experiences God's grace in her life. This question, in conjunction with the fourth question, which is how this person experiences God's judgment in her life, helps the caregiver and care seeker understand the kinds of interpretive lenses she has or automatic assumptions she makes about the value and moral goodness of her life activities. In addition, the person will generally expand along the lines of the deservedness of these experiences of grace or judgment. This helps the counselee become aware of her general approach to the world (fair, good, right, capricious, etc.) and whether she is generally optimistic or pessimistic about the direction of her life. It also helps the caregiver and care seeker identify areas where there is a confessional need or behaviors for which the care seeker needs to make or seek restitution or amends. These are very valuable articulations for caregiver and care seeker as they work together to get at the person's state of being and the problems she is faced with.

Finally, the issue of community needs to be assessed. How does this person understand herself in relation to the rest of the body? Is there appropriate connection? Appropriate emotional, physical, intellectual distance? Is there an interdependence and mutuality or is there separation and autonomy? Is there isolation? How does the body system function and how has it shaped who this person is? What is the nature of the most influential subsystem for this person and what roles and rules are carried out in this relationship? These systemic/communal questions are not separate from the ones raised earlier, but rather are another way to look at some of those questions in a more interconnected light.

There are clear connections between the themes raised as normative theological priorities for me as pastoral counselor and the assessment categories thought to be helpful for the counseling process. These questions represent one way to do a primary theological framing of the counseling task. Their theological priorities address the key elements of wholeness for people—their sense of self in relationship to God, the quality of relationship with their primary communities, and their sense of purpose, vocation, or direction.

Conclusion

The rest of the book will focus on a fourfold approach to pastoral counseling with women, with each of the first three counseling phases illustrated by a particular issue that is common in the lives of women. The four dimensions of pastoral counseling that will be used to guide the theory building of this book were developed in my chapter titled "Pastoral Counseling as an Art of Personal/Communal Activism" in *The Arts of Ministry*. Those dimensions are: (1) coming to voice, (2) gaining clarity, (3) making choices, and (4) staying connected. Each of these phases of a feminist-oriented approach to pastoral counseling with women will be discussed. In addition, the foundational assumptions discussed earlier in personality theory, counseling theory, and theological themes will undergird the following proposal and the proposals will flesh out these assumptions.

three

Helping Women Come to Voice

A recent book by Riet Bons-Storm is titled *The Incredible Woman*. The meaning of the title is twofold. It is meant to affirm women for their various strengths and their forms of resistance to patriarchal pressures. But more centrally, the title is meant to convey the fact that women are frequently "incredible"—not believable—to those around them, including, and maybe especially, their pastoral caregivers. Her argument, convincingly made, is that pastoral caregivers, steeped in the same patriarchal dominant culture as their distressed counselees, have difficulty believing the stories and experiences of women in their care that speak against or deny the "truths" of that culture.[1] In other words, it is often hard for pastoral caregivers to believe women's stories, much less to help them to gain voice and language with which to tell those stories. Rather, pastoral caregivers fall into the same traps as traditional secular therapists and find ways to label these women and their "atypical" stories as disturbed or deviant.

The purpose of this chapter is to talk about the risks to girls' and women's voices throughout their life spans, the contexts of those threats to women's voices and language, and the kinds of therapeutic strategies that best discover, support, and empower women's experiences and stories to be told. I assume, in this counseling proposal, that having language for exploring and discovering the truths of one's own experience within the web of relationships that form the context of that experience and the sense of entitlement to speak and claim that experience are important starting places for building personal and relational health. That assumption will be explored throughout the chapter.

As we turn to looking at girls and women's voices, it is important to state that there is always a risk of creating a false generic called *woman*. We, as theorists and theologians, must constantly walk the fine line between "the rock and the hard place" as defined by Serene Jones. She suggests that

> on the rock side, I place those theologians who continue to employ universalizing and/or ahistorical frames of reference to structure their accounts of human experience. . . . The advantages of these perspectives should be evident to those who engage their texts: the stability of their frameworks allow them to generate theological images which are resilient and visionary. . . . On the other hand, what they lose with this reliance on universalizing structures is . . . a place for that which "does not fit."
>
> On the hard place side of the map I locate the work of those theologians who self-consciously avoid universalizing gestures and opt instead for descriptions of experience which are historically localized and culturally specific. . . . This side is solid enough to be a hard place but its formulations are less stable than those of the rock. The challenges confronting those standing on such shifting ground are numerous: the status of normative claims, the limits and value of immanent critique, the viability of deconstructive rhetoric, and the still undecided fate of "truth" and its relation to doctrine.[2]

The tendency of feminist theory building in the second wave has certainly been to fall on the "rock" side of this dilemma. As Jones indicates, the immense risk of that is the erasure of all difference. Any experience that doesn't fit that of the "woman" being explored (and that tends to be the woman whose experience gets the most attention in both life and research—white, middle-class, heterosexual, educated, able-bodied, and so forth) is overlooked for the sake of finding adequate similarities on which to build the theoretical proposal. Fortunately, over time, the perspectives of many women who were not always included in the "dominant" perspective—women of color, lesbians, working-class women, and so on—have been brought into dialogue with the "rock" side and have been able to challenge what has often looked like a generalizable belief.

Linell Elizabeth Cady, in a recent article on identity in feminist theory and theology, succinctly captures some key issues in the rock/hard place debate:

The recognition of the depth of [women's] exclusion contributed to the turn to a distinctively female nature and experience. The articulation of women as a distinct class, oppressed in a particular way by virtue of membership in that class, was an important plank in the development of a distinctive feminist movement and politics. . . . The categories of woman and experience have served ever since as the fundamental and defining categories of feminist theory, generating many of the theoretical riddles with which it has struggled. Feminist theory, [however,] as [Judith] Grant notes, "was becoming captured by the patriarchal ideas it sought to oppose. . . . It had created a stereotypical Woman, a monolithic, abstract being defined only by her source of oppression."[3]

The answer of a constructivist perspective (hard place) to the problems of essentialism (rock) was to address this monolithic abstraction called *Woman* by acknowledging the deep and fundamental particularity of each life experience. The strength of the constructivist position is that each person's story is seen in its uniqueness and within its own particular context. Generalizations are avoided, limiting the power any one story (or cultural narrative) can have over another. In this way, the power to oppress any one group by another becomes limited. In a similar fashion, however, any chance for a shared narrative within a group and the resultant possibility for solidarity is also very limited. The weakness of the constructivist position is also seen clearly by Cady when she states that "identity is subject to fragmentation, and the political and normative voice is muted as the individual loses a sense of location from which to speak."[4]

This book makes proposals for pastoral counseling with women that will be helpful for women in a variety of contexts. Yet, because it is an attempt to build theory, draw conclusions, and make constructive proposals, it will more often risk the essentialist problems than the constructivist ones. I hope to walk the fine line between these two pitfalls—by drawing on research and experience from a variety of perspectives and by using a form of therapeutic theory that was built out of a constructivist set of assumptions: narrative theory. In these ways I am hopeful that the risks and problems of both essentialism and constructivism are minimized.

The Centrality of Voice
in Feminist Theory and Theology

The issue of language and voice has long been a hallmark of the feminist movement. Not only have many key theoretical works been developed around the rubric of voice and speech—especially finding a different voice and language than that which has been provided out of a dominant culture—but a critique of male-dominated language has been around since before the first wave of feminism and the suffrage movement.[5]

It has long been understood that language not only reflects reality but also creates it. When the language of the culture does not carry the experience or perspective of women or others of nondominant cultural status, then the culture will not operate in the best interests of those groups. And, not only are the people in these groups deprived of empowerment and full participation in the culture, but the culture is damaged too. As Jean Baker Miller says, "What I do see is that our dominant society is a very imperfect one. It is a low-level, primitive organization built on an exceedingly restricted conception of the total human potential. It holds up narrow and ultimately destructive goals for the dominant groups and attempts to deny vast areas of life. The falsity and the full impact of this limited conception has been obscured."[6] There is a great deal at stake for both individuals and the culture in new language being developed and claimed by people who have been deprived of it.

Nondominant groups are not only deprived of language but are also denied voice.[7] Most works in feminist counseling have focused on the importance of helping girls and women to gain access to their own voice. Miriam Greenspan, in the first comprehensive text on feminist psychotherapy, talks about the importance of what Nelle Morton called "hearing into speech."[8] It is not just a matter of being able to tell one's story that I am emphasizing. It is the empowerment of hearing oneself speak and learning to believe in the truth of that long-denied voice, language, and narrative. Greenspan talks about her own experience:

> The simple process of women sitting and listening to each other's stories respectfully and with an ear to the shared strengths as well as the shared ordeals had some very powerful therapeutic effects. Our relationship to everything—our bodies, our work, our sexuality, the men and women

and children in our lives—emerged in a thoroughly new light. Together we saw that the old terms used to describe politics, relationships, sexuality, power and language itself were an outgrowth of male experience and had to be reinvented from our own point of view as women. For many of us, the overwhelming sense was of seeing the world through our own eyes for the very first time.[9]

The process of losing voice may be a subtle one for girls and women, although there are many times and places where girls' voices are crushed explicitly through violence and other overt acts of harm. For the purpose of this chapter I want to talk about five contexts in which developing and having an authentic voice is challenged for girls and women in this culture. As discussed in chapter 1, there are many cultural pressures in the lives of women that shape a false cultural narrative about what it means to be female. This cultural narrative serves as the context out of which personal narratives are also built. When personal narratives are built in such a way that they do not give access to the acknowledgment or expression of a person's experience, then that person is likely to experience a variety of personal and relational problems as the meaning of experiences has to be distorted in order to fit the general framework of the narrative.

Sandra Lipsitz Bem's perspective on gender schema theory is helpful for us as we look at the cultural contexts of gender narratives before we look at the specific contexts of voice development in girls and women. Bem is most famous for her work on androgyny done in the 1970s. She has since rejected her conclusions in that work and moved to a focus on gender schema theory. This theory suggests that children, from a very young age, internalize the lens of gender polarization into their own narrative frameworks. These narrative frameworks then resist challenge from experiences that don't support them and pay attention to any data or experiences that do support them, thus reinforcing the narrative in its culturally supported direction. Bem tells us that "gender schema theory contains two fundamental presuppositions about the process of individual gender formation: first, that there are gender issues embedded in cultural discourse and social practice that are internalized by the developing child, and, second, that once these gender lenses have been internalized, they predispose the child, and later the adult, to construct an identity that is consistent with them."[10] She goes on to state that girls and boys have to contend not only with gender polarization, but also with cultural andro-centrism and with a mandate to pass this schema on through the culture from generation to generation. The kinds of cultural phenomena that reinforce androcentrism and gender polarization were detailed in chapter 1 but include things like "generic" male language (including male names becoming the "family" name), child-rearing practices, advertising strategies, entertainment themes and images, and so on. Bem argues that gender polarization and its enculturation are so ubiquitous that even feminist theory building (such as the persistent emphasis on women being more relational than men) can perpetuate their legacy.

Women and other members of nondominant groups have thus learned to interpret their own stories and experiences, needs and goals, through the lenses of the other—those they have been taught to please and appease. Often they have lost access to their truths and their honest strengths. As Jean Baker Miller says,

> Tragic confusion arises because subordinates absorb a large part of the un-truths created by the dominants; there are a great many blacks who feel inferior to whites, and women who still believe they are less important than men. This internalization of dominant beliefs is more likely to occur if there are few alternative concepts at hand. On the other hand, it is also true that members of the subordinate group have certain experiences and perceptions that accurately reflect the truth about themselves and the injustice of their position. Their own more truthful concepts are bound to come into opposition with the mythology they have absorbed from the dominant group. An inner tension between the two sets of concepts and their derivatives is almost inevitable.[11]

With these descriptions of the power of lost language and denied voice one can understand easily how feminist therapists can claim that this approach to counseling sees cultural pathology and harmful adaptation at the core of the distress that women and other marginalized groups bring into counseling. The focus is not on the intrapsychic or idiosyncratic formation of personal pathology—the focus is on internalized patriarchy and the damage that contextual patriarchy continues to do.

Laura Brown speaks of these issues with poignant insight when she talks about the counselee's loss of her "mother tongue." She says that the process of counseling is the work of counselor and counselee to come together to learn the client's emotional "mother tongue," the "native language" in which an undistorted image can be told through the freed voice of the client who is no longer silenced. There is not, in this metaphor, the necessity for an actual change of spoken language. It is more about how the client comes to rename experience, retell a narrative, in a way that no longer violates well-being, but rather empowers or liberates.[12]

In order to help a counselee move to a knowing and reclaiming of her "mother tongue" it is fundamental for the counselor to be present with the counselee as fully and respectfully as possible, validating her attempts to find language for realities that have been denied, minimized, and distorted by the dominant culture. The pastoral counselor and the counselee must work together to find the language that will authentically express the nature and power of the narrative. It is in finding that language and claiming the right to speak it that empowerment for change is made possible.

Regaining language and voice for the power of naming one's self, one's environment, and one's God has been a primary agenda for feminist theology as well. If pastoral counseling is a weave of the social sciences with primary religious and theological resources, then it is important to note that both feminist theology and feminist psychology place the power of naming at the core of empowering people and cultures that have been disenfranchised. Mary Pellauer says, in *God's Fierce Whimsy,* that "if there's anything worth calling theology, it is listening to people's stories—listening to them and honoring and cherishing them, and asking them to become even more brightly beautiful than they already are."[13]

One can see the centrality of language and naming to the theological traditions in the creation stories of Genesis. In the creation story represented in Genesis 1, the naming of each element of God's work is part of the essence of creation. As God creates day and night, the earth, and the sky, each is carefully named and evaluated. It is, in part, the naming that makes the creation real. In the creation story recorded in Genesis 2, God creates 'adam and a pleasant environment and then realizes that 'adam is isolated in the garden. As God attempts to create a companion for 'adam, part of that relationship-building process is inviting 'adam to name the new creations. As they are named, they take on meaning, and thus enter into relationship with 'adam. The one who names imbues that which is named with meaning and enters into the relationship according to the meaning given in the naming.

Traditionally *'adam* has been understood to be male, as God later makes a female out of *'adam's* rib. Although it is probably more accurate to understand that *'adam* signifies undifferentiated humanity and it is only through the splitting of *'adam*, which resulted in two human beings, that sexuality and gender were created, it is important at this juncture to recognize the attributed understanding of *'adam* as Adam.[14] Thus, in the Judeo-Christian tradition, the right to name is traced back to Adam. Male privilege has been understood to include the right to name and give meaning to the significant dimensions of culture. Women have not had the opportunity, or the authority, to participate in that naming process, despite the centrality of naming for joining that which is named in relationship. Because naming, however, is the privilege granted by God to *'adam* = "humanity," it is important that women accept the vocation of that process and learn to claim voice and language for that purpose. Women's naming of self, context, and creation is necessary for the full participation of humanity in the ongoing co-creative process with God. Helping women—and all those who have been denied the right to voice and language—to name reality in their "mother tongue" is an important dimension to the personal and cultural transformation that is the purpose of feminist pastoral counseling.

As women take on the vocation of naming themselves, one another, their contexts, and God, they are creating revolutionary change. Those things that have been assumed to be true—where the "partial has paraded as the whole"—are called into question.[15] New perspectives and realities emerge that change the world. Mary Daly says that this is the primary theological task when she writes that

> there is a dynamism in the ontological affirmation of self that reaches out toward the nameless God. In hearing and naming ourselves out of the depths, women are naming toward God, which is what theology always should have been about. Unfortunately it tended to stop at fixing names upon God, which deafened us to our own potential for self-naming.[16]

It becomes very clear, then, that authentic voice and the power to name are key elements for health—personally, relationally, and culturally—in the lives of girls and women.

Contexts Related to Women's Loss of Voice

The importance of voice cannot be overstated in terms of women's potential health. When I use the term *voice,* I am not just talking about a willingness to speak. I am also talking about the ability to find language and models that validate one's own experience and communicate a sense of entitlement to that experience as authentic and important. Joan Bolker defines the issue well when she writes, "What is 'voicelessness?' It is the inability to write or speak our central concerns. Or, to write, but as disembodied personae who bear no relation to our inherent voices: We say only what we think we're expected to say, and end up telling lies or half-truths. Voicelessness is also feeling powerless to speak and sensing that there is no one out there who speaks for us. . . . There is an epidemic of voicelessness among women."[17] To trace the loss of voice in girls and women, I will look at three of the contexts in which the ability to speak with authority, even to oneself, is threatened.

Language

Much has been written on the elements of the English language that tend to erase female experience or at least make it less important and less visible than male experience. Attention to the sexist nature of much of the English language was part of the first wave of feminist thought and it has certainly been a central part of the second wave. Most linguists would agree that language not only reflects cultural and personal realities but also shapes and even determines them. As stated earlier, narratives are created out of the language and frameworks available to them and if there is no language for an experience, it is very difficult to story it into either social or personal life. By the late 1970s there were numerous books and articles from linguistic, sociological, and theological disciplines describing the sexist implications of retaining male "generic" language. Yet despite the enormous amount of research on this topic, in the new millennium one can still listen to the evening news or a political speech and hear so-called generic male language used to represent humanity, male and female.

There is so much research available on this topic that I hesitate to explore it here. Let me just say that the large body of research from neurolinguistic and sociolinguistic perspectives has demonstrated that children and adults who hear so-called generic language like "man" or "mankind" do not think generically. In studies done of schoolchildren and adults, when words using the generic "man" are used as part of the task instruction, the male characteristic is predominant in the accomplishment of the task. For example, people asked to draw pictures of cave men tend to create pictures of prehistoric males, whereas those who are asked to draw pictures of prehistoric people create a much more equal mix of male and female pictures.[18] When girls and women consistently hear words that do not reflect or name them or their experiences, then several things happen. First, girls (and women) recognize that they are secondary in the general cultural narrative. They are included in but not as a primary subject of the cultural discourse. Second, girls (and women) do not develop adequate mental representations reflecting active, self-authoring women as key actors in the world. And third, girls (and women) learn that the they are not entitled to self-naming. This is reflected not only in generic language, but also in the use of male names for family names and in the use of male language as normative for most socially valued occupations (doctor versus woman doctor, congressman, chairman, and so forth). Not only do girls and women learn a lot about themselves by being surrounded by limited language options, but they learn a great deal about the culture and their expected roles in it. As Karen Adams and Norma Ware state, "One of the most intriguing characteristics of language is that it acts as a kind of social mirror, reflecting the organization and dynamics of the society of which it is a part."[19]

So language and—even more powerfully—imagery, available to us through our schoolbooks, our entertainment, our parents, teachers, and friends, our sermons and church school curricula—give us the raw material and the frameworks out of which we develop our personal, relational, and cultural narratives. These provide the discourses of power and position out of which we create our lives. Given these discourses created by naming males as authors, actors, and norms, girls and women run a grave risk of living in positions of subjection rather than in positions as subjects.[20] And because core narratives shape the meaning we make out of future experience, we generally have no language or framework within which to understand the issues of power and discourse at stake.

Language that does not reflect women as primary subjects in the culture and works against forming imagery that frames women as active, valuable, and entitled members of society will contribute to girls' and women's loss of voice. Bons-Storm makes this point well when she writes, "In our society one discourse is the most powerful: the discourse in the name of the Father, which means the discourse of those persons who can identify with White, well-educated, heterosexual males and their interests." She also says, "The vocabularies of women and the vocabulary of 'the proper way of speaking about one's life as a woman' are often different."[21]

Loss of Selfhood

Carol Gilligan notes that girls up to puberty are more optimistic than are boys and yet around adolescence the rate of depression (equal between boys and girls in childhood) skyrockets for girls. She also reports on a national survey by Greenberg-Lake Analysis Group in 1991, which found that "white girls tend to experience a drop in feelings of self-worth around the age of eleven, Latinas experience a more precipitous drop a few years later—around the beginning of high school—and black girls tend to sustain their feelings of self-worth, but at the expense, perhaps, of dissociating themselves from school and disagreeing publicly with their teachers."[22]

Based on the work of the Stone Center to the Harvard Women's Project, several researchers have identified a crisis period in adolescent girls' lives where they begin to lose, or at least risk losing, their voices. Gilligan, with her colleagues in the Harvard Women's Project, has discovered that adolescence is a crisis time for girls. She makes this point poignantly when she writes that

> girls' initiation into womanhood has often meant an initiation into a kind of selflessness, which is associated with care and connection, but also with a loss of psychological vitality and courage. To become selfless means to lose relationship or to lose one's voice in relationships. This loss of relationship leads to a muting of voice, leaving inner feelings of sadness and isolation. In effect, the young woman becomes shut up within herself.[23]

Ellyn Kaschak has developed an interesting paradigm, set up to stand as a counterstory to the Oedipus complex of Freud's developmental schema. In this paradigm, adolescent girls have to learn how to be "feminine" rather than female. Kaschak remarks that "becoming a woman involves learning a part, complete with costumes, make-up and lines. Learning to behave like a woman involves learning to sit, stand, and talk in the appropriate ways and to make them appear natural, to have them become natural or, more aptly, second nature."[24] Women are taught to create a false identity and then to forget that it is false.

The Antigone phase itself goes from midchildhood through adulthood. Kaschak describes its ingredients as a denial of birth and origins; danger embedded in pleasure; denial of authentic physicality that results in both invisibility and hypervisibility; overly permeable boundaries; physically based self-hatred with a focused concern on appearance as central to value; self-esteem based on self-denial; compulsively relationally oriented with one's own identity as secondary; and an identification with the "indeterminate observer," which means that she uses her eyes to see from a male's perspective.[25] These, again, are powerful descriptors of women's identity/loss of identity through the cultural rules of patriarchy.

The first point implied by the Antigone paradigms, the identification of woman and body, is extremely negative for women's lives. As Kaschak says, "In losing control of the meanings of their own bodies, of the bodies themselves, women lose even more—the opportunity to develop a well-integrated sense of self that is more internally than externally defined, that is relatively stable rather than subject to redefinition based on changes in appearance or evaluations thereof, and that is grounded in an accurate testing of abilities and skills rather than passive evaluation."[26] She goes on to say that "women, as a result, have a strong tendency to a particular sort of disconnection from their own bodies and their own cognitive/affective/physical experience—that is a tendency to watch themselves through male eyes."[27]

The second point is that of the nature of women's relatedness. Kaschak suggests that women become "compulsively related" in this developmental process. She suggests that women in this society are "driven to relatedness" by the process of alienation from themselves.[28] Lyn Mikel Brown and Gilligan, in their longitudinal study of girls moving from age eight into their early teen years, found that younger girls were in significant relationships with their peers and would speak directly and clearly about violations and injustices done to themselves or to their friends. By the age of eleven the same girls were moving away from their own knowledge, using the phrase "I don't know" much more frequently and expressing implicit and explicit knowledge of the rules they were to follow in order to be acceptable and "in relationship." Brown and Gilligan summarize their findings by saying that

> at the crossroads of adolescence, the girls in our study describe a relational impasse that is familiar to many women: a paradoxical or dizzying sense of having to give up relationship for the sake of "relationships." Because this taking of oneself out of relationship in order to protect oneself and have relationships forces an inner division or chasm, it makes a profound psychological shift. . . .Women's psychological development within patriarchal societies and male-voiced cultures is inherently traumatic.[29]

Many feminist scholars in women's development agree that adolescence is a crucial and generally traumatic life stage for women: a time of closing down. They say that adolescence is a shaky time for males, too; the difference is that men seem to emerge from their traumatic adolescence with an intact and generally positive identity, but women do not. Both the rates of depression in women and the general drop in self-esteem, especially for European American and Latina young women, demonstrate this reality.

Brown suggests that during early adolescence girls learn what it means to be a "good" woman, fearing that if they don't follow the rules of "femininity," they will experience abandonment, exclusion, or ridicule. The recent publication of books of "rules" for how young women can attract men makes these rules explicit, but my experience has been that girls and women—almost without exception—know what those rules are quite accurately. And those rules about being feminine—quiet, nurturing, relational, supportive, full of caring feelings and empathy but rarely angry, and so on—teach girls and women how to be part of the "supporting cast" rather than actors or authors with voice and authority.

When one doesn't follow the rules, there is a price to pay, often the kind of humiliation or retribution talked about in chapter 1 in Mary Ballou and Nancy W. Gabalac's paradigm of harmful adaptation. Maria Harris names the problem, saying that "this dilemma—and the choices it suggests—can be described thus: (a) either to stop or hide one's own voice in order to become, or thought of as, a 'nice girl,' and so become alienated from oneself; or (b) to refuse to be silent and take the risk, perceived and real in this society, of becoming alienated socially and politically, of being ostracized as, for example, 'brash,' 'loud,' 'aggressive,' 'bossy.'"[30]

Some girls do take the latter choice, refusing to give up themselves or their knowledge for the sake of a false identity as a "perfect woman" and the implications of that identity. Studies indicate that African American girls in particular are better able to resist the seduction of this ideal, in part because they are more aware of its falseness and because they are raised in a community that teaches girls that, in order to survive racism, they need to be able to speak out against cultural lies. For some of these young women, the resistance they are able to express to the dual realities of racism and sexism helps create possibilities of real transformation in their lives. As Tracy Robinson and Janie Victoria Ward discuss, however, there is a difference between resistance for survival, which often has short-term gains but long-term problems, and resistance for liberation. They suggest that the role of the community is to foster the kind of resistance in young African American women that will lead to long-term liberation, not just survival.[31] Beverly Joan Smith writes, "As an African American, I grew up within a particular cultural context that values voice. African American culture demands that individual voices be connected to the whole and not just to go solo and fly off somewhere." She goes on to say that African American girls "don't fall prey to the 'rules of femininity' as much as do European American girls because they don't fall victim to the myth of Prince Charming."[32] These writers feel that living in an African American community helped them to resist these cultural lies about the promise of "true femininity" because their role of voice in resisting racism was encouraged.

As discussed earlier, different girls and women experience different levels of threat to self and voice from these different contexts. African American young women seem better able to resist this de-selfing process so evident in the lives of young European American women. They are, however, more subject to threat from the next context, which I call credibility.

Credibility

Many young women learn in adolescence what it means to be a "good" woman and to "forget what they know." They give up the ability to be in authentic relationship for the sake of being related in ways that minimize the risks of exclusion and abandonment. This seems to be a mostly subtle process that most girls identify with in a positive way—claiming, in Brown and Gilligan's studies, that their previous answers (from childhood) were "stupid" and that they see things more clearly as adolescents.

Many of the young women in their study were able to identify a vague sense of disquiet, where they knew that if they expressed themselves honestly, especially in ways that might hurt other people's feelings, their relationships would be lost.[33] Even when there was no evidence that the relationship in question was that fragile, the conviction that honest expression of feelings would lead to exclusion was maintained.

Yet even when women do learn to speak their feelings and thoughts, especially ones that seem to be counter to their gender training, there is a high risk that they will not be believed or that they will be dismissed. This is the main premise of Bons-Storm's book, *The Incredible Woman*. Her data indicates that women who have gone to pastoral counselors to tell their stories of abuse, of depression, of despair with the conditions of their lives, have often experienced being perceived as sick or troubled or deceitful rather than as finally taking the risk to tell the truth about their lives. Bons-Storm writes, "When a woman tells a story about her experience from her own position and her own point of view, and in her own words, particularly when she presents herself as a rebel, she is considered to represent chaos, unreason, madness. So, she is not to be believed or taken seriously. On the contrary, she has to undergo treatment in order to be adjusted better to a father-oriented reality."[34]

This experience is especially common for African American adolescent girls, who manage to maintain a higher self-esteem through adolescence—often at considerable cost—and yet find that they are ignored, dismissed, and disbelieved in their speaking in adulthood. Joan Martin states that "we ought to understand one thing plainly. The ways in which white feminists have critiqued the 'right speech of womanhood' making all women silent, is really a critique about white women's experience and is fundamentally dissimilar to black feminists' rendering of black women's speech as speech that was 'not acknowledged as significant speech.'"[35]

The combination of racism and sexism makes it more likely that African American women and other women of color will be dismissed or disbelieved even though they maintain both voice and language to speak about their experience. Martin quotes bell hooks as they consider this problem of credibility. Hooks writes that there is a need for black women's voices "to emerge, [not] from silence into speech, but to change the nature and direction of our speech, to make a speech that compels our listeners, one that is heard."[36]

Helping women to be heard in their lives means helping women to believe that they have the right to be heard and believed. This is a difficult task. Bolker, writing about how hard it is to help empower women students to engage in creative, autobiographical writing, says that "in order to write, we have to believe someone is listening, even if it's only ourselves. Women are so often not attended to as we grow up—a phenomenon amply documented in a recent study by the American Association of University Women, 'How Schools Shortchange Girls,' that we stop listening to ourselves, let alone believing anyone else might be interested in what we have to say."[37] The issues of entitlement to voice and speech are deeply buried in the training to be "good" girls and women and in the mandate never to say anything that might risk rupturing relationships with those around you. In this, women are told they have no power and that they have enormous power—the power to single-handedly destroy the relationships in which they exist. Women believe that they do have this power because they know that their relationships have not been built, for the most part, on authentic self-knowing and self-sharing. Girls and women are in a difficult double bind here. And, as Bolker goes on to say, "The worry that the creative act of writing, or speaking out, will rupture connectedness is not a fantasy. From the inside out we know that our strong feelings may do just that."[38]

So a vicious circle is created. Girls, especially European American girls, are taught not to know what they know or say what is authentic but might be disconnecting. Girls learn to believe that their authentic voices are not authentic and they stop listening even to themselves. As they stop believing they are worth listening to, the world confirms this by disbelieving, dismissing, and ignoring them if they do attempt to say anything that is real. There are many examples of dismissal and disbelief, but one of the areas of experience most frequently affected by these is the realm of women's emotions.

Women are expected to be "emotional," especially in terms of their capacity for empathy and nurture. They are expected to be tender-hearted and sensitive. These are included in the rules for appropriately engendered womanhood. Yet the expression of even these feelings is often grounds for dismissal. Emotion is often seen as counterpoint to reason, and reason—in the dualistic system of our culture—is considered to be more accurate and useful. Women who make statements based on empathy or compassion are often affirmed as "real women" at the same time that they are dismissed as not being able to offer a valuable strategy for engaging in decision making. Dismissal, which is the reality of not being taken seriously and not being able to get a response appropriate to that which has been communicated, happens with all kinds of women's feelings and maybe especially with women's anger. As Sue Campbell puts it, "If no one takes my anger seriously by making any attempt to account for his or her behavior or to change it, but instead characterizes me as upset and oversensitive, I may be unsure, in retrospect, of how best to describe my behavior."[39] Women tend to accept the evaluation of others who dismiss them and even to apologize for expressions of strong feeling. Campbell goes on to articulate the double bind: "women who are not emotional are cold. Women who are emotional are expressing themselves in such a way as to be dismissable." This is an unresolvable problem.

Since much of what happens in the counseling process has to do with the expression of feelings, this becomes a particular problem for counselors. Bons-Storm suggests that much of the disbelief that women experience in pastoral counseling is not disbelief as such but evaluation of the stories as evidence of disturbance. She writes, "Women's stories about their confusion, anger, and depression are frequently seen as manifestations of the unbalanced and irrational way they deal with reality. The supposed irrationality of women has to be treated in order to make women 'well-adjusted' again and that means women should play the roles that are prescribed in the sociocultural narrative, where they are placed under the wing of rational men."[40] It is not uncommon for women in counseling to believe this assessment of their authentic voice and to find relief in the assignment of a "diagnosis" which at least keeps them from being invisible. Often there is this sense of resignation. A healthier response is rage at being dismissed. Audre Lorde said in 1984 that "Women of Color in America have grown up within a symphony of anger, at being silenced, at being unchosen, at knowing that when we survive, it is in spite of a world that takes for granted our lack of humanness, and which hates our very existence outside of its service."[41] Some groups of women have learned how to keep their rage alive, yet often at high costs.

These contexts of language, loss of self, and credibility exist in one form or another in women's lives. As we have seen, women of differing particularities experience loss of or denial of voice in different ways. Yet, as Bolker states, "Voicelessness is something that women share across class, race, and the many other categories that divide us, as we share the prevalence of sexual abuse and the fear of being raped. Women's silence is ubiquitous and must be broken at every level."[42] The training for voicelessness begins in childhood, as was briefly explored in chapter 1. The reinforcement for voicelessness continues through adulthood. The legacy of voicelessness is passed not just through the culture, but also from mother to daughter as she lives out her voicelessness as a model for her children. It is for the sake of multiple generations that voicelessness in women must be challenged, resisted, and transformed.

Resistance

Carol Lakey Hess, in *Caretakers of Our Common House*, asks the question, "Can caring families and communities of faith, specifically in the church, make a difference in the outcome of my daughter's development and in the development of others girls and women?" Her answer is a "resounding yes," but she warns that this will not be easy or natural. "The church has a checkered history with regard to girls and women; though Jewish and Christian history is laced with protest against misogyny, these are 'thin traditions,' which often have been repressed. Churches are too often girl-denying institutions." She clarifies this statement by saying, "It is not, however, flagrant misogyny that is the biggest threat to my daughter's future. . . . It is implicit and unrecognized 'girl-denying' that threatens the future of girls reared in mainline churches."[43]

Families, educational institutions, and churches have regularly participated in the three contexts discussed above: language, loss of self, and credibility. Today, more than in the recent past, much of the self-erasing, voice-denying, and dismissive processes are subtle and therefore harder to resist. Girls may look like they're doing "fine" and yet still be in the process of denying their own experiences and goals.[44] Girls and women learn not to know that who they are and what they speak are in conflict. Part of the process of loss of voice is not knowing that it is happening. Gilligan suggests that a patriarchal culture depends on dissociation in women: "a process of inner division that makes it possible for a woman not to know what she knows, not to think what she thinks, and not to feel what she feels. Dissociation acts through experience and memory, and when these cuts become part of cultural history, women lose the grounds of their experience and with it their sense of reality."[45] It is difficult to resist this process when any counterstory to it feels either unreal or, as Bons-Storm says, crazy and pathological.

It seems to me that there are several pathways of resistance to loss of voice and self in girls and women. And not only do they work for the empowerment of girls and women, but they also work against a girl-denying patriarchal culture.

Gilligan and her colleagues have been able to document that—at least for European American girls—there is a clear turning point as they approach adolescence where they move from being in touch with their feelings, thoughts, goals, and interests to being unable or unwilling to know or say what they have previously known. What happens at the edge of childhood that works against girls? Somehow girls learn that they will only be valuable and welcome if they are willing to take a primary role of maintaining and supporting relationships and, even then, they shouldn't count on having much of a primary role in the culture. Girls trade what they have for what seems to be more acceptable—they trade their "selves" for the possibility of being connected to the world in a meaningful way.

One pathway of resistance for girls at this developmental crisis point is actively encouraging girls to take the risk of truth telling. This sounds like an easy solution, but our expectations of "good girls" are deeply internalized. Truth telling is often confrontational, messy—even chaotic—and is rarely reinforced. We, as adults, would often rather hear what will make us feel good or happy rather than thoughts and feelings that necessitate negotiation, or face hard truths. The temptation to discourage voice in girls is as strong as the temptation to dismiss girls who don't follow the rules. Especially for adult women, who have been deeply grounded in the rules of ideal womanhood, it is difficult to encourage our daughters to do the very things that we fear will cause disastrous consequences of disconnection and chaos. As a result, deliberate choices have to be made in our school systems and in our families and in our churches to encourage girls to be truth tellers, disrupters, and active voices of resistance to kyriarchal pressures.[46] We, as parents, pastors, and educators, need to practice (and teach our daughters to practice) what Hess calls "hard dialogue and deep connections."[47] She suggests that girls and women have to learn how to support one another deeply but not to base that support on conformity to each other or to the cultural rules of womanhood. Hess calls for places of safety where women can be with one another and learn how to question and challenge their engendering while at the same time they can practice speaking their truths to one another.

In the midst of that we need to be able to teach our daughters how to engage in active resistance and we need to teach them early, before fear of disconnection and exclusion shape their ability to hear. Hess talks about two kinds of resistance—creative resistance and bold resistance. Creative resistance is the kind that uses the rules of kyriarchy in subversive ways. Kathleen D. Billman talks about Shiprah and Puah, the midwives ordered by Pharaoh to make sure that Israelite women did not safely give birth to sons and who found ways to help healthy Israelite boy babies be born by using Pharaoh's fears against him. They told him that the Hebrew women had babies so fast that the midwives often couldn't get there in time. They found ways to disobey Pharaoh without sacrificing their own lives.[48] Often it is necessary to learn to be subversive in order to both survive and develop a sense of agency. Subversion can be a very effective strategy. It may not, however, enable a stronger sense of self and self-esteem to develop.

Hess understands bold resistance to be that of direct opposition to the powers of harm. She uses the example of Rosa Parks, who made the decision to stand directly against racism by refusing to follow the rules (law) about where she could sit on the city bus. This kind of resistance builds a strong sense of self but also needs a great deal of support or the costs can be devastating. Bons-Storm states that "a woman cannot remain a rebel if she is alone, for she runs the risk of being crushed by the dominant discourse. She will be declared mad or bad, disobedient to the law of the Father."[49] Girls need lots of support, as do women, if we are going to encourage them to resist the cultural pressures that would form them into patriarchy's women.

Tracy Robinson and Janie Victoria Ward talk about two other forms of resistance drawn from their observations of African American girls—resistance for survival and resistance for liberation. They suggest that African American girls are more likely to have developed a kind of voice of resistance because they are raised in communities where resistance to oppression is a valid communal discourse. Although the support has not necessarily been for resistance against sexism, it has allowed girls to maintain and practice an authoritative voice. Because there are so many places where African American girls and women are likely to be ignored, denigrated, and dismissed, however, the resistance is often fueled by considerable anger. This, along with other complex factors, say Robinson and

Ward, may cause African American girls to choose strategies of resistance for survival that do them harm in the long run (dropping out of school, becoming pregnant, etc.). Robinson and Ward conclude that African American girls must be helped to find methods of resistance that serve their liberation in the long run. This requires an enormous commitment to young women who have difficulty seeing a positive future. As Gilligan states, "Hope is a dangerous emotion because it creates such vulnerability to disappointment and the process of change is never straightforward." The need for hope in a liberating future must be the source for helping girls and women develop appropriate and effective methods of resistance to the loss of self and voice.

A Narrative Approach
to Helping Women Come to Voice

As Bons-Storm notes, we often get bold resisters in the counseling office. Women who resist patriarchy's rules for womanhood generally pay the price of being seen as "maladjusted" (understood to be a negative state by a kyriarchal culture) and disturbed. As was said earlier, if there is inadequate support for resistance, then it is hard for a resister to maintain a healthy sense of self. Resisters may come to counseling to find out if they are well.

Nonresisters also come to counseling. Nonresisters are often in much more psychological and spiritual trouble than are resisters, but they look healthier. Nonresisters are often depressed. They may also be victims of domestic or sexual abuse. They are generally silenced and know little about having an authentic voice.

There are also semiresisters—women who have played by the rules for the most part but have never entirely lost the knowledge that they are playing a role that isn't entirely them. These women come to counseling in hope that they might find a way to become whole again—to reunite self-knowledge and outward behavior.

Counseling can be helpful for each of these groups. There are also other ways for them to find health. There are many forms of "corrective action" that don't require a counselor's office.[50] Friends, consciousness-raising groups, truth-telling church circles, eye-opening educational experiences—all of these may serve as corrective action for the silencing process of the culture. Yet with a culture that is increasingly unwilling to provide listening ears, it is often difficult for a woman to find a context that helps to "hear her into speech."

Narrative Theory

A narrative approach to pastoral counseling with women is a significant resource, particularly in the context of the need to find empowering stories to resist oppressive narratives. Narrative counseling theory is grounded in a constructionist set of assumptions. This means that people construct meaning and that it is the meaning that people attribute to themselves and their experiences that constitute both identity and the development of resources for living life. We make meaning and live our lives through the stories that we have created to give our lives coherence. Those stories come from our families, our institutions, our histories (personal and social), and our culture. As the dominant discourses of the culture intersect with our own experiences, a core narrative is formed that shapes the way we understand and build each new experience into the story. Problems in our lives gain force when our guiding narratives do not give us the perspective or the resources we need to move our lives in directions that we would prefer. Wendy Drewery and John Winslade say, "Often it seems to us, problems are such because we feel unable to move them—we have lost agency in our life. What is happening is that the stories we are telling ourselves about what is happening are disabling. These are stories in which the client is positioned, or subjected, she is not the actor but the passive recipient of the given positioning."[51] This does not mean that life circumstances are not real but that in facing those life circumstances the person's core narrative does not provide the meaning that would allow novelty or creativity in resolving or resisting those circumstances. Our interpretation of reality and the meaning we make out of it are socially constructed, according to narrative theory. Therefore we have the capacity to shift meanings and thus change the options available to us in dealing with life circumstances. The new reality offers a way of resisting the problem that has felt irresistible because it has been so deeply rooted in the narrative. A person comes for counseling most often because her current narrative is problem-saturated or too narrow to see a future with positive options.

 ; a particularly significant issue for people who have experienced
lization and oppression within the dominant discourses of the

culture. As we have noted, women do experience living within a patriarchal and kyriarchal discourse that challenges, damages, and dismisses their voices in a variety of ways depending on other particularities in the woman's life. A narrative approach, which is based on helping the counselee to find voice and self-authoring and, thus, different meanings and possibilities for life, is a powerful resource. Drewery and Winslade state that "the narrative counselor looks for alternative stories that are enabling—that allow the client to speak in her own voice and to work on the problem herself. This process can be described as repositioning, or reclaiming the voice of the client. We often use the terms speaking and voice as metaphors for the agency of the client. We believe that stories that are spoken in the voice of the client are experienced as more enabling than stories that tell the client's story for her. The narrative therapist's objective, then, is to reposition the client as the speaker or teller of her own story."[52] A therapeutic strategy, which minimizes the external authority of the counselor and maximizes the agency and authority of the counselee, will be most useful to women who live with constant challenges to voice and credibility.

Before I go on to talk about the process of deconstructive listening I want to emphasize two points about narrative therapy that were made in chapter 2. First, narrative therapy is not primarily a set of techniques or a science of behavioral change. It is a philosophy grounded in a belief that deep within their own stories people have the resources and possibilities to create less problematic and more productive lives—often called preferred narratives. The narrative-oriented counselor has a strong conviction about the authority and agency of the other. The primary stance of the counselor in narrative therapy is of a compassionate, curious, and respectful listener who pays very careful attention to the story in order to find subplots that assist the counselee in resisting problem-saturated narratives and oppressive discourses. The counselor believes in empowering agency in the counselee and thus creates a counseling environment in which the counselee has primary agency in the therapeutic relationship.

Second, narrative therapy assumes that people are not problems. The most basic truth of this approach is that people are people and problems are problems. A counselee has a relationship with a problem but she is not the problem. The whole premise of deconstructive listening is to help the counselee separate herself from the problem so that she can better resist it. The work of deconstructive listening is to take a strong advocacy stand with the counselee against the problem. The counselor unhesitatingly ascribes the problems in the person's life not to a diagnosis of deficits in that person, but to the strength of the problem that seduces the counselee into forgetting the kinds of resources she has to resist or resolve it.

These two fundamental premises of narrative counseling—that people have within them the knowledge and the resources to create a preferred narrative and thus a new life, and that people have relationships with problems but are not problems themselves—form the basis for deconstructive listening. This form of listening does two important things for counselees seeking to find voice and agency. First, it creates a safe, respectful place with a person who has no other agenda than to listen very carefully as an advocate for the counselee. Second, it immediately functions to displace and challenge dominant discourses that have labeled the person as the problem and her resistance to the culture as pathology. So narrative counseling with women begins with feminist listening—a combination of empathic, validating listening and deconstructive listening.

Feminist Listening

When a girl or woman has learned to distrust either her voice or her ability to be credible, she loses confidence in her own judgment and in her own sense of self. She is vulnerable to being named by others and to living out her life as dictated by the script of dominant cultural discourses that have not been formed with her best interests in mind. For a counselor (or anyone) to listen deeply to one who has been deprived of voice or authority, believing whatever she says and allowing her to name and define the problems that she experiences, creates a novelty that in itself empowers and strengthens. The power of listening has long been known in feminist circles. Morton's famous phrase, "hearing one another into speech," and the documented effectiveness of women's consciousness-raising groups confirm the usefulness of the listening context.

The key elements of this kind of woman-affirming listening are belief, affirmation, and education. The woman is believed because her dominant experience has often been that she is not believable. This is a vital aspect of the counseling process. We, in the counseling fields, have tended to listen to people with more of an ear to disbelief, or at least to flaws and inconsistencies as symptoms of a problem. Drewery and Winslade point out that "the success of Western psychology has become its limitation: in the mental health area in particular, we have learned to focus on personal deficits in ways that speak of failure rather than accomplishment, that produce social hierarchies (experts who often appear to know more about people's lives than they do themselves), and that erode our sense of communal interdependence and common purpose."[53] Yet belief in what the counselee is saying is fundamental to helping someone gain both voice and agency. Alan Parry suggests that being heard and believed in the counseling room means that the counselee's unique perception of things is being validated. The novelty of this experience, he suggests, "tends to be corrective for someone whose life has been one of invalidation involved in any relationship in which the other's description overrides the person's own experience of a given event."[54] Bons-Storm says boldly that, for a feminist counselor, it is worth the risk of being deceived to believe in one's women counselees. If a lie is told, then it becomes part of the story and the question of why the lie was needed becomes a question the counselee must struggle with.[55]

So believing the counselee is a necessary starting place for the pastoral counselor of women. It is also necessary to affirm the woman's labor of gaining voice and resolving problems in her life. This affirmation is not a cheerleading process. Rather, it is based on the belief that the counselee has the resources she needs within her own narrative. She has survived and struggled against the problems she is facing and the resources she has used in those struggles are still available to her. In narrative theory, the contradictions and inconsistencies of the narrative are not used to identify deficits, they are used to affirm gaps in the problem narrative and thus possibilities for alternative stories that are less full of problems. Affirmation of the counselee's work as well as affirmation of her infinite resourcefulness in making meaning and creating new directions for herself are central to this work.

So narrative counselors are not neutral in their work with counselees. They take a strong stand with the counselee against the problem. And they are very willing to help a counselee look at the dominant discourses of the culture that have served as a framework for problem-saturated narratives. Mary Sykes Wylie says that for David White, the founder of narrative therapy, "the personal is and must be, deeply embedded in the political. The stories of the people he sees are of personal struggle and transcendence, no doubt, but in White's eyes they are also unmistakably tales of power politics, the 'politics of local relationship' as well as the larger social politics of gender, class, professional, and institutional dominance."[56] Narrative counselors feel free to bring up the nature of dominant discourses as they function against the best interests of the counselee. Although the counselor does not operate out of an expert position, she or he does serve as a co-author with the counselee in investigating problem narratives and with constructing alternative narratives out of the substories of the person's life.

Deconstructive Listening

Deconstructive listening is a way of joining with the counselee by paying careful attention to the story that she tells. It means listening in a believing, affirming, and culturally alert way. But it also means that the counselor is listening to the story not in order to solve the problem, but to discover the problem as the counselee describes it and to find ways to disempower the problem by empowering the resources of the counselee. This kind of listening has several phases. First, deconstructive listening works intentionally to externalize the problem from the person. This means that the problem is changed from being an adjective that describes the person (e.g., "I'm a depressed person") to being a noun that plagues the person (e.g., "I struggle with depression"). This seemingly simple linguistic shift has profound implications. The problem narrative often has such a grip on the counselee that it and the counselee have become one ("I am depressed," "I am alcoholic," "I am no good"). Externalizing separates the counselee and the problem in such a way that the counselee and counselor join together against the problem. This kind of process shakes loose the hold of the problem narrative and almost immediately makes room for a host of alternative frames for the counselee. Deconstruction is the process of investigating and unpacking ideas that have been taken for granted as truths. In order to do that, gaps have to be created in the narrative so that there is space to look at what has been assumed.

The second part of the process of externalizing is naming the problem. For some it is enough to label it merely as "the problem" or "trouble," but for others it can be helpful to personify the problem with a name or a characteristic. One author described a client who was in a life and death struggle with "Al" (alcohol and the culture of alcohol consumption), who was a charming and seductive "guy" from whom she needed to get a divorce.[57] The more that the problem can be externalized, the more likely the counselee can generate resources to resist it. Jill Freedman and Gene Combs say that they "believe that listening with an externalizing attitude has a powerful deconstructive effect. It biases us to interact differently with people than we would if we saw them as intrinsically problematic. It creates a different 'receiving context' for people's stories, one in which we can work to understand their problems without seeing them as problematic or pathological. In this kind of context, the content and meaning of people's stories almost always becomes less restrictive."[58]

The third element of deconstructive listening is looking for places where there is a "unique outcome" to the problem narrative. In other words, the counselor looks for times when the ruling discourse was resisted or where actions predicted by the narrative weren't taken. For example, if the discourse suggests that this person is too overcome by depression to take action on her own behalf, yet she comes to a counseling session deliberately seeking help for the depression, there is an inconsistency in the narrative. The narrative counselor would note that by asking a question about it like, "How were you able to get up the energy to come into the office today given the power that depression has been exerting over your life lately?" Narrative counselors ask a lot of questions in the listening process—questions that emerge out of places where the listening has revealed a potential resource or alternative story. This kind of listening demonstrates a high level of counselor commitment to the life of the counselee. The listening is very focused and alert to any new possibilities. Drewery and Winslade suggest that this approach requires "intentionality on the part of the therapist, skill in language use, and systematic attention to the hidden assumptions in the ways people tell their stories."[59]

These three elements of deconstructive listening—externalizing, naming the problem, and looking for unique outcomes or deconstructive possibilities within the story—work together to plant the seeds for gaining voice, agency, and authority in the naming of one's own life and in the meaning making of life experiences. Problems are resisted or resolved as new narratives are built that tell the story of a person successfully able to move toward her preferred life. And these new narratives are built out of the counselee's experiences that have not had a place in her core narrative because they were dismissed or ignored when they didn't fit with the dominant discourse. This emerging narrative (which will be discussed further in chapter 5) doesn't eliminate the harsh realities that she may need to face, but she can now face them with a sense of being a subject in her narrative rather than a character written and manipulated by outside forces. This is what gaining voice is about.

In the post-modern sensibility, the story is set free to perform as simply a story that allows for re-invention as the story teller finds a voice rooted in the person's own experience and in the connection of her story to those of others, and to larger stories of culture and humanity. The realization that we are all characters in each other's stories as well as in our own reminds us that our stories go forward as we act in ways that also forward the stories of others. A hermeneutics for such therapy validates and questions all points of view so that they do not harden into stories that are assumed to be objectively true.[60]

In other words, this is not an individualistic kind of counseling theory. It is helping people to actively lay claim to voice and participation in the larger stories of the culture. The opposite is also true. Any person's private story of oppression, marginalization, or harm becomes a story of the culture and limits the possibilities for that culture to be whole. Working to loosen dominant discourses of oppression and dismissal in the lives of women also works to loosen the power of the dominant discourse in the society as a whole. The purpose of gaining voice is not to drown out those other voices in the community, but to enable all to be co-authors and co-creators with each other and with God. We are not only carriers of our own stories, we are part of each other's stories within an ultimate story of God's ongoing narrative of creation.

four

Coming to Voice in the Context of Intimate Violence

Nowhere are the issues of women's loss of voice, language, and credibility as clear as they are in the dynamics of domestic or intimate violence. As we saw in chapter 1, we live in a culture that is saturated with violence of all kinds. We are troubled by the unpredictability of street crime and we worry about being its victim. Yet for women the worry is not on the street—it's in our homes. Women are more likely to be assaulted in their own homes by someone with whom they have or have had a trusting, caring relationship than they are to be assaulted on the streets in the most violent American cities.[1] A study by the United States Justice Department reported that child abuse and domestic violence account for one-third of the total cost of crime.[2] According to the Bureau of Justice, intimates commit 13 percent of all rapes, robberies, and assaults where most of the violence is assault. Men are more likely to be the victims of violent crime in general, but women are more than ten times more likely to be the victim of violence by an intimate.[3] Most of us have seen these kinds of statistics. But there has been an overwhelming silence in response to them in most of our churches and communities. Somehow, we believe these numbers don't have much to do with us or with those we know. We don't want to know that they may be much closer to home than we think.

Judith Lewis Herman, in her work on trauma, suggests that facing the realities of intimate violence and its usual traumatic consequences is much harder than staying blind to it. She says, "It is very tempting to take the side of the perpetrator. All the perpetrator asks is that the bystander do nothing. He appeals to the universal desire to see, hear, and speak no evil. The victim, on the contrary, asks the bystander to bear the burden of pain. The victim demands action, engagement, and remembering."[4] We, as a culture and as a church, have consistently made the decision to side with the perpetrator through our silence. In order to do that we have also had to silence the victims of intimate violence, usually through disbelief. By making the victims of intimate violence either invisible or incredible we revictimize them. One of the keys to recovery from the traumatizing effects of intimate violence is the ability to remember and tell the truth about these experiences of betrayal and *to be believed*. Without that community of belief, the trauma does not get resolved.

Herman points out that there are a variety of tactics that the perpetrator uses to encourage bystanders to ignore or disbelieve the victim. Those tactics include secrecy as a primary strategy. Most victims of intimate violence are coerced or threatened into silence about their abuse. Whether we are talking about child sexual abuse, wife battering, or partner rape, secrecy is always the starting point. If secrecy doesn't work, perpetrators move on to attack the credibility of the victim. This can happen through blaming the victim, denying the occurrence, or explaining or rationalizing why it wasn't an act of violence or abuse.[5] And as a culture we are all too ready to accept this process of discrediting the victim. Carol J. Adams notes that "women and children are 'appropriate' victims in our culture, which sees the adult (white) male as the normative person. We can find cultural definitions of women and children as male property; for that reason, fathers and husbands believe they have the right to control and punish."[6]

As I worked on this chapter I heard a news story on television, a story that is not uncommon on the evening news. In the report, a twelve-year-old girl had told her parents that her pastor had been forcing her to have sex with him for the past two months. She finally broke through the fear and pressures for silence and told her parents, who took her to the hospital for treatment. The reporter then interviewed five members of the pastor's congregation. Each one supported the pastor without a word of care or concern for the child. One said, "The pastor has a beautiful wife. Of course he didn't do this." Another said, "This man has done so much good for this community. I don't know why someone would spread such vicious rumors about him." A third reported that he was busily engaged in raising money for the pastor's legal expenses. This, unfortunately, is a familiar example of the principles of secrecy, silence, and of siding with the perpetrator by not being willing to even hear the story from the victim's perspective.

The church has participated in many ways in this process of silencing victims of intimate violence. It has used theological justifications, particularly the sanctity of the family, to justify its silencing of domestic abuse victims. It has been in unquestioning collusion with patriarchy in terms of assuming the normativity (and believability) of males. And it has not wanted to participate in the kind of upheaval that it would cause to actively advocate on behalf of victims, especially since it is often the perpetrators who have the power and authority within local churches. For example, Marie M. Fortune warns pastors that when a woman comes in to tell them that her husband, who is also the chair of the board of trustees, an active church school teacher, and a substantial donor, has been battering her,

> you will not be able to believe her. No matter how well-intentioned you may be, what she is describing to you runs counter to your experience of that individual. What you have to keep in mind is that your experience with that individual is true and real for you and is public. Her experience with that individual is true and real and is private. Now with most of us, in the conflicting face of experience and information, we go with our experience. But, remember that in cases where someone is disclosing abuse by someone you know, there is another piece to this story that is the private person. Oftentimes the typical abuser has an exemplary public persona and yet in private engages in all sorts of behavior that seems unbelievable to you. Knowing that, our job is to press ahead and to believe that person—even though it doesn't fit with what we know about the abuser—so that we can be present to the victim and ultimately to the offender.[7]

It is usually more difficult for us to side against a person whom we wish to believe is innocent of this kind of behavior than it is to believe that the accusation is a lie.

It's important to look at some of the issues in the church that get in the way of being able to help make abused women both visible and believable in that context. Looking at some of the potential resources in the church to help us be witnesses for those who have been harmed is helpful as well.

Intimate Violence and the Church

Pastors, on the whole, have not been very useful to women and children who have experienced abuse in their families. Most studies about the usefulness of clergy in situations of domestic abuse find that they are rated as both the least-used resource and the least-helpful resource compared to family, friends, psychotherapists, family doctors, and social service agencies. In a recent study, researchers found that clergy effectiveness is consistently low and they speculated that this was probably due to clergy endorsement of traditional teachings concerning the sanctity of marriage. In addition, a research group sent out a two-page questionnaire to 5,700 pastors and fewer than 10 percent of the questionnaires were returned. The researchers concluded that pastors lacked interest in or were hostile to the notion of domestic abuse. They also noted that the clergy that did return their questionnaires seemed to be concerned about battered women, but indicated that they were torn by theological perspectives that seemed to be in conflict with the best interests of the women.[8] These are very serious issues if indeed clergy are feeling that they are not able to be very helpful to victims of intimate violence, especially wife battering or spousal rape, because they are trapped by theological doctrine that mandates patriarchal power. It is interesting that women who rated their pastors helpful tended to be from churches that normally addressed social problems in general and that created an environment where women felt safe in coming forward with their stories. They were also more likely to rate their pastors as helpful if they were willing to take action to intervene in the violence, not just to listen passively to the victims.[9]

Women who are committed to their religious traditions often turn to pastors for help when they experience problems in their families. Yet it is also true that women who have experienced intimate violence are much more likely to leave their religious practices and affiliations than are nonabused women. This is partly because they have experienced revictimization through silence and silencing and partly because they experience the church's betrayal as symbolic of God's betrayal. It's important to look at some of the doctrines and popular understandings of theology that work against women's safety and against justice when they have been victims.

Theological Issues

In chapter 1 several theological issues were raised that have been important in developing a feminist approach to pastoral counseling. When we look at these and other theological tenets in the concrete contexts of intimate violence, it becomes even more clear that theology and the pastoral care of a person are deeply linked. I will briefly explore a few of the most relevant theological problems here as a way to gain insight into better directions for pastoral care for victims of intimate violence.

We have already talked about problems related to an image of God that works to represent men as more godly and more normative than women, so I will not explore that further here except to say that the image of God as male or father is often a serious spiritual issue for women who have been abused by fathers or male authority figures. Helping women to explore new possibilities for their God imagery may well be an important dimension to their regaining access to the divine in their spiritual lives. Women who have been taught that God the Father is in control of the world and of their lives may have only two ways to understand God's participation in their abuse. Either God is on the side of the father(s)/husband(s) and against them for good reasons, or God is as helpless or invisible as they are and not of much use. It is vital to allow the full richness of God's presence and meaning—as evidenced in the stories of the Scriptures, the experiences of the mystics, the narratives of people of faith over time, and her own story—to be part of an abused woman's healing experience.

These issues around the image of God rather naturally lead us into another issue: what Carole Bohn calls a "theology of ownership," which she says is often grounded in a misinterpretation of the Genesis creation stories. A theology of ownership suggests that humanity was granted dominion over creation by God and that dominion was interpreted to mean ownership. Along with ownership is the tendency to objectify that which is owned so that the needs of the owner are considered primary and the purpose of the owned (or object) is to serve the needs of the owner. It is easy to see how we have gotten into trouble with this in terms of our ecological crises. But part of the ownership paradigm came from the conclusion that there is some sort of natural hierarchy that determines authority and rule. God is at the top of this hierarchy and men, who are closer to God than women, come next. Women follow, and children are after that. They are followed by animals and then other groups in nature. People who are different from those who are seen as the norm (and this includes a lot of people—especially people of color, people with disabling conditions, people with nonheterosexual orientations, and aged people) lose their place in the hierarchy and tend to be even more objectified and marginalized than their place would have made them. This chain of ownership and control has grounded much of the entitlement to abuse women and children in the name of discipline and order.

Carole R. Bohn suggests that most of us would absolutely reject this notion of ownership and yet it is extremely common for women or children who have been the victims of intimate violence and who seek counsel from pastors to receive some form of advice that reflects the minister's belief in a theology of ownership.[10] I personally have heard reported a minister saying that a woman should stay with her battering husband because he's going through a hard time and needs her support or that a young woman who was being sexually abused by her father should seek her father's forgiveness for her role in this sinful activity or that the woman who is being battered must be doing something to bring on her husband's battering or discipline and she should attempt to change her behaviors. These are reflections of a theology of ownership.

Another theological issue that has been pursued by both male and female theologians exploring the dynamics of intimate violence is that of the glorification of suffering sometimes culled from our theologies of atonement. Feminist theology in particular has demonstrated a heavy investment in exploring, deconstructing, and re-imagining Christian understandings of Jesus' death and resurrection.[11] The investment has hinged, at least in part, on the recognition by many women and men of the epidemic levels of abuse against women and children and the use to which Christian theology has been put in allowing that abuse to occur. Feminist theorists have long been aware that abused women and children frequently receive messages from their pastors, from Christian husbands and parents, and from "well-meaning" Christian neighbors that there is divine meaning in their experience of abuse, that the abuse itself is salvific or a means to deeper spirituality, that it is their place to suffer, that husbands or parents know best, that they are somehow at fault, or that it is a sign of deep Christian charity to tolerate being abused by a "loved one." The stories about these kinds of messages told by battered women, incest survivors, and others are legion. Annie Imbens and Ineke Jonker conducted a study in the Netherlands of eighteen women who had experienced childhood sexual abuse and who had been raised in Christians homes to find out how the abuse and the Christian upbringing might be related. They heard over and over again that Christian images of women, the God-given authority of fathers, and the mandates of humility, forgiveness, and submission were contributing factors to both the occurrence of abuse and the difficulty they had in recovering from it. In their interviews, they also heard of the correlation sometimes made by these women between God's relationship with Jesus and their fathers' relationship with themselves. Imbens and Jonker recount the following:

> Several of the incest survivors told us that, as children, they had been sad about Jesus' crucifixion; they did not understand why he had not come down from the cross, or why God, his Father, allowed him to be crucified. The combination of the way they often experienced Jesus (as loving, good, close by, and providing security) with this torturous death (often explained as God's will in order to redeem the sins of humankind) gave these survivors a terrifying image of God: the image of a sadistic father, someone hungry for power. "God and my father were a lot alike," says Joan.[12]

These studies and stories convey some of the motivation behind feminist and profeminist theologians' exploration into theories of atonement. Obviously, these issues around Christology and the way suffering and redemption are understood are of great consequence in pastoral care work.

Another significant theological issue for this discussion is a little harder to frame concretely, but has to do with the variety of qualities that have been defined as valuable for Christians and have especially been applied to good Christian women. As Mary Daly once said, "The qualities that Christianity idealizes, especially for women, are also those of a victim: sacrificial love, passive acceptance of suffering, humility, meekness, etc. Since these are the qualities idealized in Jesus 'who died for our sins,' his functioning as a model reinforces the scapegoat syndrome for women."[13] Imbens and Jonker, in their study of Christian women survivors of incest, discovered similar reports from the women they interviewed. They validate, out of women survivors' experiences, what feminist theologians have been writing about over the past few decades, but these are not theologians, these are wounded women. The problems these women named from their Christian backgrounds that affected their experiences of abuse include:

- The images of women in the Bible and in the church are generally negative. They are seen as either sinful and evil (Eve, woman taken in adultery, Potiphar's wife, Lot's wife, Bathsheeba, etc.) or weak, silly, crying (these are their words). The women saints are seen as valuable because they allowed themselves to be martyred or to suffer for God's glory. The saints mentioned most often were those who suffered pain or death (rather than lose their virginity in one case) and didn't complain. Their reward was in heaven. These are powerful messages to all girls; they are devastating messages to girls experiencing sexual abuse.
- The message that women are to be submissive to males and silent. This meant that the girls who were being abused were confused about whether they had the right to say no to their abuse. Many assumed that since the males had God-given authority, what was happening must be their fault.
- The message that women are to be humble, to turn the other cheek. This message often kept the incest victims from telling anyone about the abuse. Often the abusers had the dual role of protector and abuser and the young women found ways to make allowances for their behavior.
- The paradox of being valued for their sexuality at the same time they are responsible for all sexual sin. All of these women had learned that they were responsible for men's sexual misconduct with them. Virginity was esteemed, motherhood after marriage was essential, but don't say no to your father and suffer in silence. These are difficult paradoxical messages.
- The Christian mandate to forgive the offender. Many had heard this from their pastors when they did finally break their silence and it silenced them and made them guilty again. We will look at this issue of forgiveness again in a moment.
- The mandate to honor your father and mother. The message was frequently given in conservative or fundamentalist Christian households that parents are not to be questioned. The message was often reinforced by the girls' experience of their fathers being seen as pillars of the church.
- Various biblical values of obedience, humility, vulnerability, being last, the sin of pride, glorification of suffering, and so on that contribute to the victimization.[14]

It is important to note that all of these women (with one exception) had to turn their back on the church in order to heal. The majority of offenders, however, are still involved in the church. Half of them still occupy an official church position. This is true with James Newton Poling's research on child sexual abuse also.[15] It is destructive and useless to tell these women that they have misinterpreted their religion and that God and creation really aren't like that. This is, however, the common interpretation that they have internalized, as have most women and children and men, and this is the reality we need to address. Imbens and Jonker say that "for these incest survivors, the prevailing views on women in our Christian churches have deepened their despair and guilt rather than providing them with safe shelter."[16] A large number of women in Europe and in the United States have validated the experiences of the women of this study. Many women who were not sexually abused have also said that their experience of Christianity was similar to these stories and that it has affected their lives in very negative ways. It is the role of pastors to help their congregations explore our biblical and theological traditions responsibly so that they do not contribute to justifications for intimate violence.

The theology of forgiveness is an important issue as well. Churches have had a tendency to urge victims of violence—especially intimate violence—to forgive their abusers. Those who do so are seen as more Christian, more holy. Yet, as Marie M. Fortune suggests, forgiveness should probably be the last step in the healing process rather than the first. Using a helpful exploration of the biblical understandings of forgiveness, Fortune finds that without justice, forgiveness is an empty exercise. She says, "Forgiveness before justice is cheap grace and cannot contribute to authentic healing and restoration to wholeness for the victim or the offender."[17] Forgiveness as the church has tended to understand it often is in contrast to holding the perpetrator accountable for his or her actions. Fortune proposes that forgiveness be the last step in the process that includes confession, repentance (which is *metanoia*—a fundamental change of heart and mind), and restitution (making amends for the damage caused). She notes that in the Christian Scriptures forgiveness comes from the one with power to the one without power, as in forgiving a debt. To ask the powerless one to forgive the one with all the power is antithetical to our biblical witness. These challenges are helpful theological shifts that give us a way both to hold perpetrators of violence accountable and to help empower those who have been victims of violence. Fortune and Poling tell the story of twenty-five incest perpetrators sitting in a circle during their treatment. "They said, 'Tell the clergy for us that they should not forgive us so quickly.' Each of them upon arrest had gone to their ministers and had been prayed over, 'forgiven', and sent home. Each of them said it was the worst thing that could have been done for them. That cheap grace had allowed them to continue to deny responsibility for their abuse of others. It in no way indicated their repentance or their treatment."[18]

We must consider these theological issues as we develop a pastoral counseling approach to women and children victimized by intimate violence. Without challenging some of the "traditional" doctrines that support a patriarchal power system, pastoral care cannot appropriately provide a safe and healing environment for abuse victims. Nor can it appropriately call offenders to account. The church will continue to be known by its silence in the face of abuse and by its collusion with those who do harm. Larry Kent Graham and Marie M. Fortune say that the church needs to be known as a place where "we hold perpetrators accountable and we are on record as religious communities that abuse is not tolerated. When offenders are held accountable, we can become a safe community to heal."[19]

Many women find their spiritual resources, often built out of quite traditional theological doctrine, to be of central importance in surviving their experiences of violence. It is not uncommon for women to report that they prayed to God that they might live through their rape or survive their battering and it was only that connection to the divine that gave them any hope. Many also feel that their prayers have been answered when they are not killed in their violent or abusive experience. Women's spirituality is often rich with deeply personal connections to the divine and their confidence in God's presence and faithfulness is a cornerstone of their narratives. The theological issues discussed above do not denigrate or deny the potency of spirituality in many women's lives. They only question whether the traditional doctrines, commonly understood by churchwomen, serve as vehicles of resistance to intimate violence or whether they may even make it more likely that intimate violence will occur.

So it's important for us to look within Christianity to see what resources our faith traditions hold for us as we seek to become a community where accountability, prevention, and healing are possible in the context of intimate violence.

Theological Resources

It seems to me that our tradition does hold resources for those of us attempting to care for survivors of intimate abuse and prevent future abuse. I think there are several theological resources that can deeply and positively inform our pastoral directions with people who have experienced or are experiencing these kinds of violence. Let me explore just two of those.

The first theological resource I would name is the nature of justice as understood in the Scriptures, especially in the prophetic traditions. Many would suggest that the core principle that runs throughout all of the Scriptures is the notion of justice. John Dominic Crossan suggests that justice is not just a quality that God manifests or chooses. He says that the essence of God is justice—justice is who and what God is.[20] This theme permeates the expectations and experiences of the biblical writers. Particularly in the prophetic literature, we find this emphasis dominates all else.

The prophetic tradition carries the notion of bearing witness. Not only did prophets critique the dominant and oppressive culture, they also served as witnesses to the harm that was being done to those who were being abused or marginalized. Paula Cooey writes, "Indeed, generations of prophets and judges from Moses and Deborah to Jesus have been admonished by God or have admonished the people of God to use their senses to bear witness to injustice, or conversely, they have been threatened with the 'hardening' of the senses as a punishment for injustice."[21] One of the mandates the prophetic tradition puts upon those of us who offer pastoral care to those who have been oppressed and abused is to bear witness. This not only means believing their stories. It also means that we speak in whatever ways we can that make it more likely that their voices will be heard and that the voices of the oppressors will not be heard. The witness-bearing tradition of the prophets works in direct contradiction to the silencing and denial that have been more typical of the church's response to victims of intimate violence.

One of the ways that this prophetic tradition can be used is by carefully listening to those who have not been heard. These are the voices that are privileged in working with people who have been victims of intimate violence. As David Tracy says, "The prophetic voices of our present may be found best, as they were for the ancient prophets and for Jesus of Nazareth, in those peoples, those individuals, and those new centers most privileged to God and still the least heard in the contemporary Western conflict of interpretation on naming the present: the suffering and the oppressed."[22]

Cooey agrees that the voices of the suffering and the oppressed have both "epistemic and moral primacy" and need to be heard. This means, she says, that in order to let them be heard we have to challenge the primary symbol systems in our religious traditions that separate voice and body in such a way that abused women and children (and other marginalized people who are abused) can speak fully for themselves. She also suggests that we need to challenge doctrines, like some of those named earlier, that seem to legitimate and normalize abuse—doctrines like the atonement, glorification of suffering, and unhelpful formulations of sin and evil. Finally, she proposes that the church spend energy developing theological resources to resist violence and bear witness for those who are at risk.[23]

A second theological resource for us is the consistent biblical mandate of hospitality—hospitality to all, but especially to strangers. And in this context when we are talking about strangers we are talking about those who are the most vulnerable. As Fortune and Poling write, "The hospitality tradition called upon the community as a whole to protect the widow, the sojourner, and the orphan. These were the persons in the community who had the least resources and were the most vulnerable to exploitation by others."[24] This religious tradition does not allow us to respond to the victims of violence only with comfort and care. It requires that we do not allow this harm to keep happening and it requires this of the whole community on behalf of all who are vulnerable. The theological mandate of hospitality will not allow us to call intimate violence a private matter or a family matter into which we cannot intrude. It calls instead for us to make sure that families are safe havens and that the structures of domination and oppression with which we are familiar in the culture at large are not reproduced in families. Families cannot be private sanctuaries where violence can occur behind closed doors—they must be held publicly accountable and family members must be helped to know that they do not have to experience violence against them just because the abuser is a member of the family. Perpetrators must come to know that they will not be allowed to do harm to people with whom they have covenants of responsibility and care. We are all part of a larger body, a larger family of God, which means that we are responsible to those who are made vulnerable in places where there should be covenants of trust.

Having equipped ourselves with both a prophetic commitment to bearing witness and a mandate of hospitality, we can now turn to a discussion of intimate violence itself—its dynamics and proposals for pastoral care and counseling for its victims.

Intimate Violence: Definitions and Contexts

When I refer to intimate or domestic violence I am specifically including battering or sexual assault by a spouse or partner; incest or sexual abuse of a child by a family member or a trusted caretaker; physical or emotional abuse or neglect of a child or children; abuse or neglect of a vulnerable adult (vulnerable through age or mental or physical disabilities) by a family member; and homicide by one family member of another, or by a partner. Due to space and the goals for this chapter, I will to limit my consideration to battering, rape by a nonstranger, and sexual abuse of a child by a person in a significant position of trust and the recovery from that experience, which is often delayed until adulthood. Each of these experiences is unique and has its own specific dynamics of harm and processes of recovery. Nonetheless, they have much in common, especially the traumatic fracturing of relationships of trust and the effect of that on victims' frameworks of meaning.

Trauma

Not everyone who experiences one or more forms of intimate violence ends up with harmful effects. Some women are able to go through rape or battering or even child sexual abuse without being significantly traumatized. Yet studies indicate that women who have been victims of childhood sexual abuse demonstrate about twice as much impairment as women who haven't been similarly victimized.[25] In like fashion women who have been raped are nine times more likely than nonvictims to attempt suicide; women who are in battering relationships are also at higher risk for suicide attempts.[26] Studies have also found that women who have been raped are more likely to use alcohol and drugs, develop eating disorders, and become subject to anxiety disorders.[27] These are a few of the consequences of the traumas of intimate violence. Yet despite these heavy costs, fewer than 20 percent of victims of intimate violence show significant psychological problems.[28] They find ways to function and even thrive as adults through varieties of coping skills and the strengths they have developed through having to survive these traumas. Several articles by psychotherapists note how often women who are functioning quite "normally" in their lives come for psychotherapy because of the disorganizing and fragmenting nature of their experiences of violence. They both function well *and* bear the burden of the harm they have experienced.

Women who are abused by people with whom they are in a trusting relationship generally experience a sense of betrayal and a deep challenge to their own meaning-making systems. Despite the realities of the culture, girls are not raised to expect violence against them in their homes. They are much more likely to be raised believing that "their men" will take care of them to such an extent that they are free to focus their own care on others. They are taught through fairy tales, romance novels, and other forms of gender training that their role in life is to care for important relationships, becoming deeply empathic and sensitively responsive to others, and they will be protected and cared for in return. This is particularly true for dominant culture women, who are protected in many ways from seeing the flaws of this mythology. Many African American women, as noted in chapter 3, are taught early that those myths about women being cared for and protected by men are unlikely to be real and thus they are better able to develop the resources they need to take care of themselves. Sadly, this does not protect them from intimate violence. Battering rates for African American women seem to be approximately the same as for European American women and, despite their frequent invisibility in the studies, Lenore E. A. Walker reports that African American women have been described as most at risk for rape at some point in their lives.[29] As we have noted before, it is crucial to discover the way women have understood their experiences by carefully listening to their stories and believing them. This minimizes generalizations across different particularities.

Maria P. P. Root suggests that trauma permanently changes its victims' personal construction of reality. Those principles by which one has lived and organized experience, what we have called one's narratives, have been radically challenged by the trauma of intimate violence.[30] In order to heal from trauma it is necessary somehow to integrate this alien and fragmenting experience and rebuild a narrative that allows meaning to be built out of it. It is also necessary to rebuild the narrative in such a way that hope is present—hope in a life of meaning and purpose, not just survival.

Root describes three kinds of trauma that may overlap in women's experience of intimate violence.[31] First, there is direct trauma. This is the kind we are most familiar with and for which victims are most likely to get some kind of care or support (although, as we have seen, not always in experiences of intimate violence). Direct trauma occurs when there is an observable experience of harm that occurs to a person (or persons) as a result of intentional aggression, a natural disaster, an accident, and so on. Second, there is indirect trauma. This experience of trauma occurs when a person is affected by a direct trauma against someone else. This kind of secondary trauma may occur when, for example, a child watches her mother being battered or even when women hear the stories of other women being harmed by family members. Finally, there is what Root calls insidious trauma. This is trauma that is experienced by people because of a bias against them for reasons of their social status or identity, which isn't valued by the dominant culture. In our culture, for example, people of color, gays and lesbians, poor people, and women are among those who experience insidious trauma because of their identities. Root points out that "while its impact shapes a worldview rather than shatters assumptions about the world [as the first two forms of trauma do], over time it may result in a picture of symptomatology similar to that of direct or indirect trauma, particularly involving anxiety, depression, paranoia, and substance abuse."[32] What is interesting about this schema is how it demonstrates that most intimate violence takes place in the context of all three of these forms of trauma. Since trauma recovery depends in part on the victim's state of health and empowerment at the time of the trauma, this means that women, who generally live with insidious trauma due to being female in an antifemale culture, have fewer resources with which to resist the fragmenting effect of this kind of traumatic betrayal.

Thus, the trauma of intimate violence is a complex one, with overlapping layers of betrayal, powerlessness, loss of control, and fear. Consequently, many theorists of intimate violence talk about the danger of post-traumatic stress disorder (PTSD) for those who have experienced intimate violence. Initially, rape trauma syndrome was the first intimate

abuse to be explored in light of trauma and post-trauma. As further research was done, however, it became clear that child sexual abuse and the
experience of wife battering also lead, in many cases, to a post-traumatic
stress disorder. Herman describes this research:

> A wide array of similar studies has now shown that the psychophysiolog-
> ical changes of post-traumatic stress disorder are both extensive and
> enduring. Patients suffer from a combination of generalized anxiety
> symptoms and specific fears. They do not have a normal level of alert, but
> relaxed, attention. Instead, they have an elevated baseline level of arousal:
> their bodies are always on the alert for danger. They also have an extreme
> startle response to unexpected stimuli, as well as an intense reaction to
> specific stimuli associated with the traumatic event. It also appears that
> traumatized people cannot "tune out" repetitive stimuli that other people
> would find merely annoying; rather, they respond to each repetition as
> though it were a new, and dangerous, surprise. The increase in arousal
> persists during sleep as well as in the waking state, resulting in numerous
> types of sleep disturbance. People with post-traumatic stress disorder take
> longer to fall asleep, are more sensitive to noise, and awaken more fre-
> quently during the night than ordinary people. These traumatic events
> appear to recondition the human nervous system.[33]

Women who come for pastoral counseling who have experienced intimate violence in their lives may need to be understood within this
PTSD framework. Even, as is so often the case, when women come to
counseling without identifying intimate violence as an issue in their
lives, post-traumatic factors may well be involved. Given the statistics,
the possibility of violence in women's lives needs always to be considered
when a woman comes to the pastoral counselor's office, even though we
often don't want to consider this possibility.

Despite all of these forms of intimate violence having similar effects on
their victims—namely, a sense of fragmentation in one's system of meaning as well as various forms of fear, helplessness, and sense of loss of control—it may be useful to define and discuss each of them briefly before
turning to proposals for care.

Incest

Child sexual abuse has been defined in a variety of ways. The National Center on Child Abuse and Neglect defines child sexual abuse as

> contacts or interactions between a child and an adult when the child is being used for the sexual stimulation of the perpetrator or another person. Sexual abuse may also be committed by a person under the age of 18 when that person is either significantly older than the victim or when the perpetrator is in a position of power or control over another child.[34]

Incest is generally understood to fit into this definition and occurs when the perpetrator is either a family member or an adult who is in a trust or caretaking relationship with the child. Because we are talking about the betrayal of trust relationships in this chapter, we will focus on incest.

Like all of these forms of intimate violence, it is very difficult to estimate the prevalence of incest. For one thing, the silence and silencing that surround intimate violence, especially with incest, suggest that a very small percentage of occurrences are reported. In addition, that there are differing definitions of incest makes it difficult to compare one set of statistics with another. Nonetheless, the estimates range between 20 percent and 45 percent of women and 10 percent to 18 percent of men having been sexually abused as children. Several studies suggest that at least half of those incidents of child sexual abuse are incest.[35]

The consequences of incest vary greatly depending on many factors such as age at abuse, length of abuse, relationship with the abuser, other kinds of concurrent trauma, cultural factors, other support systems, and interpretation of the experience at the time. Yet some aftereffects are held in common by victims of incest. An important study by Susan Morrow and Mary Lee Smith suggests that girls who are victims of incest universally experience hopelessness, powerlessness, loss of control, and a deep sense of threat or danger. Girls' response to that is to develop strategies that directly resist these feelings. They do this in a variety of ways that include: dissociation (splitting the mind and spirit off from what is happening to the body); forms of amnesia; substituting one set of feelings (like rage) for another (helplessness, fear); discharging or releasing feelings (drawing, journal writing); numbing themselves; rationalizing or explaining the trauma, including the common strategy of self-blame, so that it is less important or more manageable (if I behaved better this wouldn't happen or he's just trying to make me feel special); attempting to control other areas since the incest wasn't under her control (becoming perfectionistic, becoming a caretaker of others); seeking confirmation of her experience from others (usually done subtly); and finding ways to resist (running away, attempting to avoid being alone, locking a door). These strategies are used to deal with overwhelming feelings of fear and powerlessness.[36] Often they make the experience one that can be survived.

The biggest problem with these strategies is that they often become deeply built into the child's, and then woman's, narrative in such a way that they feel like they are inevitable aspects of her personality. An adult woman often comes to counseling because these strategies, which served as important resources for her as a child, are now creating problems in her life. Without understanding the context of abuse, however, neither the counselor nor the survivor can find ways to develop appropriate alternative narratives. The naming of the context and the resistance to silencing are a crucial part of the healing process.

Women also come to counseling when memories of their childhood abuse begin to break through the years of denial that they had put in place in order to survive. The memories may come as much as twenty, thirty, or more years after the abuse has ended and may be precipitated by a change in a close relationship or a family life cycle change.[37] If memories break through (or the anxieties and fears associated with the experience break through without there being clear memories), the person may experience extreme discomfort. Her symptoms may well lead counselors to believe that she has a psychiatric disorder when, in reality, she needs support to move through and integrate her experiences of childhood harm.

Rape

Rape is not easy to define. The definition needs to be specific enough to be useful but broad enough to include the variety of coercive sexual activities. The definition that I find most useful is that rape is any activity where sexual activity is forced or coerced upon another and where usually some part of the victim's body is used for the sexual gratification of the perpetrator. The National Crime Victimization Survey, which is a household survey done by the United States Census Bureau, found that there were 171,420 rapes in the United States in 1991.[38] This number is low compared to the results discovered by the National Women's Survey;

they discovered that 13 percent of the women surveyed had been victims of completed rape and that 39 percent of those women had been raped more than once. Only 16 percent of rapes had ever been reported to the police. And the vast majority of rapes (78 percent) were committed by people known to the women.[39]

Often when a woman is first raped, she is dazed. She has been through a life-threatening experience and she has been violated in almost every vulnerable way. Her body has been violated through her sexual vulnerability. Cultural values about women's bodies often make women feel deeply shamed and exposed in this experience. A woman has been violated through losing all control of her life in the experience. She has often been intentionally humiliated and her sense of herself has been violated. Her life has been threatened and so her human existence has been violated. And any sense of the world being a safe place has been violated. This is generally an overwhelming experience. The woman may believe the myths of rape at the emotional level even if she intellectually knows differently. Consequently she may feel responsible and guilty at the same time she feels violated. She may try to deny that it happened, try to minimize it, or be in acute shock and fear. In addition she may fear (legitimately, in many cases) the responses of the people around her. How she is received by the people around her makes a huge difference in the way she is able to process this traumatic event. And since partner rape is one common form of rape, it is important to note, as Judith Herman says, that "when the rapist is a husband or lover, the traumatized person is the most vulnerable of all, for the person to whom she might ordinarily turn for safety and protection is precisely the source of danger."[40]

Walker gives five major ways of coping with rape: avoidance and expressive, nervous/anxious, cognitive, and self-destructive coping. She suggests that those women who are able to use their cognitive resources and are able to express their feelings are usually able to cope best. One of the most important aspects of beginning to heal from a rape is regaining a sense of control.[41]

Judith Worrell and Pam Remer propose six phases in moving through a rape experience. First, they talk about the pre-rape experience. This includes the fact that most women spend considerable psychic energy fearing rape. It also includes the victim's engagement with the rape myths of the culture. The second phase is the act of rape itself from right before its occurrence to immediately following the rape. The coping skills used by the victim to survive the rape are part of this phase. The third phase is a time of crisis and disorganization. Rape victims often experience a sense of helplessness, a loss of control, and shame. This is a vulnerable time in terms of how the victim will construe the rape. Worrell and Remer suggest that any implicit or explicit blaming will have a significant effect on that process. Phase four, they suggest, is made up of an outward adjustment and calm, a desire to get on with life and not give the experience any more attention than she has to. She attempts to minimize and suppress the feelings from the experience. Phase five usually happens when the denial or minimization stops working and she begins to have intrusive thoughts or flashbacks, nightmares, and anxieties. Finally, in phase six, she is able to make meaning out of this rape so that it can be integrated into the rest of her narrative.[42] She is changed by the experience, but if this phase is successful, her new narrative will reflect a sense of the strengths and resources she used throughout this process and how it has been integrated into her life.

There are women who have been raped who have managed to suppress their experience of rape for a period of years, never moving into the fifth phase. If those memories or anxieties surface, the woman may move suddenly into this fifth phase and re-experience the rape as if it were a current crisis. The person who can't work through a rape crisis until later may well experience the symptoms of post-traumatic stress syndrome. In that case she, like the woman who is in the acute phase of grief recovery, will probably experience intrusive memories, nightmares, anxiety problems, and possibly alcohol or drug problems.

It's vital for the pastoral counselor to understand the cultural myths of rape (which are an extension of the myths of patriarchy) in order to help the woman put her rape in an appropriate framework of meaning. It is also important to move with the woman through her phases of recovery at her pace.

Wife Battering

Pastors in general report that dealing with wife abuse in the church is one of the most difficult pastoral problems that they face.[43] They feel torn between their theological beliefs, their personal experiences with people accused of violence, and their sympathies with a victim. Even those who have additional training in domestic violence tend to blame the victim. Wood and McHugh found in their research that only 12 percent of the pastors responding to a survey recommended arrests for batterers and only 8 percent recommended a protection from abuse order.[44]

Wife battering is a serious problem—one might even say an epidemic. Some of the statistics were given in chapter 1. Estimates suggest that around four million women are assaulted by male partners every year and that somewhere between 30 percent and 50 percent of all female murder victims over the age of fourteen are killed by a current or former spouse (compared to 4 percent of men).[45] In addition, between 30 percent and 50 percent of all homeless women are trying to escape domestic violence.[46]

Spouse abuse includes direct harm from one spouse to another as well as threats of violence in the context of prior violence and violence against children, property, or pets as a form of threat or control. Although spouse abuse can be female to male or between partners of the same sex, the vast majority of battering is by men toward women. Studies that claim a significant amount of battering of husbands by wives generally ignore the fact that most of that violence is in response to or in protection against husband-initiated violence. Also, much more injury results from male to female violence.

Women who are abused often attempt to try at first to understand the violence within their existing frameworks of meaning. They may blame themselves, rationalize why this is an exceptional experience, or minimize the violence. Over time, women tend to stop blaming themselves but have difficulty perceiving options to get out of the violent situations. Many pastors, at their best, feel that the only possible solution is for the woman to leave her battering partner. In fact, it is not uncommon for pastors to base their help on the condition that the woman leave her partner. Yet, as Walker notes,

> research demonstrates that leaving does not stop the violence. Instead, it continues, often escalating at the time of separation to life-threatening proportions. Some women have also become so dependent on the batterer that they believe they cannot survive without him. An important point regarding battered women, moreover, is that they may actually be physically safer staying with the abuser, over whom they still have some influence, rather than being alone and unprotected without the ability to calm him down. Many men who batter women stalk and harass them. They do not let the women go. . . . It is important for the therapist not to make leaving the battering relationship a treatment goal. Rather the goal

must be to live in a violence-free environment. This may be difficult or impossible while living with the abuser, but it may be equally difficult or impossible while living apart.[47]

When women are battered, there tends to be a somewhat predictable cycle. Walker has developed a proposal based on her research about this cycle. She suggests that there is a time of tension buildup in the relationship followed by the actual battering and abuse followed by a time of calm, maybe even remorse and care. One of the problems is that with the amount of denial and silence about battering and the general lack of support for battering victims, the violent spouse during the calm period may be the victim's best source of nurture and care.

Some researchers have questioned whether there is normally a time of calm and remorse, suggesting that it is just a time period between violent incidents. Walker acknowledges that the periods of calm and contrition may well get shorter and shorter as time goes on. One thing that all researchers acknowledge is that violence in domestic relationships tends to escalate in both frequency and severity over time. Women's lives are often at risk. The other thing that most researchers agree on is that spousal battering is not about a loss of control, but reflects an obsessional need for control. Battering is about controlling and manipulating a partner, making sure that she meets the partner's needs. It is not, usually, about catharsis or a lack of anger management.[48]

Worrell and Remer suggest that a victim of domestic violence needs to find safety, to get information and support for regaining her own perspective in order to make decisions about her life, and find resolution and restructuring so that her life can become violence-free.[49] This process may take a long time because it involves rebuilding a sense of self, a sense of entitlement to safety, and a recognition of strengths and resources after becoming convinced by her batterer that she has no resources or strengths.

Although there are many common dynamics for women who have suffered these kinds of abuses, there are also many differences. Some women will seek out counselors in the midst of crisis, but many women come for counseling without any real consciousness that their suffering is related to abuse they are either currently suffering or have suffered in the past. Women need to be helped to find their voice, to be believed, and to be supported as they seek to heal from the significant harm that results from the trauma of intimate violence.

Helping Women Come to Voice
in the Context of Intimate Violence

There are three major approaches to caring for women who have been victims of intimate violence. First, there are short-term crisis needs for women or children who are in the midst of intimate violence where the focus must be on the victim's safety, and the perpetrator's accountability. This is an area where, by and large, church pastors have not done well but where the needs are great. All pastors need to know how to offer pastoral care to women and children (and their abusers) when they present in crisis.

The second dimension for pastoral care in this context is how to care for women who present for pastoral care and counseling not in the crisis of violence, but as they seek to recover from the trauma of having been victims. These women, as we have seen, often come to pastoral counseling without revealing, sometimes not even knowing, that there is a link between their distress and a history of abuse. Consequently, any pastoral counseling with women who have problems with relationships or who experience depression, anxiety or phobias, eating disorders, addictions, or a host of other seemingly unrelated symptoms needs to assess the possibility of a past history (or current experience) of intimate violence. There has been a great deal of debate about the risk of implanting false memories of abuse for people who have symptoms but no real memories of harm, especially in the case of child sexual abuse. J. L. Herman, Walker, and many other well-respected feminist researchers of women's trauma suggest that it is unlikely that therapists will implant lasting memories that aren't accurate. They suggest that, over time, women will reject "memories" that aren't real for them. Nonetheless, women should be allowed to discover and name their own experiences and give narrative to the often fragmented, nonverbal memories of abuse as they are able. Walker writes that "most clinicians who work with women who are survivors of childhood sexual abuse understand the need to go slowly in helping clients to retrieve lost memories."[50] Yet that shouldn't make counselors afraid to ask questions about the counselee's history of symptoms and to give clear signals that they will support the counselee if she has a history of abuse that needs to be explored and integrated.

The third issue is that of prevention and resistance. Individual pastors as well as churches themselves need to take a strong stand against family violence, starting with naming it as abuse and holding perpetrators accountable at all levels. All three of these approaches to pastoral care in the context of intimate violence work together to bring individual, relational, and societal healing to one of the most damaging and costly problems of our time.

Crisis Care in the Context of Intimate Violence

There are some basic principles in crisis care for each of these forms of intimate violence. The guiding principles, however, are safety and support. Many children and women who are in the midst of violent relationships, for some of the reasons named above, are unlikely to report their problems directly. Studies indicate that most women who have been battered, for example, have not reported their violence out of fear of reprisal from their batterers, self-blame, or a sense that it wasn't worth being taken seriously (she recognizes that there is a strong chance that she is not going to be believed, and thus the consequences of reporting are too great to take that chance). In addition, women who are battered have often been so isolated that they don't even know whom to tell. Children who are being abused are also often afraid of the consequences of reporting. They usually have been threatened in a variety of ways in order to make sure that secrecy is maintained. They are also aware that they depend on their families for their day-to-day survival as well as for whatever emotional nurture they are able to get. This, again, makes the stakes of reporting the violence, if indeed it even occurs to them, very high. And rape victims, especially victims of date or partner rape, are highly unlikely to report, often for fear of not being believed. The point is, of course, that many women will present themselves to their pastors for help without volunteering the information that they have been harmed in an intimate relationship. It is up to the counselor to make it as safe and as easy as possible for a victim to reveal her experience of intimate abuse.

Rape

The counselor who encounters the rape survivor immediately after the rape must do several things. First, she or he needs to treat the experience as a crisis and make sure the safety of the counselee is assured. She may want to not be alone. If it happened in her home, she may not want to stay there. It may be helpful to offer to stay with her or go with her to a place of safety if she chooses. She should be encouraged to seek medical care, especially if there are injuries. It's important that the pastor know of emergency centers that are trained to deal helpfully with rape victims. Calling someone from the rape crisis center to accompany the victim through this process is often helpful, but it may still be important for the pastor to be available as well. It is important that the victim know the process that she will be going through with the medical center and the police. Control must be returned to her in as many ways as possible. Well-meaning paternalism (or maternalism) that takes over for her is misplaced kindness. One victim reported having her friend in the emergency room ask if she would like a cup of coffee. When she said no, the friend brought her a cup anyway and even that small act made her feel that her choices (which were taken from her in the experience of rape) continued to be ignored.

It is important that the counselor provide nonanxious support for the survivor and that she or he not be overwhelmed by the story. Many feel that men should not counsel with women who are raped. Sometimes, however, a male clergyperson will be the primary support resource available. Some women who are raped may react with extremes toward men—often feeling anger toward all men, but sometimes feeling that only a male can protect her (one of patriarchy's myths). These are natural reactions. If a male clergy is the main resource person for the rape victim (and even if the clergy caregiver is a woman), it might be especially important for her to be in a support group of women survivors or have a female conversation partner or advocate, services that are often offered through rape crisis centers.

It's important to know that acute reactions to rape may include an aversion to being touched in any way as well as anxiety, shame, and possibly rage. All of these feelings are appropriate and need to be supported by the caregiver. As the recovery process unfolds, the pastoral role continues to be support, belief, and co-authoring her work at making meaning out of the experience.

Incest

When a pastor receives a report from a child or an adolescent that she or he is being sexually abused by a family member or caregiver, it is her or his responsibility to report that abuse to the appropriate child protection authorities. Most experts agree that this is a legal responsibility as well as a moral one. In addition, if the pastor has good reason to *suspect* sexual abuse (or, indeed, physical abuse) of a minor, she or he is responsible to report that as well. In other words, the pastor is expected to take initiative in situations where sexual abuse of a minor is (or probably is) occurring. This is a difficult position to be in for a pastor who wishes to maintain his or her pastoral connections with all members of a family. But the most important issue is to stop the abuse. The child needs to know that you, as pastor and representative of the church, stand with her or him in the face of this enormously destructive experience. Even if the intervention ends up not protecting the victim, for the child to know that she or he was believed and supported may make an important difference in her or his healing as an adult. Fortune writes, in response to an ineffective intervention into incest, that "when that child is thirty years old, in therapy, disclosing the experience, she or he will remember you and remember that there was one person who believed him or her. And, that will make all the difference in their healing. The importance of your day's worth of work with that child—even if you can't affect anything else about how the child is responded to—made a difference for that child. That is all we can do sometimes, because we are up against a system that is not there to protect children."[51]

In addition, it is important to try to stay connected with the family members as they go through the legal processes and investigations. The primary pastoral role is to support the family members and hold the perpetrator(s) accountable for the violence. There is rarely a completely happy ending to this kind of event. Often the child is taken out of the family, at least temporarily, for her or his safety. The other family members may continue to deny the reality of the abuse, which can be very painful and fragmenting for them. It also means, however, that the victim of the incest needs a great deal of care and support.

Partner Battering

The crisis elements of spouse battering are very clear—the primary agenda is safety from harm. Yet, as noted above, many victims of battering are unwilling to leave the batterer for a variety of reasons, including: a fear of reprisal, the safety of the children, child custody problems, problems of economic support, dependency on the batterer, a minimizing of the problem, putting others in danger, nowhere to go, fear of public opinion, as well as many other possible roadblocks. If a woman refuses to leave the batterer (and notice how the burden is on the victim to build a new life while the perpetrator can live consequence-free), the pastoral counselor needs to work with her to maximize her safety. Walker suggests that it is important for the counselor to hear about four battering incidents: the first, the most typical, the worst, and the most recent. These four stories give a good clue about the patterns of violence. The woman can be helped to take note of the signs that indicate an acute battering incident is about to happen. Usually there are somewhat predictable signs that the victim can learn to recognize. She can be taught how to leave before the battering actually begins.

The most important aspect of this crisis care—other than believing and supporting her—is helping the woman develop an escape plan that is both detailed and realistic enough to get her out of the house in an emergency. She should be asked to draw a basic plan of the house and to identify rooms where the violence usually begins. She should then map out an exit plan from that room (and other likely places) that has at least two options in case one escape route is blocked. She should also have available to her any important papers, extra money, and car keys where she can get at them without searching. If she has young children, she needs to figure out how to get them (for both their safety and for custody reasons) and, if the children are older, she needs to arrange where and when to meet them after they all leave the house. If there are items of value in the house or pets that the woman wants to protect, she may want to take care of that ahead of time—asking someone else to take care of the pet or to store objects for her. And, as Walker concludes, the plan needs to be practiced and memorized so that it becomes automatic when she needs it.[52]

Every pastor should have this kind of knowledge and the ability to use it effectively in crisis situations with victims of intimate violence. Pastors need to have done their homework so that they are not scrambling to find resources (like women's shelters, legal resources, rape crisis lines, support groups, etc.) during the crisis moment. All pastors need to have a thorough referral list with resources they have personally evaluated so that they can be free to pay attention and tend to the needs of the person in distress. These are basic crisis procedures for victims of intimate violence. It is common, however, for a woman to come for pastoral care or counseling, not in the crisis of the violence itself, but as a result of the longer-term effects of the trauma.

Recovering from the Trauma of Intimate Violence

When we talk about the process of helping people move through the healing process of trauma recovery, it's important to remember that the pastor may play many roles. First of all, healing care is not limited to formal pastoral counseling. Second, the pastor is not the only agent of healing in the church. And third, the pastor needs to be able to work in concert with appropriate community resources for the good of the care receiver. If the church gives clear messages through its education programs, sermon topics and illustrations, support group structures, and use of money (such as having a discretionary fund to help pay for healing resources in the community), then it is more likely that all three of these structures of healing will be able to work together for the good of the victim of intimate violence.

In keeping with both narrative theory and feminist principles, it is important in the healing process to focus on women's strengths and resources rather than assessing deficits and pathology. This is easier said than done. For one thing, counseling has been so steeped in a medical model of sickness and a behavioral model of problems that it is "natural" for caregivers and care receivers alike to approach counseling with those two lenses. But women who have been victims of intimate violence generally are not in distress (even years later) because they have characterological or even behavioral deficits. They are in distress because (1) they have had minimal opportunity to process and integrate a traumatic history into the rest of their lives and (2) they have skills and strengths that were of great help to them in surviving the violence but that now get in their way. In regard to the first reason, it is important for the caregiver to find ways to best hear the story of the violence, believing and supporting that story fully (rather than use a pathology model, which might look for inconsistencies and errors in it for the sake of symptom assessment), and helping the care receiver to make sense of it and meaning out of it for her ongoing life narrative. In regard to the second reason, the caregiver needs to assist the care receiver in discovering ways that her strengths can be used appropriately for their current context so that they do not cause further distress. Narrative theory is helpful for both of these goals.

As a deconstructive method, narrative theory works to understand the sources of the beliefs and assumptions built into any person's narrative, especially those aspects of the narrative that are causing distress. In other words, it immediately asks the question, "What discourses serve as the context for this narrative?" This means that narrative theory always has cultural analysis built into it and that cultural analysis is shared between counselor and counselee as they work to co-author a preferred narrative. Intimate violence and its damage can only be understood in the context of a culture that uses a variety of methods to normalize it. It is within this cultural analysis that the rest of the goals for trauma recovery are set.

Judith Lewis Herman talks about several criteria for the resolution of trauma, particularly the trauma resulting from intimate violence, in a person's life. She names seven criteria for assessing that resolution:

The distressing feelings and behaviors for which she came to counseling have become manageable.

The person is able to bear the feelings associated with the traumatic memories.

The person has authority over her memories—she can elect both to remember the trauma and to put the memory aside.

The memory of the traumatic event is a coherent narrative, linked with feeling.

The person's damaged self-esteem has been restored.

The person's important relationships have been re-established (as she chooses).

The person has reconstructed a coherent system of meaning and belief that encompasses the story of the trauma.[53]

Herman suggests that all of these criteria are being addressed throughout the entire caregiving process.

The primary starting place for this caregiving work is in listening deeply to a care receiver's story and joining her in giving it voice. This is the process of co-authoring. For so many women who have been either childhood or adult victims of intimate violence, there have been no words and no story for this experience. For women who have survived incest, depending on their age, there may never have been words associated with the sexual abuse, only images and sensations. And, even for adult victims, trauma memories often are recorded in visual or sensory images without a coherent narrative to hold them together.

Not only have words and voice been missing, but credibility has also been absent. For those who tried to get help or to talk about their experience, there has often been a culture of disbelief surrounding them, for all the reasons discussed. As Fortune states, while talking about childhood abuse, "An adult who begins to remember (or, I would add, has an environment where remembering has some purpose) and acknowledge experiences of childhood sexual abuse and is ready to speak about these experiences to someone else is on the way to becoming a survivor. Justice means believing the victim's story, though the facts may seem muddled and confused. The truth is the reality of that person's experience of being victimized."[54] In other words, truth is not external, but rather subjective. The counselor has no need to investigate or figure out how much of the story is "real." The story *is* real because it is real for the person telling it. The caregiver's responsibility is to help the story to be told and, in the process of its telling, help the person to explore the assumptions and frameworks that have made this story—with its negative implications about her worth, goodness, and potential—truth for her. The story needs to be told, in its fullness, while being heard by both caregiver and care receiver in a nondeterminative way. She will need to wonder about who taught her that the abuse is her fault. She will need to look at why she was unable to get help. That is part of the deconstructive process of the story, which then makes room for her to look at parts of her story that hold the potential for finding a self that is not overwhelmed by fear and powerlessness. She will be able to find what parts of her were able to resist and survive the violence being done to her and how those aspects are still available to her in her current story.

The counselor has to walk a fine line in this work between deep hearing of the story as the care receiver tells it and not reinforcing the fear and helplessness deeply ingrained in the victimized trauma. The care receiver must know that she is fully believed and that the caregiver has empathy for the deeply traumatizing effects of the experience without affirming her permanent status of victim. The care receiver's need for catharsis must be held in tension with her need to develop a less problematic understanding of herself and her possibilities. The work of deconstructive listening has the capacity to help the counselor and counselee walk these fine lines.

So, in helping the counselee move toward the healing criteria listed above, the counselor works hard to listen with appropriate empathy, maintaining the boundaries between the counselee's story and the counselor so that the narrative doesn't take over the counseling process. The listening allows the counselor, where appropriate, to externalize aspects of the story that have been unhelpfully internalized. For example, one might note, as part of the reflective listening process, that as the counselee talks about being a terrified child, she had to fight fear on a regular basis. Rather than the counselee understanding herself as fearful, the counselor externalizes fear from being an essential part of the counselee, to being an outside force constantly threatening her sense of well-being. Again, this line between empathic hearing and deconstructive externalizing becomes a fine, but important, one to walk.

Another helpful aspect of deconstruction comes through asking the counselee, when appropriate, where she learned to believe certain assumptions she may have about herself—for example, asking her, "who first taught you that you had to honor your father even though he was abusing you?" Helping her to explore those kinds of sources for problematic aspects of her narrative offers doorways into a familial, cultural, and theological analysis that will help put the counselee's story in the context of the larger stories of harm. They may also help her begin to find alternative resources.

A third aspect of deconstructive work is looking for places where there are exceptions to her problematic narrative in the midst of it and being curious about those exceptions. For example, "I'm interested in why you found yourself feeling stronger when you were talking with your grandmother," or "I'm curious about how you were able to help your sister get out of her violent marriage? What resources did you offer her?" In more traditional counseling approaches it is common for the counselor and counselee to focus almost exclusively on the coherent, dominant, and problematic narrative. This often has the unwitting consequence of "thickening" or strengthening it. The emphasis in a narrative orientation to counseling is on the exceptions or "unique outcomes" in the narrative and giving them enough focus so that they might become sources for a preferred direction. This doesn't mean that painful memories aren't allowed to surface and be named. That is a key aspect of the care for victims of intimate violence. It just means that those memories aren't allowed to stand alone when there may be resources for coping with them that were buried along with the memories in the narrative itself. This process shouldn't be rushed, but deconstructing the problematic narrative along with looking for unique outcomes should always be a part of the counselor's process. In this, as in all good counseling, however, the pace of the counselee should be what sets the pace of the counseling. The counselor should never carry the agenda of "getting somewhere" but rather use her or his knowledge and skills to assist the counselee with healing from, and integrating the problematic aspects of her life that are the consequences of, trauma.

Prevention and Resistance

Throughout this chapter we have discussed some of the problems that work to maintain the reality (and normativity) of intimate violence. We have discussed theological problems that seem to support violence rather than its victims. We also named some theological resources to aid us in overcoming those problems. We have discussed a patriarchal culture that makes children and women "appropriate victims" because of their lesser status and power in the society. And we have discussed the reluctance of people and institutions to take up a stance of advocacy for victims and resistance toward family violence.

It is clearer to me in talking about intimate violence than in relation to any other topic that the gender training with which we indoctrinate our children must be challenged. I am firmly convinced that we train our children in ways that make intimate violence—at least in heterosexual relationships—likely, if not inevitable. We help our boys form narratives of ownership, of entitlement, of no "sissy stuff" (gender polarization), of focusing all feelings into either sexual expression or anger, of "getting ahead," and of other male mandates that put all boys and men at risk of a variety of problems and make them likely candidates to initiate violence. Bell hooks writes that even black men, who are deprived of access to a white dominant culture's male power at every point, learn that their one commonality with white male power may be in sexist behaviors. She writes that "black males, who are utterly disenfranchised in most every arena of life in the United States, often find that the assertion of sexist domination is their only expressive access to that 'patriarchal power' they are told all men should possess as their gendered birthright. Hence, it should not surprise or shock that many black men support and celebrate a dominant 'rape culture.'" She goes on to say that there are those black male voices who stand firmly against this kind of violence against women, but they tend to be ignored by the dominant culture. She also suggests that women have learned to structure their attraction to men around how "masculine" men are and thus feed into the continuation of male violence against women.[55] This system of attraction is built out of male and female gender training and its reinforcement throughout life. Hooks suggests that women have to find ways to challenge that structure of attraction (which looks to evidence of traditional masculinity) as part of our resistance to intimate violence.

The reality is that no girl or woman seeks out violence or finds it attractive, but hooks is accurate that there is a structure of gender training that creates a false "complementarity" between men and women that heightens the likelihood of intimate violence. As has been discussed throughout this text, girls are gender trained to be responsible for the success and nurturing of relationships and to believe that, without successful relationships (whatever the cost), they are at risk of isolation and harm. Women are also trained to do mind reading—to develop forms of feeling empathy, which makes them hypervigilant to the possible feelings and motivations of those in primary relationship with them. They tend to use that "empathy" to offer sympathetic rationalizations for men's violent behavior against them. Girls are also taught how to be depressed rather than angry, which takes away much of the energy that could be used for resistance. And, finally, girls are taught that they are not entitled to the use of overt and direct power; their influence is to be more subtle and channeled through expressions of nurturance. These gender-training dynamics predispose women to be less able to resist intimate violence used against them.

Given the power of this gender training to make intimate violence likely between men and women in families, one of our key areas of preventive work needs to be with our children, making sure each gender has the tools to build strong and nurturing relationships and each has the tools to resist harm aimed against them.

Prevention and resistance have to do with dismantling patriarchy at its very heart so that our own personal, familial, institutional, and societal narratives do not contribute to the likelihood of intimate violence. Consequently, when I talk about pastoral care as offering support for alternative narrative possibilities as they occur, what I mean by support is institutional, relational, and personal efforts to affirm and encourage the development of these alternative ways of being and interpreting while not denying the ambivalence in that process. That means we have to be willing to deconstruct our own violence-laden assumptions—psychological, theological, linguistic, relational, vocational—and be held accountable when we act out of them. Preventive pastoral care will involve deconstructing and being held accountable for our own violence-laden core narratives (as leaders of the church) and helping, then, to support the development of exceptional nonviolent narratives in persons, church, and society. And knowing how these more overtly violent narratives are interwoven with more subtle strands of stereotypical gender training (e.g., our various forms of entertainment and some of our theological interpretations) helps us to do this deconstruction and restorying at the deep, integrative levels required for change.

The work of prevention and resistance also means not being willing to tolerate intimate violence in our congregations and holding people accountable actively and with initiative. Adams writes that "church leaders must acknowledge that they know sexual violence exists in society and, therefore, in their congregations. Are they prepared to offer helpful responses? When clergy do name violence from the pulpit or in their other capacities as church leaders, they report surprise at the number of people who come forward who have been personally affected by sexual violence." She concludes by suggesting that clergy, as leaders, must be ready to name violence just as people attempting to heal from intimate violence must be ready to name the violence done against them.[56] I think it is appropriate to ask, as we explore the development of voice in the context of intimate violence, whether or not we as leaders in the church are ready to develop our own voices, even at the risk of credibility and respect, so that we might stand counter to the epidemic of harm against women and children found in intimate violence.

five

Helping Women Gain Clarity

The process of coming to voice is a vital dimension of becoming and staying healthy as a woman. The cultural pressures to diminish women's voices and selves, to make women invisible through language and sex-stereotyped places of belonging, and to make women incredible by disbelieving their experiences in patriarchy are powerful and developmentally cumulative. Women who come to pastors with a sense of *dis*-ease or despair about their lives often first need to be helped to speak about their experiences and to know that they will be believed. This involves several processes. Some women have so dissociated from their own truths that they have to be helped even to know what they know. Jeffrey Zimmerman and Victoria Dickerson suggest that this is particularly true for adolescent girls. They write,

> The work with adolescent girls involves attention to a first step, prior to self-authoring, perhaps a pre-authoring. Carol Gilligan's appreciation of "voice" for women and her discussions with adolescent girls have suggested that adolescent girls are "losing their voice" or coming to "not know what they know." This loss of voice has implications for the therapist working with families with adolescent girls in that before the girls can begin to narrate their own stories, they must first "know what they know" in order to understand that they can even have an authentic story.[1]

This, in part, involves helping girls and women who come to counseling learn how to consider their own truths without fears about what they "should" be saying in order to maintain relationships and avoid harm. It requires a safe environment, a supportive and believing pastoral presence, and encouragement for the counselee to pay attention to her own feelings and experience. Obviously, a person can't explore her own narrative, much less re-author a preferred narrative, without feeling entitled to her own voice and language.

Yet it is not just a matter of getting in touch and speaking with one's own voice. Individual and communal narratives are formed within a larger context that shapes the available discourses out of which those narratives emerge. So women and men form their personal narratives in a context of cultural patriarchy as well as cultural white racism, classism, ableism, heterosexism, and ageism. This means at least two things. First, it means that the experiences that tend to be brought into a person's core narrative and given language and meaning are those experiences that fit the dominant formative discourses, moderated only to the degree that one has been taught and encouraged to maintain narratives of resistance (as in some African American communal experiences). Second, it means that a woman usually shapes her experiences in such a way that they fit the dominant narrative in some way that causes a minimum of cognitive or relational dissonance. Women learn to lie to themselves in response to the lies about women and women's place within which they have been raised.

Riet Bons-Storm gets at these problems when she talks about women's "unstories." She says, "In our society, an experienced event tends to turn into an unstory if that experienced event cannot be put into a self-narrative considered appropriate by the dominant belief system. An unstory usually contains roles for women and men that clash with the proper roles. The sociocultural narrative presents specific models of what the roles of women and men in all relationships ought to be. If women have 'unfitting' experiences, there are no 'good' stories about them."[2] The dominant stories about the way we are to live as men and women (and as people of various skin colors, sexual orientations, ages, and physical abilities) have been quite narrow in our culture. The stories of the dominant culture have featured, and continue to feature, white, heterosexual, educated men as the main actors. This does not mean that all men are considered powerful, nor that they all feel powerful. Most men do not experience themselves as primary actors in determining the shape of the culture. It does mean, though, that those who have had the primary power to shape cultural discourse have been dominant-culture men. This means that many stories and experiences that do not fit well within these dominant-culture stories, or that contradict them, are lost, discredited, or twisted to fit better. Gaining voice is the process that resists and dismantles women's invisibility and incredibility or the tendency of their discourse-challenging experiences to remain unstoried. But there needs to be another therapeutic process that helps "untwist" or deconstruct and reshape the experiences that have been shaped to fit the dominant discourse and therefore create a system of lies within the narratives of most women.

Gaining Distance from Problematic or Untruthful Narrative Strands

It becomes clear, then, that while a deep hearing of the story is crucial to helping women gain voice, a different kind of help is needed for the process of gaining clarity about a narrative created within a patriarchal context. This kind of help, which emphasizes separation from and deconstruction of belief systems that have felt like truth, has an anti-intuitive feel or a suspiciousness of intuition that can be uncomfortable for both counselor and counselee. In fact, one of the most helpful things to know about a feminist perspective on pastoral counseling is that much of it is "counterintuitive." I use the term *intuitive* here cautiously, because what is often called "intuitive" has been deeply distorted by internalized patriarchal biases and externalized reinforcement for following through with those biases. When counselors rely primarily on experience and intuition in pastoral counseling, they are very likely to collude with toxic value systems and exclusionary assumptions. When they gauge other people primarily by their own experiences, they find that they are only able to work effectively and healthily with people who are enough like themselves not to challenge their deeply held truths about life. Pastoral counseling that intends to participate in personal, familial, and cultural transformation needs to be willing to question anything that seems to be a "truth" of the dominant culture.

Gaining clarity in the counseling process requires considerably more than telling and hearing the story. It requires seeing the story through a variety of meaningful lenses and routinely asking the epistemological question, "How do we know what we know?" It means that, although gender is a crucial category that life experience is organized and interpreted around, it does not always have to be the starting place in a feminist approach to pastoral counseling. Sometimes the appropriate starting place is with race or class or sexual orientation as the dominant category of oppressive experience. The counselor must be well informed about the power dynamics within this culture around gender, race, class, age, sexual orientation, and able-bodiedness. This requires more than extrapolation from personal experience. Although various systems of dominance and subordinance in this culture have a great deal in common, they cannot be exchanged for one another in terms of assumptions about the ways they affect people's lives. Pastoral counselors who practice out of a feminist, multicultural, multiple-analysis context need to research multicultural perspectives, seek out colleagues and consultants of different races, classes, and sexual orientations than her or his own, and explore her or his own internalized and external contexts of privilege and disenfranchisement. They need to explore how they respond to their own experiences of privilege in the culture—knowing that they are probably in categories that make them both oppressed and oppressor in the variety of situations they live in.

Julia A. Boyd says that, "in doing therapy with women of color, feminist therapists must recognize that they will again become students. . . . Making the assumption that prior mental health training or feminist politics will transcend the necessity to comprehend the ethnic and cultural lines of survival for women of color will place both the client and effective treatment in serious jeopardy."[3]

These issues are especially important for the egalitarian relationship required by a feminist perspective. In an egalitarian relationship, power differences are acknowledged and minimized to the extent possible for the counseling relationship to function. If power is shared to the degree possible, then it is important to be able to analyze and acknowledge the kinds of power and privilege that exist in that relationship. People who have experienced themselves as relatively powerless in many settings (and this may include many clergy in general) are often unable or unwilling to see the arenas in which they are granted power and the nature of the power they exercise. For many women, at least, power has such a negative connotation that they are unwilling to claim it. Consequently, the very real power that does exist is used in an indirect manner that makes accountability for it difficult.

Counselors need to be able to do appropriate cultural analysis. They need to know the kind of information discussed in chapter 1 and they need to keep current with what's happening in dominant cultural discourses. This information doesn't make them experts on the counselee's life. She is the expert on that experience and her narrative is the primary source of information for the counseling. But the lenses of power analysis are a primary part of the resources that the pastoral counselor brings to share with the counselee as appropriate for the sake of clarification.

This means that part of the pastoral counselor's task is to be able to look at and question the truthfulness of any and all assumptions that dominant systems of understanding have put out as truths. Much of that work is being done in the deconstructive projects of feminist, womanist, and other liberationist approaches to psychology, theology, and counseling practice.

Mary Ballou and Nancy W. Gabalac, in their paradigm of corrective action, discuss the process of separation as a first phase of counseling. They suggest that, in order for women to find themselves and develop authentic voice and narrative, they must separate from the definitions of and beliefs about themselves that have been developed as part of the process of harmful adaptation. This can be a very anxiety-producing process because what has seemed certain, even if it causes misery, is at least familiar and secure. It is a significant time of "unlearning" what has seemed unquestionable.[4] I think that the more feminist and womanist critiques pervade the culture, the easier it will be for a woman to question the "truths" of harmful adaptation, because at least there will be some alternate realities (or counterstories) that aren't entirely alien. But, at a personal level, this kind of change is difficult and frightening.

One woman who came to pastoral counseling revealed that she had been depressed for most of her seventeen-year marriage, even though her treatment for depression had only begun with her suicide attempt several months earlier. In her hospitalization, Mary had been told that her depression would improve with medication and so was able to understand the depression as an illness. This had been reassuring to her, because unpacking her life circumstances and questioning the way she understood her purpose and her roles would have been too painful and disruptive. Mary's depression, however, did not significantly improve over time and she entered into pastoral counseling. As we explored her current family situation, which included very traditional roles for family members, a sense of her own powerlessness, and threats of domestic violence and ongoing emotional abuse, she began to realize that taking medication was not going to bring her to a sense of her own health and wholeness. This was very distressing for her and she said one day in a counseling session, "I'm afraid of all the things that may change if I get over my depression." The stakes are high for women who come to counseling and who realize that their world doesn't reflect who they are or who they would want to become if they could live in a world that was equally healthy for all of its members.

This kind of deconstructive and reconstructive work has two primary resources. One of those resources is learning where the damaging assumptions and beliefs about the counselee's self and her potential come from. This is an educational process that relies on cultural analysis and listening openly to the stories of other women. The other resource comes from within the woman's own experience, the kinds of experiences that have challenged the dominant discourse rules but that have been left unstoried in the core narrative because there was too much dissonance or discouragement to pay them adequate attention. Narrative therapy theory is very helpful for using both of these resources.

We have explored the task of cultural analysis in previous chapters. Therapeutically, the counselor does not do a lot of didactic presentation in order to convey the world as she or he knows it. Instead, the counselor helps introduce other possible interpretations for the assumptions the counselee may have made about herself and the world. More important, the counselor helps the counselee look at her own history in terms of where she learned her limiting or oppressing beliefs about herself and the world. Ballou and Gabalac suggest that

> when a woman can make the very power systems which limited and controlled her the objects of study, she can gain some distance from them. She can lessen the hold that the power systems have had on her through their teachings, by beginning to examine and decode their messages, identifying the needs, goals, and uses for women that underlie the values that the power systems wish her to accept as her own. As she contrasts the promised rewards with the actual social, economic, and psychological consequences of the chronic self-denial and dependence that are recommended to her as a lifestyle, she starts the critical analysis that can protect her from the internalization of external prescriptions and norms.[5]

One place where this kind of analytical work can happen is in support or counseling groups of women. Because women often have been taught to pay more attention to, and have more empathy for, other people's stories than their own, a woman may be able to hear the experiences that another woman has with more critical distance and advocacy than she gives to her own. Women are more likely to generate alternative interpretations of negative self-images and assumptions for other women than they are for themselves. After a while, though, it becomes evident that they can make use of what they are saying to each other for their own stories. Cultural analysis and deconstruction become a natural outgrowth of these kinds of truth-telling women's groups.

The second resource for gaining distance comes out of women's own experiences and stories. As the counselor carefully listens to the stories and experiences being revealed, she or he asks questions about those experiences, such as, "Where did these beliefs come from?" or "When were things different?" When a woman begins to question all aspects of the stories she tells, she may well find gaps in her own interpretations because she has never been given the opportunity to stand back and examine her experience from an affirming point of view. Parry explains the process by saying that

> to question and challenge a story even as one listens respectfully to it is to introduce unrealized or forgotten connections between that story and the stories and events which, as seemingly unconnected, have left the person experiencing guilt or powerlessness as she attempts to make her story proceed according to her intentions. . . . Intrinsic to the validating role of the therapist with respect to the person finding her voice, is that of offering within a series of challenging yet respectful conversations, words that give voice to hitherto inchoate experiences. Such words are never imposed from some "knowing" point of view, but put forth as if only to demonstrate that such experiences can be described and shared through the magic of language.[6]

It is by the discovery of stories that don't fit the dominant narrative— examples that show where a woman was self-sufficient or extraordinarily successful or stronger than she usually sees herself—that the hold of the dominant and damaging narratives are loosened. In other words, it is within the woman's own life experience that the hopeful future resides— not in changing her but in helping her find the creative possibilities that have always been a part of her but that the dominant discourse and oppressive power structures have discouraged her from finding. One of the key assumptions of a narrative approach to counseling is that those alternative or unique stories are abundant and can be found with minimal difficulty. Those are the stories, then, that get therapeutic attention. Rather than focusing exclusively, or even mostly, on the negative stories and experiences (i.e., "getting to the root of the problem"), the narrative counselor focuses at least equally on the stories and experiences that will change the core narrative by being included.

These resources—the ability to do cultural analysis, especially by forming truth-telling communities, and the ability to find alternative stories within one's own experience even when they have been constricted or invalidated by a dominant discourse—find form in the notion of counterstories.

Counterstories

A counterstory is defined by Hilde Lindemann Nelson as "a story that contributes to the moral self-definition of its teller by undermining a dominant story, undoing it and retelling it in such a way as to invite new interpretations and conclusions."[7] Defined in this way it is clear that a feminist counterstory can be formed and told by any individual as she seeks to resist a destructive dominant story that is interwoven within the core narrative. A counterstory is always a rebellious story—emerging when the counterstory is recognized to be more true than the dominant story and serving to resist that dominant story. It is a moral story in that it leads its teller to take action—action that is intended to continue resisting the dominant story as it empowers the teller to restory her life. It gives strategies for resistance and strategies for reconstruction. In addition, counterstories attempt to hold in careful and creative tension the dual realities of women's victimization in a patriarchal culture and women's strength, resiliency, and creativity in resisting that victimization.

Although feminist counterstories can be told and heard by an individual woman as she seeks to deconstruct a problematic narrative and reconstruct a healthier one, it is important to be aware that a counterstory that attempts to undermine a dominant patriarchal story can prove hazardous to the teller unless it is told and heard in a safe community. As we noted in chapter 3, "A woman cannot remain a rebel if she is alone, for she runs the risk of being crushed by the dominant discourse."[8]

Consequently, counterstories that deliberately seek to undermine and deconstruct patriarchy's narrative are best generated, told, and used for action in feminist communities of choice. Nelson believes that feminist communities of choice make room for counterstories that not only resist dominant culture stories, but also create the space necessary to generate morally preferable narratives that will enhance the culture and its members. These communities have the potential not only to recognize difference, but to put faces on difference in such a way that stereotypes and negative judgments are avoided. The stories that are told are both personal and political and they allow each to be known even as the community develops a shared counterstory. The hope is that the stories of each are heard carefully and that they cause each member to examine her own narrative in ways that are both accountable and empowering.

The counterstories formed in feminist communities of choice become, as Nelson says, "narratives of resistance and insubordination that allow communities of choice to challenge and revise the paradigm stories of the 'found' communities in which they are embedded (the pre-existing contexts in which we belong such as neighborhoods, families, work, etc.). The ability of counterstories to reconfigure dominant stories permits those who have been excluded or oppressed by a 'found' community to gain fuller access to the goods offered there. Feminist counterstories in particular can be used to reclaim the wider community for its marginalized members."[9] Feminist counterstories, as defined by Nelson, create the bridge between personal and cultural narratives—they provide access to both deconstruction and restorying for individuals and for the culture.

Theological Resources

The development of counterstories is not unlike the dynamics of the parables told by Jesus. This form of discourse, which appears to be authentic to Jesus in the Scriptures, can be an important methodological resource as pastoral counselors attempt to help people gain clarity about their lives and relationships. There are several dimensions to the parables that might be useful to consider for the work of clarification in feminist-based pastoral counseling.

First, many of the parables deal with the ordinary. There is a general respect for ordinary events in the ordinary people of the time. These are often stories about marginalized people going about their daily business. And yet in the middle of those daily events, radical insight breaks in and nothing remains the same. God's spirit and wisdom are present in what might otherwise seem like a routine moment and the characters in the parable are transformed, as is the culture that hears about this transformation. The parables are about people having their ordinary lives respected and valued as a way to experience God. When talking about the parables that are oriented toward the domestic life of women, Nicola Slee says,

> the parables suggest that within the context of the domestic the unexpected, the wholly gratuitous and unlooked for, erupts—but in so doing, the very world of the everyday is irretrievably shattered, irreversibly transformed. This provides no easy solution to the conflicts women experience between the domestic and the professional, home and work, family and society, and others, but it does hint that to discover the presence of God within the confines of the mundane and domestic is radically and explosively to transform these realities—and this may be as uncomfortable as it is unexpected.[10]

Also, the transformation experienced in the private, everyday sphere has radical implications for the listeners and for their world. Transformation is never merely a personal experience.

Second, the reframing that happens in the parables may give guidance to the pastoral counselor. The assumption of many of the parables is that the realities accepted by the dominant culture obscure truth. People have learned to believe lies and, thus, to put their own lives in danger or distress. This is also true for most of the people who come for pastoral counseling—they have lost themselves in attempting to live according to false definitions of who they are and what their world is really like. So one way for the truth to be revealed is by turning things upside down and, in the chaos of that, allowing new perspectives on truth to emerge. Counseling is risky. People come to counseling because their lives are not manageable any longer with their current narratives. And many people come to the counselor without the ability to imagine life in another way. They often come asking to be helped to return to "normal," even though "normal" was the precursor to their experience of extreme distress. I worked with a thirty-eight-year-old woman struggling with depression and suicidal ideas who wanted to be helped to get back to normal. When I explored with her what she was like before she was depressed, she was unable to locate any time in her adult life when she was not depressed. Is it ethical, much less feminist, for me to help her return to a state of functional depression? Counseling is risky because lives and relationships and contexts change because of it. Coming to and believing in a new kind of clarity may be frightening.

A third dimension that serves as resource to pastoral counselors is one pointed out by Donald Capps in his book *Reframing*. Capps suggests that it is the storyteller, or, in this application, the pastoral counselor, who provides the story's frame. In other words, the content of the story belongs to the people who experience it, but the frame through which that story is seen is provided by Jesus in the parables and by the pastoral counselor in the counseling process.[11] The framework, therefore, can be shifted in such a way that more authentic and life-giving truths emerge from the story than they did through its original framework of meaning. The parables gave new directions to their hearers in situations that seemed stagnant and absolute. The same is true for the process of reframing in pastoral counseling when it is done for the sake of finding more life-giving directions.

We should note that the process of gaining clarity moves alongside the process of gaining voice. It is not a distant, objective, analytical experience to identify the counselee's problems so they can be solved. It is a coming to new awareness—a transforming awareness—for the sake of empowering the self and enriching and reversing a culture that has been and continues to be toxic to many people. It is a searching from within the ordinary, the whole life experience of the counselee and her relationships, for re-orienting moments that open pathways to truth that have been hidden by dominant and damaging scripts. Coming to voice and gaining clarity help people move toward the ability to engage in authentic response to God and to others. They help people become able to seek and follow their vocations without the chains of falsehoods about the self, about their places in the world, and about their gifts and graces for the betterment of God's "kindom."[12]

Counseling Resources

It seems to me that narrative therapy theory is especially useful when helping a woman gain clarity about her experience and vocation. In the last section on coming to voice we talked about the importance of careful listening on the part of the pastoral counselor—a listening that comes from a place of unknowing and that trusts that the counselee has the resources she needs for health. This kind of listening provides a safe and hospitable environment where a woman can move from being incredible to herself and others to being credible. She can learn to know what she knows and to speak that knowledge with confidence. Coming to voice helps a woman overcome the societal forces, which have often become internalized, that have told her she has nothing to offer and no right to her own story. She learns to trust herself and her interpretation of her experience.

Unfortunately, our core narratives are formed within the context of the culture's core narratives—about gender, about race, about sexual orientation, about appearance, and so on. Our own personal narratives are generally formed so that they do not create unmanageable cognitive and emotional dissonance with the familial, institutional, and cultural stories we live within. Of course, we choose elements of the family and societal stories with which we will identify, but many of those choices are made early and without much critical awareness that they may well be distorted. Thus, when we come to voice we may recognize elements of our own stories that are in conflict with cultural or familial truths and we may seek support for exploring those in the face of the familial or cultural resistances we will encounter. This is an important part of feminist-oriented pastoral counseling—helping to support counselees as they name and claim personal and communal counterstories that better guide them through life as whole and authentic people. There are also times, however, when counselees live with problems that don't seem resolvable because the often false claims of the family or culture don't allow a preferred and healthier narrative to surface. In these situations it is important to find ways to deconstruct the problematic narrative in such a way that more authentic and useful truths may emerge.

Narrative theory has a strong deconstructive/reconstructive emphasis. One of the most important elements of narrative counseling is separating the problems or issues that the counselee brings for counseling from the person herself. A person is helped to move from being, for example, a "depressed person" to a person who struggles with (or against) depression. As Joseph B. Eron and Thomas W. Lund suggest, in creating this form of counseling, narrative therapists "spoke about problems and therapy in a profoundly different way than their predecessors or contemporaries. From the idea of thinking of people as 'having problems' (or being problems), they moved to the idea of problems 'having people.' Problems were oppressive, alien invaders that took over people's lives and prevented them from being who they wanted to be."[13] Thus, it is often important for the counselor to move from a stance of empathic listening, so central to the process of coming to voice, to a stance of deconstructive listening. This not only separates the problem from the person, it also facilitates the counselee's exploration of where certain previously unquestioned narrative beliefs came from. Once those destructive beliefs that were once held to be truths are seen as one possible interpretation out of many, then new meanings that work on behalf of the counselee and her relationships may begin to emerge.

Before moving on to the work of constructing alternative narratives, a case example here might be helpful. Jennifer came to her pastor for some counseling help because she had been in a relationship that had been moving toward marriage and that had become derailed. This had happened to Jennifer before, and in both situations she had broken the relationship off because she didn't trust her boyfriend's commitment to her and love for her. She suggested to the pastor that "she was a mistrustful person and needed to get over it." The pastor listened carefully to Jennifer, affirming her right to make decisions about her relationships and her feelings of insecurity and worry. As they talked together, the problem seemed to emerge as one of not being able to tell which situations she should be trusting in and which ones she should be mistrustful of. She had been raised in a home where it was safer and more accurate to distrust what she was told by her parents, who were both active alcoholics and abusive to her. Unfortunately, she had internalized the label of "mistrustful person," in effect blaming herself for what had been good judgment in her youth.

Together, Jennifer and her pastor worked to name the problem as "self-doubt." They framed the issue as one where Jennifer tended, when in intimate relationships, to have to struggle with self-doubt about whether she was accurately reading the relational situation. This introduced the possibility that there were times when Jennifer's mistrust was an accurate judgment about a relationship's credibility and times when it might not be the best interpretation. In the process of exploring this problem (named "self-doubt"), which seemed to creep up on Jennifer when she was in an intimate relationship, Jennifer was also able to identify numerous situations when she had made a good judgment about the trustworthiness of a friend or colleague. In fact, it became clear that in both of her intimate relationships, Jennifer's judgment of mistrust was an accurate one. She was able to identify several people who would not name her as mistrustful the way her two boyfriends had. Once she began to identify times when she had accurately judged trustworthy relationships, she also realized that self-doubt seemed to have the most power in her intimate romantic relationships. She experimented with developing certain criteria by which she could measure trustworthiness in these relationships and she experimented with voicing her expectations and concerns with a romantic partner. In doing this, self-doubt was disempowered and Jennifer was able to see that she had good powers of discrimination and, in fact, an acute sensitivity to people who weren't trustworthy. She learned how to claim that gift of sensitivity and eliminate her self-label of being a mistrustful person.

This case demonstrates the importance of finding an accurate name for the problem and separating it from the person so that the problem can be adequately resisted and lose its centrality in the counselee's core narrative. Once Jennifer was not operating by a strong narrative theme of seeing herself as a mistrustful person, a whole new set of experiences, which were more accurate and more helpful, began to emerge. Deconstructive listening is naming what is doing harm to the person from within a central place in the narrative, and separating it from the person so that it might be disempowered and replaced.

Once a problem is named and separated from the core narrative, thus losing its power, exceptions to the problem can be named and restoried. People have many experiences that either contradict or don't fit into a central narrative. The way people cope with that generally is either to not remember the exception or to distort the experience and its meaning in such a way that it doesn't engender cognitive or emotional dissonance and, thus, can be integrated into the narrative. In the case above, Jennifer was able to remember times when she wasn't mistrustful at all, but rather had formed numerous close relationships with friends and colleagues. The counselor avoided buying into the problematic narrative and believing that this internalized label of "mistrustful" really represented Jennifer's core self. By opening up the framework and finding the more significant problem of "self-doubt" and then separating that from Jennifer's self-definition, new stories that served as helpful allies in fighting off self-doubt became available. This story again illustrates the absolute importance of the pastoral counselor operating from a position of not-knowing. The counselor does not try to "diagnose" or look for pathology or lead a person to the "right" perception. The counselor's primary function is to help open up the framework that is holding a problematic narrative in place so that exceptions and previously ignored stories may find their way into the person's meaning-making processes. The counselor is able to raise questions about the power and place of the problem and explore with the counselee how the problem might best be resisted. It is after deconstructive listening and deconstructive questioning have separated the problem from the person and have relativized its interpretive claims that the processes of looking for narrative exceptions and restorying possibilities can take place.

This work of restorying is not an individualistic process. A feminist approach to pastoral counseling affirms that a person's story is always an engendered story and that gender is one of the culture's key narrative themes. Gerald Monk writes that, "far from being simplistic, narrative counseling is based on the understanding that problems are manufactured in a social, cultural, and political context. The newly born child is instantly bathed in a cultural 'soup.' From a narrative perspective, problems may be seen as floating in this soup. The problems we encounter are multisourced, they are developed over a long period of time, and they come together through the medium of human language to construct and produce our experience."[14] Restorying involves remembering and giving credibility to stories that had no place in the problematic narrative but that serve to both resist problems and form meaning that help the counselee move to a healthier personal story within a healthier cultural story. Deconstruction and restorying/reconstruction are both personal *and* political acts.

Five Rs for Helping Women Gain Clarity

I find it helpful to think of this narrative process of gaining clarity through five Rs. These fundamental processes in feminist-oriented pastoral counseling are theologically motivated in that they seek to help empower authenticity and strength for women counselees and for a culture struggling to resist patriarchal and kyriarchal forces that destroy its members.

The first R is for *remembering*. One of the characteristics of problem narratives is that they tend to make it difficult to remember anything that doesn't fit their "truths." Thus, it is important to find ways to re-member those experiences and people who hold alternative and pre-ferred truths for the counselee's narrative. Since the counselee frequently can't remember those things that would cast doubt on a problematic strand of a core narrative, it may be important for the counselor to ask about others who might have seen things differently. For example, ask-ing Jennifer about who might not have thought she was a mistrustful person elicited memories about relationships that were full of mutual trust and satisfaction. There are generally trustworthy people in a coun-selee's life that have seen through the lies of the problematic narrative and thus will stand as witnesses to alternative truths. I had a grandfather, for example, who consistently countered my self-narrative of being a person who disappoints others. He would challenge that narrative whenever he got the chance to whomever was reinforcing it at the time. This served as a very important counterstory for me in my formative years. Generally a counselee can find the exceptional person who holds the exceptional narrative strand. That person will help her to remember new truths.

The second R is for *reframing*. Reframing is a gentle process that takes the content of a story as accurate and truthful and then offers new angles from which to see and make meaning out of that content. Any action or event has numerous possibilities of interpretation. In fact, these multiple possibilities of interpretation are often the source of enormous conflict between people who see the same event but give it different meanings depending on how the event fits into their own narrative frameworks. Narrative theory affirms that language is reality—how we interpret and make meaning out of events becomes the truth of those events. Narrative counselors attempt to support new, nonproblematic or less problematic frameworks as possible avenues for interpreting and making meaning out of experiences that have been storied within the problematic narra-tive. In some ways this listening for the purpose of discovering new frameworks for interpretation is the point of a narrative approach. Wendy Drewery and John Winslade talk about the listening style of the narrative counselor and suggest that, "Unlike the Rogerian therapist, whose active listening is intended to reflect back the client's story like a mirror without distortion, the narrative therapist looks for hidden mean-ings, spaces, or gaps, and evidence of conflicting stories . . . listening for what is not said."[15] The purpose of this is not to diagnose pathology but rather to provide a potential framework for what has not been said and to facilitate the new, preferred narrative.

Reframing invites a relativizing of prior problematic assumptions. Usually, a problematic narrative is problematic because it offers no acceptable pathway to a solution to the problem experienced by the counselee. The purpose of reframing is to offer an alternative way of thinking about the experiences or feelings that have motivated the counselee to seek counseling. It attempts to offer an equally or more plausible alternative to the current interpretive strategy. And it attempts to provide multiple pathways for new directions, whereas the previous interpretation led to a dead end. At the very least, a good reframing response by a counselor introduces a credible possibility that there is more than one way to understand what's going on. A reframing response must be plausible and truthful. It must represent a valid possibility for interpretation or it will not be useful and, in fact, will be seen for what it then is—a manipulative, counselor-driven expectation for the counseling.

To use an example I have cited elsewhere, Mary had viewed her depression initially as a moral weakness and as a failure to her family. When she had been hospitalized after a suicide attempt, the medical team credibly reframed her depression as an illness—something she could not avoid but could be treated. This brought Mary great relief—a new way to understand her experience that gave her some hope. Unfortunately, it also took away her role as an agent. She felt like a helpless victim and was no more empowered to address her general despair than she had been previously. In addition, the medication was only marginally effective. In our work together, both of her interpretive frameworks (moral failure and disease victim) led her to dead ends in terms of creating a satisfying life for herself and her family. What I heard in her story, that which was unsaid but present, had to do with her sense of disempowerment and invisibility. After helping her come to voice in telling her story and being deeply believed, I suggested a reframing for her depression. I suggested to her that I could not imagine a better way she could have gotten her family's attention than by "going on strike" through her depression. This reframing, although shocking to her in some degree, also held a note of familiarity and truth. It led us to explore ways in which she could develop a different kind of agency in her family that would not be so hard on her and on her relationships. The reframing allowed new narratives to emerge.[16]

The third R for helping women gain clarity is for *reversing*. Here I am drawing on Mary Daly, a theologian who powerfully redefined the grounds of theological conversation from a radical feminist perspective.

Although direct reversals of interpretation are not always helpful, when narrative strands are grounded in and intertwined with the lies about women of patriarchy, often it becomes important to suggest that the reverse value may be the more accurate one. Sometimes it is only in the starkness of a proposed reversal that the falsehood of patriarchy's claims becomes apparent. Daly offers some insight into that process in the radical theology and philosophy of *Gyn/Ecology,* where she talks about the primary rule of patriarchy as being that of deception. She suggests that in order for us to gain clarity it is necessary for us to re-reverse the great reversals of patriarchy. Her assumption is that if most of the values that patriarchy holds dear and assumes as truths were reversed, those reversals would represent much greater truth for women's lives.[17] In her thorough analysis of a sexist culture Daly also demonstrates the rather amazing power of language and the need for women (and for all whose language has been either eliminated or co-opted) to create language that more accurately and powerfully describes their authentic experience. Reversals can be offered as tentative hypotheses when patriarchal claims are so deeply interwoven with self-interpretations that self-destructive actions are the only seemingly viable options. For example, a woman who has experienced battering by her husband over time cries out, "But a good Christian woman does not break her marital covenant. She supports her husband and tries to understand him." An appropriate reversal response might be, "Could it be that the covenant was broken with the first blow?" or "Maybe a good Christian woman is called to stand against her husband's sin." The problem with reversal responses used in one-to-one counseling is that they tend to elicit a desire to defend the original interpretation. Reversals that are most effective seem to come out of a group context where a group member can speak out of her own experience in a way that challenges the absolute claim of the counselee. It is particularly true, though, that theological or faith claims may sometimes have to be subjected to the strategy of reversal in order to open them up to exploration and novelty.

The fourth R in the work of gaining clarity is that of *re-imagining.* Over the years of working with feminist-oriented pastoral counseling I have become convinced that imagination is one of the most important and effective resources available for helping women gain clarity and imagine new directions and choices. For our purposes, I am defining the image as an internal experience that integrates perception, feeling, and meaning into a new whole. The use of imagination unleashes the creative, integrative power within each person to find out what symbols open her up to more meaningful connection with God, with self, and with creation. By defining the image in this way, it becomes clear that an image is much more than an internal or mental picture, although this is how it has sometimes been understood. It is, instead, an experiential reality in and of itself—one that integrates thought, feeling, and meaning inside the self and in the social context. Thomas A. Droege states that "the imagination is a natural resource that we all have for a fuller, more effective life. Rather than escaping reality, the imagination has access to the inner world of our experience and can give a deeper-than-intellectual expression to that reality."[18]

One of the primary reasons that imagery is so helpful in counseling is the paradoxical reality that images are autonomous in and of themselves, having a life of their own while still being under the control of the imager. One of the most powerful characteristics of imagery is its autonomy. Even in the process of induced or guided imagery an image takes on a life of its own, tapping into knowledge and perceptions through a nonlinear, nonintellectual route. Experiencing the power of this autonomy in imagination work can have a profound effect on the client. And yet even in the intensity of this process, the imagers know that they are engaging in a behavior that involves choice. They can manipulate the image in terms of setting and process. They can watch the imagination process as if they are standing outside of it. In fact, it is the safeness of this control, the "I" being able to observe the "me" in the image, that allows the imager to participate in the power and novelty of the imagery experience. It is this paradox of novelty and controllability that make using imagination a powerful tool in a narrative approach to pastoral counseling with women. The integrative power of imagination allows new narrative possibilities to emerge that come out of authentic self-experience and yet takes the various contextual realities of the woman's life into consideration. Whether it is through the use of a powerful image or metaphor that serves as a vehicle for generating new views of self, or an imaginative rehearsal of creative possibilities, or even an extended fantasy process that produces a larger scope of life choices, the use of imagination in pastoral counseling is a key resource for the development of life-giving narratives.[19]

Finally, the fifth R for gaining clarity is that of *restorying*. Restorying is the process of taking those unstories that have existed in experience but that have not been able to be claimed, and building them into the core narrative. The purpose of a core narrative is to take the cumulative set of experiences one has had and make integrative meaning out of them. The core narrative is what serves as the integrative lens. It is only when the problematic strands of the core narrative have been adequately challenged with new meaning-making lenses as they become available that unstories can find their way into the core narrative and play their own role in shaping the person's hermeneutical assumptions. Restorying is taking back into oneself those things that represent authentic truths and making them a part of the ongoing narrative. The narrative regains a sense of continuity and meaning, which can be communicated to the self and to others in ways that lead to a more abundant and faithful life.

Restorying often requires that others be exposed to these new aspects of the self-story so that they do not continue to live according to the scripts of the old problematic narrative. Narrative theory is a systemic theory in that it recognizes that people have many other players in their stories. Narratives are not individually owned but rather formed, played out, confirmed, and denied in the many systems we are a part of. As individuals gain a different sense of self and a new clarity about the truths they wish to claim about themselves in the world, others who have known the person in the context of the former narrative need to be introduced and integrated into the new pathways generated by the new narrative. This may take the form of couple, family, or group counseling or it may involve coaching a counselee in exposing others to new narrative assumptions. In the encounter of the person with the new narrative with those who still operate within the parameters of the former narrative, their mutual or relational narrative is also reshaped. A negotiation of truths and meanings is introduced into the relationship in ways that may not have been present before. This can be difficult and stressful for the counselee and her relationships and yet is necessary for the integration of her new directions and meanings. The counselor can help this process by helping people in relationship to look at their shared narrative and re-examine assumptions they had previously held in common but that are no longer mutual.

Restorying is a process that occurs at individual, relational, institutional, and cultural levels. It is an ongoing endeavor. Women who are beginning a restorying process may need a great deal of support and validation for the changes they have made as they engage these changes with important worlds of meaning that existed before the counseling work began. Communities of choice where counterstories (to the destructive dominant narrative) are generated and supported may be a very important part of the re-integration of the counselee's "new worlds" and old.

Gaining Clarity as a Multifaceted Process

It is important to note that these five Rs are not limited to one-on-one pastoral counseling. Much of this work is done in women's lives through friendships and intimate partners, through educational experiences or group conversations, and through everyday encounters with events that challenge core assumptions. Pastors can participate in the process of building preferred narratives and disempowering problem narratives for people and for culture through their preaching, their education courses, the modeling they do, and the groups they make available, as well as through the work of pastoral care and counseling. Pastors need to be willing to engage in the deconstructing of patriarchal and kyriarchal narratives in all dimensions of their work so that the constructing of personal, familial, institutional, and cultural narratives may be healthier for all.

six

Gaining Clarity
in the Context of Depression

It is not an exaggeration to say that the most common request for counseling to a pastor comes from women who are struggling with depression. That is not to say that depression will always be the presenting problem. Many women who are struggling with depression come to the pastor with issues that do not immediately seem linked to the depression. A woman may ask for marital counseling or for help in addressing other relationships. She may want to talk about her work, her boredom, her lack of spirituality, or her guilt. But the reality is that in many cases these counseling requests are a symptom of, or even a cause of, an experience of depression. And it can be easy for a pastor to miss the depression in her or his eagerness to address the presenting problem. Thus, it is important for pastors to understand how prevalent depression is in women, as well as its symptoms and effects.

Defining Depression

There is a variety of definitions of depression. In fact, some writers suggest we should never talk about depression, only depressions.[1] There are several complicating factors when we try to define depression. First, it is a word of common usage. Most people periodically experience what they name to themselves as "depression." That can mean that they are experiencing a sense of having low energy or being bored, in a down mood, or restless. Or it can mean that they are experiencing familiar symptoms of an overwhelming lethargy that drapes itself over them periodically and saps their interest in living. Or it can be any number of symptoms or experiences between these two ends of the spectrum. Some experts define depressions as just that, a spectrum of symptom configurations that have similarities but differ in duration, intensity, and triggers. Others suggest that there are distinct kinds of depression that may or may not be related to each other in terms of their causes or their treatments. This is the second complexity. Various kinds of depressions may exist that call for different understandings or treatments, but there is much debate about what those different categories and treatments might be. Some scholars of depression claim absolute biological roots for depression and, thus, absolute biological treatments for them. And there are people of equal expertise who claim that depression, at least in most forms, is primarily, if not absolutely, a response to life events and environmental factors. Although there are numerous scholars who now talk about depression as a "bio-psycho-social" problem (or even a bio-psycho-social-political and sometimes even spiritual, problem), it seems as if many are using this complex name with a great deal of uncertainty about what really leads to depression and what can help people resist it. The only thing that seems pretty clear in the literature is that depression is a serious problem for contemporary Western culture and that women suffer from it at a rate of at least two to one over men (some say as much as four or even six to one). We can't talk about pastoral counseling with women without focusing significantly on depression.

Although most of us "know" what depression feels like, it is a misleading knowledge. When we are in the midst of depression, it seems to steal our energy, our ability to experience pleasure, our plans and goals for our lives, and even our hope. Yet when we are no longer feeling depressed (or have never experienced it) it is very difficult to remember what it was like or even to have much sympathy for others experiencing it. There is an amnesia-like experience when one is experiencing depression about what it was like not to be depressed and that emotional amnesia seems to go both ways. So we can describe depression but it is hard to imagine it and its enormous power unless we are experiencing it or have done so recently.

Depression is a total experience. It involves the mind, the spirit, the body, important relationships, casual relationships, work, family, leisure time, and so on. There is no aspect that depression leaves untouched when it enters a person's life. Susan Nolen-Hoeksema describes the common symptoms of depression as including "loss of motivation, sadness, low self-esteem, physical aches and pains, and difficulty concentrating. The depressed person often talks about 'not caring any more' and shows decreased interest in the activities she used to enjoy. She may lose her appetite or she may begin eating more. She may have trouble sleeping, or she may want to sleep all the time. People struggling with depression are slowed down in movement, in speech, and in thought. Very common to depression are thoughts of worthlessness and guilt, and some people experiencing depression attempt to commit suicide."[2] These symptoms vary in duration and in intensity. Some suggest they vary in cause.

Most often people divide up types of depression by these three factors—duration, intensity, and etiology, or cause. Most people suggest that there are two major forms of depression—unipolar and bipolar. These, as their names suggest, are delineated by their cycles. People who struggle with unipolar depressions experience the symptoms of depression consistently, while people with bipolar depressions experience a cycle of depressive symptoms generally followed or preceded by symptoms of mania. Mania involves a sense of extreme well-being and enormous energy that impairs judgment, discipline, and impulse control. People who experience mania tend to do everything in an accelerated fashion. They tend to need to be moving all of the time, to talk fast and continuously, to make dozens of plans and want to follow them all immediately. People experiencing mania often get into trouble with the law or in relationships by acting impulsively and extravagantly in whatever they do. Like depression, mania can vary in duration and intensity, ranging from mild "highs" to psychosis. Just to confuse things a little further, there are some forms of bipolar disorder in which only one side (usually the depression) exhibits itself and yet it is still understood to be the depression that "goes with" the normal bipolar experience.

Within the two broad categories of unipolar and bipolar depressions there is a variety of other distinctions. *The Diagnostic and Statistical Manual,* 4th edition (DSM-IV: the diagnostic "bible" of psychiatry) represents the most detailed categorization of different types of depression. Some find that this diagnostic process interferes with the care of people with depression more than it helps. Others find that having these categories with detailed distinctive symptoms for each is helpful in making treatment decisions. For our purposes here I will list several kinds of depressions usually delineated when categories of depression are used.

1. MAJOR DEPRESSIONS. These are often called "clinical depressions." They are unipolar and are characterized by significant physical,

emotional, and relational symptoms. A person who is experiencing a major depression has had continuous symptoms for more than two weeks and finds herself feeling helpless, hopeless, sad, and joyless. Usually she experiences eating disturbances (eating significantly more or less than usual) and sleep disturbances (sleeping significantly more or less than usual). She may well experience a sense of self-hatred or guilt or despair. She tends to evaluate herself, her current life, and her future in very negative terms. And she has little hope or anticipation that her experience with depression will ever end. Major depressions often last six months or more and once a person has experienced a major depression, it is common for them to return with even greater intensity in the future.

2. DYSTHYMIA. This is a more mild and chronic form of depression. Many of the same symptoms are present but they are not as incapacitating or intense as in major depression. This kind of depression, as with major depression, is more common in women, people with inadequate financial resources, and people without adequate relational support. This kind of depression becomes so present that it can begin to feel like it is a personality trait rather than a form of depression.[3]

3. BIPOLAR DEPRESSION. This variety comes in two forms. One is commonly called manic depression and it is the major form of this depression. It involves swings in mood from major depression to mania and seems to have a strong biological basis. There is a variety of medications used to control the symptoms of this problem that mute the extremes of both depression and mania. A milder and more chronic form of bipolar depression is cyclothymia, which, again, can be so chronic in a person's life that it is hard to distinguish it from a personality trait.

4. MINOR DEPRESSION. There are also milder and less chronic forms of unipolar depression labeled in a variety of ways. Little real research has been done on these. Some people feel that they are very similar to major depression, only in a shorter or milder form and so should not be distinguished. These would be called minor depression (same duration as major depression but with fewer and less intense symptoms) and recurrent brief depression (severity is the same as major depression but only lasts for two to four days at a time, recurring at least once a month).[4]

5. SEASONAL AFFECTIVE DISORDER. This category of depression is defined by the experience of being recurringly depressed at a specific time of year, usually in the fall or winter. This is treated primarily by biological means using light therapy. Some argue that because this depression is

so clearly responsive to light therapy it should not be classified with the depressions.

6. HORMONAL DEPRESSIONS. There is significant debate surrounding these depressions, which are categorized hormonally for women. The first is premenstrual dysphoric disorder and the second is postpartum depression. For a diagnosis of premenstrual dysphoric disorder the symptoms must be severe enough to interfere with daily living. The symptoms listed in the DSM-IV are both physical and emotional—tiredness and bloating as well as anger, hopelessness, and anxiety. Angela Mitchell, however, says that "one study found that about forty percent of women have mild symptoms but only two to three percent have symptoms severe enough to truly disrupt their lives."[5] Many feminist scholars are concerned about this tendency to equate women's biology with psychopathology and there is a great deal of evidence that with both a diagnosis of premenstrual dysphoric disorder and postpartum depression, the hormonal changes only amplify depressions that already existed for other reasons. As Nolen-Hoeksema says, "One reason researchers may be having such a difficult time finding consistent evidence for various explanations of premenstrual depressions is that these depressions may not represent a distinct form of depression. Rather they may simply be exacerbations of an underlying or chronic depressive disorder. Very few women who show depressive symptoms during the premenstrual period show symptoms only during this period."[6] Similarly, women who experience postpartum depressions (depressions immediately following the birth of a child) may well have both hormonal and environmental factors at work in the depression, but women who have had prior depressions are much more likely to experience postpartum depressions than women who have not. As Mitchell says, "While there is probably a biological underpinning to the illness, women who have significant life stresses like money problems are more at risk. So are women who have serious marital or relationship problems."[7]

The reality is that these labels can be helpful or hurtful to the people for whom we care. We can use labels to help us better understand, normalize, and counsel with the women who come for pastoral counseling or we can use them to objectify, simplify, and dismiss them. Diagnostic criteria for depressions are useful insofar as they lead us to a better ability to connect with those suffering with them and help us to build a better set of skills for helping them resist depression in the present and the future.

The main thing for pastoral caregivers to know about working with people who are struggling with depression is that they experience it at every level of their existence. Depression creates (or is caused by) a set of cognitions or hermeneutical narrative lenses that shape all experiences into negative meanings. Psychologically, people feel powerless, confused, and despairing. Physically, people feel tired, achy, sleep and eating disordered, and as if their brain and body have stopped working for them. Relationally, people tend to experience more discord and isolation. And theologically, people lose a sense of the goodness of life or the possibilities for the future. For people who are depressed, God may well feel absent or uncaring or insignificant. Life may lose its value, even to the point of suicide. Depression, whether it is a major depression or minor or brief or postpartum, feels like a gray fog in which one lives and breathes and has one's being. Depending on the severity, the fog may periodically lift or the sun may shine through, or the fog may be so dense that a person becomes completely disoriented, but the fog is common to all who struggle with depression.

There is no agreement on what causes depression. There may be different causes for different types of depression. For example, bipolar disorder has long been thought to have genetic, biochemical roots. It is safe to say, however, that while there may be biological components in most depressions, depression cannot be understood entirely or, in my opinion, even primarily in those terms. One way to begin getting at the causes of depression—so that we can be engaged in prevention and not only care—is to look at who gets depressed. When different populations experience different levels and frequencies of depression, it helps us see root causes by looking at the differences between those groups.

Who Gets Depressed?

Because the term *depression* can describe so many different phenomena it is hard to get an accurate estimate of how many people suffer from it. Nonetheless, various surveys and studies estimate that at least 10 percent of the adult population (eight million people) of the United States is depressed in any given year. According to Howard W. Stone, "depression accounted for 565,000 hospital admissions, thirteen million visits to medical doctors, and seven-and-a-half million hospital days per year [in

1993]."[8] And according to most experts, depression in the United States (and in much of the world) is on the rise. Throughout the developed world, at least, there are consistently many more women than men who struggle with depression. With the exception of four populations, we see this large gender difference in depression. Those populations where there are no clear gender differences are elementary-age schoolchildren, college students, the recently widowed, and the elderly. In addition, it has been assumed that these gender differences only exist in unipolar depression, but Nolen-Hoeksema writes that "in a review of the literature on bipolar disorder, Clayton showed that both bipolar disorder and unipolar depression are more prevalent among women than among men."[9] If this is true, then there are no types of depression equally experienced by women and men except in the four populations mentioned above. It is worth exploring these gender differences in order to draw some tentative conclusions about causes of depression, especially in women.

Although there have been relatively few studies that empirically explore the nature of sex differences in depression, some work has been done in this area. Nolen-Hoeksema wrote a book titled *Sex Differences in Depression*, where she reviewed all of the relevant literature on this topic. The various studies have generally been created to explore one of the particular hypotheses of this sex difference. Those hypotheses include biological explanations (hormonal and genetic), psychological explanations (personality traits in women make them more susceptible), sociological explanations (undervaluing by society, minimal role satisfactions, role overload theory, and help-seeking differences in men and women), and political explanations (discrimination, both overt and covert, and violence against women). Nolen-Hoeksema explores each set of hypotheses and looks at them in the context of women's life cycles.

She begins by looking at children and adolescents. It is well known that sex differences in depression do not emerge until adolescence. As Nolen-Hoeksema writes, "Before adolescence boys show more of almost every type of psychopathology than girls, including adjustment reactions, antisocial disorders, learning disorders, psychotic disorders, and affective disorders. Only with anxiety disorders and affective disorders, however, do we see a switch in the ratio of boys to girls with the disorder during adolescence."[10] She explores this adolescent shift through a variety of theoretical proposals and concludes that there are probably only two certain explanations for it. First, "the rates of sexual abuse of girls increase substantially in early adolescence and many abuse victims continue to be abused throughout their adolescent years. . . . It seems plausible then that at least some of the increase in rates of depression in adolescent girls can be attributed to increases in the fear of abuse and in actual rates of abuse."[11] Numerous studies show a greatly increased risk for depression and suicide in girls and women as a result of physical and sexual abuse. Second, the development of secondary sex characteristics is generally viewed quite negatively by girls. "Girls do not like the physical changes of puberty and they have poorer body images than do boys. In addition, there appears to be some increased vulnerability to negative life events in girls during some period of pubertal change, although it is unclear exactly when this period of sensitivity occurs."[12] These two events, violence and increasing development of negative body image, seem to be the events most clearly linked to the development of adolescent sex differences in depression.

After going through the studies of each category of explanation, Nolen-Hoeksema concludes several things. First, she concludes that hormonal and genetic explanations are not supported by the literature as causes for the sex differences in depression. She writes:

> The biological explanations of sex differences in depression have not been well supported. There is no evidence that women have a greater genetic predisposition to depression than men, and the hormonal explanations have received mixed and indirect support at best. . . . Finally, the biological explanations of sex differences in depression, as a class of explanations, cannot explain the absence of sex differences in certain subgroups, such as university students and the recently widowed. Certainly the women in these subgroups have the same biological make-up as women in groups that do show sex differences in depression. Social and environmental factors cannot be ignored as we try to explain the variations across groups in sex differences in depression.[13]

She also concludes that neither help-seeking differences in men and women nor personality traits explain these sex differences. Although she clearly feels that much more research needs to be done to better explain these global sex differences in rates of depression, Nolen-Hoeksema does identify several well-supported theories of difference. First, women experience more intimate violence (both rape and battering) than do men and this has a significant effect on rates of depression. Second, women experience overt and covert discrimination pervasively in the culture and this negatively influences both self-esteem and affect. Third, inequalities in marriage are a source of women's greater vulnerability to depression. And finally, women tend to respond to depression differently than men, ruminating on it excessively, whereas men are more likely to distract themselves from the depression, resulting in shorter depressive episodes. While this fourth issue is of particular importance in exploring how to best help women struggling with depression, the other three explanations center on the consequences for women of living in a patriarchal culture. As Susan J. Dunlap writes, "Multiple indicators suggest that what accounts for the differences in rates of depression is differences in access to power."[14]

Women's Experiences with Depression

As we can see, many women suffer from depression. Estimates range from 5 to 9 percent of American women being depressed at any given time and as many as 25 percent or more of women becoming depressed sometime in their lives, again depending on how one defines depression. Some data suggests that the rates are lower among African American and Hispanic women,[15] while some researchers find similar rates across racial and ethnic lines.[16]

According to the American Psychological Association's National Task Force on Depression and Women, particular life circumstances can trigger depression. Those circumstances include overwhelming stress, victimization (especially childhood sexual abuse, rape, and battering), inadequate income, alcohol and drug abuse, and violence. And although all women are at high risk for these experiences, as Mitchell states, "These events are disproportionately represented in the lives of Black women."[17] People who experience poverty, violence, and other forms of powerlessness are at higher risk for depression.

In general, women begin to experience higher rates of depression around age fourteen or fifteen. Those rates continue to rise, peaking between the ages of twenty-five and forty-four. The rates then seem to remain fairly stable, possibly dropping somewhat during older age. Contrary to popular thought, women don't seem to experience higher levels of depression around "empty nest" or other transitions of midlife (like menopause).

Kay Rawson and Glen Jenson conducted a significant study measuring levels of depression in women at midlife. They discovered that there were no significant differences in rates of depression among women ages thirty-four to forty-four, forty-five to fifty-five, and fifty-six to sixty-six.[18] The researchers concluded that "the departure from home of the last child is significant, but is not a traumatic event; that ambivalent feelings are normal; and that the women generally viewed midlife as a positive time." They go on to say that "two cultural myths about empty nest in the literature, (a) that depression is inevitable, and (b) that full-time home-makers will experience more distress than women who have outside work, remain unsupported."[19] It is important that the myths about women's depression be debunked as we seek to find accurate information about those things that make women most vulnerable to depression. Factors that do seem to make women vulnerable to depression, some of which have already been alluded to, need to be explored.

Victimization

Violence against women was discussed at some length in chapter 4. It is, however, worth noting again that women experience very high rates of intimate violence in their lives. Over 25 percent of all of the violence women experience is intimate violence, compared to only 2 percent of the violence men experience.[20] Somewhere between two and eight million women are assaulted each year by their partners. There are more than half a million rapes every year of women and almost two-thirds of the women do not report the crime to the police.[21] And more than one-half of the women murdered in the United States are murdered by their partners or former partners.[22] Intimate violence has a significant effect on mental health in women. Women who are battered experience depression at very high rates, some studies showing as many as 80 percent. Women who are battered are also at very high risk for suicide attempts, as many as 25 percent or higher having made attempts.[23] In addition, one of the most significant predictors of married women's depression is spousal aggression, especially when it is physical aggression.[24] Rape victims are also at significantly greater risk of depression and suicide attempts in the year following the rape. Donald Meichenbaum suggests that women who are raped often experience post-traumatic stress disorder, which includes anxiety and depression as part of its profile.[25] The linkages between intimate violence and depression are such that any woman who comes to a pastor about depression should be asked about experiences of violence in her life.

Marital Conflict

Numerous and contradictory studies have attempted to explore the relationship between marriage and women's depression. What seems to be clear is that married women are significantly more depressed than married men. Unmarried men, however, are more depressed than unmarried women. In other words, marriage in general is very good for men's mental health and variably good for women's.[26] We have already explored some of the reasons that marriage can be problematic for women—unequal division of domestic labor and childcare, threats of violence, inequity of decision making, and so forth. Marriage can also be helpful and healthy for women. The key issue is the nature of the marital relationship. In an interesting study on martial discord and depression, researchers discovered that there were several predictive factors for depression in the women partners, while there was only one for the men. For depressed married men, the only significant variable that correlated with their depression was their level of problem-solving skills. For women, however, the level of depressive symptomatology was highly correlated with spouse-specific assertiveness, problem solving, and occupational status. In other words, the more a woman felt that she couldn't be assertive with her husband (even though she might be assertive in other dimensions of her life), that she didn't have adequate skills with which to solve the marital problems, or that she was unemployed, the more likely she was to be depressed. Additionally, physical abuse by the partner against her was also a significant predictor of depression. Also, there were two belief systems (out of ten tested) that correlated with depression in women: a belief that "mind reading is expected" and a belief that "disagreement is destructive."[27]

This study has significant implications for exploring depression in women. We have already discussed the implications of domestic violence on depression. All of the other factors that correlated with depression had to do with issues of agency or power. If a woman didn't feel that she could say what she wanted or needed from her husband (assertiveness) or that she couldn't ask him what he wanted or needed (expectation of mind reading), she was more likely to experience depression. In addition, if she didn't feel that she had the skills to solve the problems herself or she felt that to disagree or argue with her husband would be destructive, she was more likely to experience depression. These are issues of agency. When women feel relatively powerless (possibly compounded by the extreme powerlessness of physical or sexual abuse) in a marriage relationship, which exists in a larger culture also working to disempower her, they are more likely to become depressed. Issues of power are central to women's depression, whether they are in the family, in the workplace, or in larger cultural structures like the media and advertising.

Life in a Sexist, Racist, and Classist Culture

As was discussed at great length in chapter 1, we live in a culture that organizes power, in part, around certain dualisms like male or female, white or "colored" skin, heterosexual or homosexual, and so on. These power arrangements disadvantage the second of each of these pairs (and anyone who doesn't completely fit the first member of the pair is assigned to the second). Women, in general—and women of color, lesbians, and poor women to an even greater extent—live with constant reminders that they are not valuable members of the culture. Mitchell writes poignantly about the experience of many African American women:

> Research points to the connections between living in a racist society and these illnesses. Common sense tells us that living in a society that places little value on our Blackness or our femaleness must take its toll on our psyches as well as our bodies. Research asserts that poverty and loneliness lead to isolation and depression; common sense says we are more often poor and alone, isolated and depressed. Research concludes that people in psychological pain often self-medicate with whatever is available: sex, food, drugs. Common sense points out that we would not need the salves we so often choose—unhealthy relationships, food, cigarettes, alcohol, and drugs—if our minds and souls were not pained.[28]
>
> To be sure, things have greatly improved since the 1960's when the only media representations of people of color were demeaning caricatures. . . . But Black women and girls frequently pick up on quiet, subtle messages of inadequacy, inferiority, and uselessness in their daily life experiences. Demeaning myths about Black women abound. While we may not be more biologically predisposed to depression than others, we are, by

our race, more often than not predisposed to a dubious reception from a
world that, in general, has little positive use for Black people.[29]

It is this kind of persistent and pervasive undermining of self-esteem and
purpose that contributes to women's vulnerability to depression.

Most feminist theorists take the realities of cultural patriarchy as an
underlying cause of women's depression as an assumption. For example,
Miriam Greenspan, after listing typical depression symptoms, writes,
"The obvious reality is that in a woman-hating culture it is normal for
women to hate themselves. Depression is, for one thing, a survival strategy adopted by women in a society that devalues women while demanding and idolizing femininity."[30] These are powerful words. Along with
others who focus on the effects of patriarchy, she realizes that the culture
has been and continues to be damaging to women. It is important to continue to remember that we live in a world that is, in many ways, hostile to
women. Women live with a certain level of pervasive fear as well as with
a lowered sense of self-esteem due to the violence toward them in the
world. They also live with the realities of role and work overload, work
segregation and harassment, and the constant threat of poverty. These are
all vulnerability factors for depression as they work together to take away
women's power and women's agency.

Self-Esteem

Strong links have been made between self-esteem and depression. The
statistics discussed in chapter 1 give a sense of the systematic attack on
women's self-esteem from the time of infancy through adulthood. Linda
Tschirhart Sanford and Mary Ellen Donovan have done an extensive
study on women and self esteem. They conclude that:

1. Low self-esteem is primarily the result of being female in a male-
   dominated culture.
2. Low self-esteem is at the root of many of the psychological problems that women experience and attempts to cure these problems
   without addressing the causes of low self-esteem lead to other
   problems.
3. Low self-esteem and the resultant psychological problems continue the problem because women are easier to "keep in their
   place" when they are depressed and feeling powerless.

4. It is necessary for women to develop self-esteem as individuals and as a group in order to be able to challenge the oppressive status quo.[31]

Women who experience low self-esteem are vulnerable to external evaluations of their goodness and value. In a patriarchal culture these external evaluations are likely to be less than authentically affirming. This becomes a vicious cycle, one that is depressogenic. If the culture prescribes "feminine" traits for positive evaluation but sends paradoxical counter messages that those "feminine" traits are not really valuable, there is no real way for a woman to build adequate self-esteem. Dunlap writes, "Dependence, helplessness, passivity, accommodation, self-sacrifice—all of these qualities are considered feminine in our culture and all of them have been identified as conducive to depression. To relinquish one's sense of agency and control, to mold one's feelings and opinions to those around you, to see one's worth as derivative of those you serve, all of these are part of this culture's definition of the feminine and all of them are clinically depressogenic. To be truly 'feminine' is to be vulnerable to depression."[32] Helping a woman to resist depression requires more than helping her to regenerate her energy and hope. It also means helping her find ways to personally and communally resist these worlds of meaning in which she lives that contribute to her and other women's disempowerment.

Suicide

Not all depression in women leads to suicide or suicide attempts. In studies of sex differences in depression, for example, researchers find that while men who struggle with depression are characterized by indecisiveness, somatic concerns, lack of satisfaction, and suicidal feelings, women tended to experience self-dislike, crying, irritability, fatigue, and distortion of body image.[33] Men are more likely than women to take lethal action against themselves in the face of depression (and other experiences of hopelessness). Women tend to ruminate about the things at issue in their depression and tend to be more willing to experience helplessness in their wake. It's important to know, though, that although men kill themselves at much higher rates than do women, (1) that rate differential varies over the life span, and (2) women attempt suicide on average at three times the rate men do. In terms of the rate differential, women kill themselves at half the rate of men when they are each in their early twenties but at one-tenth the rate when they are each in their sixties. The same kind of differential applies in reverse to suicide attempts. Adolescent women attempt suicide at ten times the rate of their male peers but much less often as they reach older age.[34] In addition, men's suicide rates increase over their life span—it is low in adolescence and peaks at around age sixty. For women, suicidal activity peaks around age twenty and stays fairly stable throughout their lifetime.

Charles Neuringer has identified what he feels to be a key configuration of traits that distinguish between suicidal and nonsuicidal women. He writes:

Suicidal women were found to have a set of intense negative emotions and orientations not matched by other women. Compared to other women:
- they feel that life is duller, emptier, and more boring
- they are less interested and responsive to people and events
- they feel angrier, they have less interest in and are more dissatisfied with their work
- they report that thinking is a great effort; their thought processes are slow and sluggish
- they feel their ideas lack value, and they lack intellectual self-confidence
- they feel more guilt-ridden and less self-approving
- they feel inadequate and helpless
- they feel more depressed and weary.

He adds that the final move with suicidal women is to a "nothing matters to me" attitude that leads to an almost inevitable suicide attempt.[35] Neuringer's configuration of attitudes and behaviors of the suicidal woman may be more a matter of intensity of depressive symptoms than a unique set of feelings. His point, however, is that once women have moved to the extremes of depression and apathy, they are at high risk for suicide.

Suicide in women crosses all race and class lines. Whereas there is a myth that African American women don't kill themselves, this is not true. Mitchell writes:

As bell hooks points out, Black women are killing themselves daily in both obvious and not so obvious ways. Black women actually have a lower completed suicide rate than other demographic groups (white women commit suicide at three times the rate of Back women, the rate for Black men is eight times as high, and for white men it is fourteen times as high). . . . And for every Black woman who takes her life in a moment of despair, there are probably hundreds who are killing themselves slowly with drugs, alcohol, and overeating. Add to that the numbers of us who are killing ourselves with malignant neglect—ignoring those chest pains, that lump in the breast, that cigarette-induced hack—and we have a true crisis.[36]

When we consider the variety of ways that women have had to choose to resist oppression, domination, and violence that are self-destructive for them, we have a suicidal crisis in women. In addition, Neuringer suggests that there is growing evidence that female suicide deaths are increasing at a faster rate than male suicidal deaths and that suicide attempts by older women, even though they are fewer, are more likely to be successful.[37] It is important that pastors pay attention to women who show any signs of suicidal thinking or behavior, which might include giving their belongings away, talking about life in the past tense, using euphemistic language about death, or engaging in actively self-destructive behaviors.

Pastors must know what to do when they suspect suicidal risk in a counselee. Most depressed people have had thoughts of suicide. But if a person is able to identify stronger reasons not to live than to live, then she is in danger. If she has thought about how she would commit suicide and can tell the counselor her plan, and if she has the means to carry out that plan, the pastoral counselor needs to question whether or not she is asking to be in a safe environment. It is useful for the counselor to ask people directly if they are thinking of hurting themselves or if they are thinking about suicide. Often people are relieved to have their feelings spoken out loud. If suicide is a likely option, the person should be referred to a psychiatrist who can facilitate medical supervision or to a pastoral counselor or psychotherapist trained in working with suicidal situations. Of course, the pastor should make sure that the suicidal person has followed through with the referral. If a psychiatrist or trained pastoral counselor or psychotherapist is not immediately available, then it is desirable for the pastoral caregiver to go with the depressed person to a hospital emergency room and help her to be admitted and kept safe until she can work through the suicidal danger.

Addiction

Given that not all self-destructive behavior associated with depression falls under the category of active suicide attempts, it is useful to look at the topic of women and addiction (especially alcohol addiction) in the context of depression. It is often proposed that the addictive use of alcohol is related to attempts to self-medicate the symptoms of depression. This has more often been proposed for men as a way to explain their lower rates of depression, but it is also relevant for women. We could also talk about women's use of other substances (food, caffeine, and other prescription and nonprescription drugs) as related to depression, but that is beyond the scope of this chapter. It is fair to say that some of these other substances may well be used in attempts to comfort and console the self (especially food), but they do not have the same global consequences the use of alcohol does (and prescription and street drugs). So this section will focus on alcohol use and addiction as it relates to depression.

In 1995 Wilsnack and Wilsnack surveyed the literature about drinking habits of women in the United States. The research was sometimes contradictory but did draw certain conclusions. For example, whereas women's drinking had become more acceptable in our own culture (and some others), the proportion of women who drink did not seem to be significantly rising. Their survey indicated that the proportion of women who drink alcohol in the United States fell slightly in the 1980s and that those who drank had fewer episodes of heavy drinking than in the prior decade. They also found that—despite major media concern about women's drinking that emerged in the 1970s—the rates of alcohol consumption during that period were relatively unchanged. In addition, women's rates of drinking continued to lag behind men's rates.[38] It appears that most authors conclude that the ratio of women problem drinkers is somewhere between one to two and one to three women to men. Yet it is important that we do not let this information make women who have drinking problems invisible or marginalized. We are still talking about significant numbers of women who experience drinking problems.

In terms of some particular populations of women, Jahn Forth-Finegan has discovered that Hispanic women tend to abstain from alcohol more often than non-Hispanic women. L. E. Gary and R. B. Gary found that African American women tend to abstain more than other ethnic groups but that when they did drink alcohol they tended to do so more heavily than other groups.[39] In general, Moira Plant reports, women of color are no more or less likely to have a drinking problem than their white counterparts.[40] Similarly, Forth-Finegan reports that problem drinking in women seems to be unrelated to socioeconomic level.[41] In terms of other particularities, a Chicago study by D. J. McKirnan and P. L. Peterson in 1989 found that lesbians reported more alcohol problems than nonlesbian women, although they did not report being heavier drinkers. Studies report that lesbians, in contrast to non-lesbian women, tend to increase their drinking quantity as they age. In one major study, 3 percent of lesbians who were between the ages of seventeen and twenty-four reported daily drinking compared to 21 percent of lesbians aged fifty-five and older.[42] These number differences might be related to changes in the culture for young lesbians today as compared to thirty years ago and consequent drinking patterns due to living with intense homophobia rather than a longitudinal shift in drinking patterns for individuals over time. Again, it's important to note that the research on women and alcohol includes very little that looks at different groups of women by their cultural or racial or ethnic particularities. Much more work needs to be done in this area.

Women who work outside the home make up a higher proportion of problem drinkers than nonemployed women, but this is probably due to access to alcohol rather than for reasons of stress. In fact, contrary to prior theories, it appears that women who are role deprived are more likely to drink than those who have multiple roles. And women probably drink for the same reasons that men drink—to enjoy themselves, feel a part of the group, relax, or treat themselves. Most women drink in moderation without a lot of problems. But significant numbers of women do end up with physical, emotional, and relational problems related to the abuse of alcohol and it is important to note that those women who are alcoholic often get missed by those who could help them, partly because there are fewer numbers of heavy-drinking women than there are heavy-drinking men. In addition, women's symptoms of addiction are often dismissed by physicians because of their stereotypes about alcoholics either as men or as obviously fallen women or because women who become addicted and experience problems because of their drinking often drink considerably smaller quantities of alcohol than men with similar symptoms.

Finally, women's alcohol abuse is often missed because women tend to drink or take drugs alone. For example, Sheila Blume reports that 84 percent of 116 alcoholic women studied in depth did their drinking at home.

Married women, employed women, and upper-socioeconomic status women were most likely to drink alone. Many of their families and friends were unaware of the seriousness of the drinking problem until it was significantly advanced.

Women's problem drinking is overlooked for all of these reasons of stereotype, smaller quantity, and secrecy. In fact, women's misdiagnosed symptoms from alcohol abuse are often treated by giving them other addicting drugs to deal with problems like nervousness, insomnia, stomach upsets, ulcers, and so on.[43] And to complicate the problem, women rarely present themselves for treatment, partly because of the stereotypes and stigma, and partly because of the kinds of family responsibilities they have that would be threatened by admission of a need for treatment.

A significant amount of research demonstrates a connection between women's mood disorders and addiction. When studies look at predictors for alcohol abuse in children, girls who turn out to be at risk tend to have low self-esteem and an impaired ability to cope with day-to-day life. These factors are related to the experience of depression. This profile was not true for boys, who were best predicted by aggression, low anxiety, poor school success, and antisocial problems in junior high and high school.[44] Furthermore, in a variety of studies, women alcoholics tended to have higher levels of anxiety and depressive symptoms and lower self-esteem where, again, men more often displayed antisocial trends.[45] Plant suggests that "in relation to problem-drinking women, there is a suggestion from some research that females are more likely than males to use alcohol to change negative mood."[46] College-age women who scored highest on feeling adjustment scales (which indicated that when they drank it was to relieve shyness or to feel happier) had the highest level of later drinking problems and, in fact, better predicted addiction likelihood than did actual drinking problems in college.[47] Blume reports that

> in the general population sample, nineteen percent of the women who fulfilled diagnostic criteria for alcohol abuse or dependence at some time during their lifetime also fulfilled criteria for a lifetime diagnosis of major depression [compared with five percent of the men]. The rate of lifetime diagnosis of major depression in alcoholic women was nearly three times the general population rate for women of seven percent. Comparing men and women with both alcohol abuse/dependence and major depression, J. E. Helzer and T. R. Pryzbeck reported that depression was primary in sixty-six percent of women but in only twenty-two percent of men.[48]

There are a couple of important implications from this research. The first and most obvious implication is that depression in addicted women needs to be taken as seriously as the addiction itself. The second implication has to do with treatment strategies. As I have indicated throughout, feminist research in general suggests that depression in women is best treated by helping women to find their own voices and to challenge their gender training—especially in regard to self-image and self-esteem—which they received in a pervasively sexist culture. This approach to depression implies that a confrontive approach to addiction, one that asks women to focus first on their faults and shortcomings, and then on giving up control, may well increase those self-perceptions that contribute to the depression. There are several important feminist works on women and addiction that challenge the traditional twelve-step approach to treating women with addiction problems. Pastors should become familiar with these.

Caring for Women
Struggling with Depression

Throughout this chapter, in keeping with narrative theory, I have talked about depression as a noun rather than as an adjective. Women are not depressed—depression and women are not synonymous and depression, even when it has entered a woman's life, doesn't define her. Too often, though, we allow depression to serve as an adjective in a woman's life instead of recognizing it as an enemy. It is important for pastoral counselors to recognize that women encounter depression, risk being overcome by depression, and struggle with depression. If we allow depression to be an external problem that is given access into women's lives through a variety of physical, psychological, relational, and cultural pathways, it will be much easier to keep sight of women's agency. It is crucial for women's success in fighting depression that they regain a sense of agency in their lives so that they might be active agents in resistance to depression. Women experience so many vulnerabilities to depression—intimate violence against them; pervasive attacks to self-esteem; disempowerment in families, at work, and in the culture at large; racism and heterosexism; role overload; and so on—that gaining clarity about those vulnerabilities and agency in choosing how to respond to them are crucial elements in fighting depression. The role of the pastoral counselor is to use whatever resources are available to help women gain clarity, agency, and power in their fight against depression.

The issues raised in the first part of this chapter help us to determine the key elements needed to help women who are struggling with depression. First, it is important that we see depression as a multifaceted, total-person attack. When women encounter depression, it affects them at every level. As we have noted, there are physical, emotional, intellectual, relational, and spiritual symptoms that give depression its power. We have noted that when women are in the grips of depression, it is hard for them to remember the possibility of not being depressed and it is almost impossible for them to find the energy to experience visions or hope for the future. In addition, the tasks of daily living are generally accomplished only with significant effort that leaves the woman with little energy for relationships, work, or self-care. Depression may well feel like a cocoon that cannot be shaken off. In the midst of that depression, it is difficult to imagine fighting successfully to get rid of it. In fact, the lethargy, sadness, and self-contempt may be experienced as essential and permanent. At best, the counselee may only want to talk about how bad she feels about feeling bad and to want to explore her story from within the hermeneutical lens of the depression itself. This can be very seductive for the counselor, who can be drawn into the depression with the counselee and, in the process, be a collaborator in its victory.

It is very important for pastoral counselors to recognize these dynamics as a part of the depression and not part of the resistance to it. Counseling methods that focus primarily on insight or even on the nature and symptoms of the depression may well feed into reinforcing and strengthening its power. The focus on depression as a noun, as an externalized problem that can be resisted by the essence of the woman herself, is a crucial component for successful resistance. The two temptations of the counselor in working with someone experiencing depression are (1) to cycle down in the depression with the counselee, or (2) to become impatient with the person for not "shaking it off." In both cases, the important boundary between counselor and counselee has been compromised. The counselor needs to remember that she or he is shoulder-to-shoulder with the counselee in attempting to find resources for the counselee's fight against depression, even though it is the counselee's depression, not the counselor's. It is the counselee's agency that needs to be mobilized in this process, not primarily the counselor's.

A variety of studies cited throughout this chapter give us key information for helping to care for women struggling with depression. Nolen-Hoeksema's exploration into gender differences in depression found that one trait that intensifies and lengthens depression in women is their tendency to ruminate about their sad and negative feelings and thoughts. As Nolen-Hoeksema writes, "I have argued that one determinant of the duration of a depressive episode is the type of response people engage in when depressed. People who ruminate when depressed tend to remain depressed and may become more severely so than people who try to distract themselves from their depressive symptoms."[49] Women tend to write in journals, to talk to friends about how bad they are feeling, and to move inside themselves to process the feelings and thoughts. While these skills are crucial and positive in much of women's lives, working well to enhance and nurture relationships and to nurture self-growth, they work against a woman struggling with depression. These behaviors work to further *internalize* the experience of depression in her life rather than to *externalize* it so it can be resisted. Good pastoral counseling will not help women struggling with depression to further ruminate on their experience; it will instead work to externalize depression so that it can be described, delineated, tracked, and resisted. Cognitive-behavioral approaches to counseling with depression do this, to a certain extent, and narrative approaches are specifically formulated to do this work of externalization and resistance.

Second, the literature also suggests that counseling with women experiencing depression needs to find ways to deconstruct the diminishing and disempowering messages fed to women that destroy self-esteem and agency and work in a myriad of ways against the possibility of abundant life for women. It is important early on in the counseling process to begin asking women where they got certain depressogenic ideas that they have taken as given. Asking where the belief has come from helps to begin relativizing that belief and diminishing its power. If an assumption—such as women are supposed to be self-sacrificing in the face of the needs of others—can be examined, then it can also be measured against other ways of making meaning out of life experiences. Once other ways of selecting and interpreting life choices are an option, then counterstories, either out of previously unstoried experience or out of countercommunity participation, can be generated.

Dunlap talks about "resistance discourses" in ways that are similar to the way we have defined counterstories. She writes:

The hope lies in "resistance discourses" that would subvert, do "battle" with, the patriarchal truth-of-woman discourse. This resistance discourse, this web of ideas, institutions, practices, psyches, an apparatus much bigger than simply a concept or idea that constitutes a "truth" operates in a variety of ways. This discourse might emerge in the concepts of feminist theory and feminist theology, or in the esthetic realm of visual arts and music. It might emerge in the strategies of women organizing for better health care, for safe streets, adequate housing, for access to safe and affordable abortions. It might emerge at the level of the interpersonal, in the painful re-negotiation of household and child care duties within a family, or at an emotional level in a newfound rage against sexual harassment or the joy of mutual friendship. Resistance discourses, and all the multivalence of the web that they imply, offer an alternative version of the vision and practice of what is true of woman. They are also present along with patriarchal truth-of-woman discourse, engaged in the struggle for truth. Thankfully, one can discern a resistance discourse that speaks of woman as powerful, competent, entitled to pleasure that is embodied in alternative communities.[50]

Dunlap helps us to see the importance of developing counterstories that serve to resist what has passed for truth in the general cultural discourse about women. Fortunately, there are more resources out of which to build these resistance narratives or counterstories in our culture today than ever before. Although some of the material may represent tokenized examples, there are women CEOs and women's sporting events and television role models in ways that there have never been before. Although women have always found material for counterstories as tools for survival and as resistance to the lies and violence of patriarchy, there was rarely enough material to counter the patriarchal discourse. There may still be a scarcity of material in the culture to build adequate resistance discourses out of, but when women are also encouraged to find their own truths in community with one another, resistance to patriarchy and to depression will be supported.

A third clue from the literature on women and depression helps us to develop appropriate counseling resources, and that is the evidence that depression is predicted in women when certain family narratives and behaviors combine in conflictual marriages. It is important to note that for marriage to be nondepressogenic for women, it has to work against the kinds of power arrangements that get carried over from the culture (and often the church) into the family. Whether it is in the equitable division of domestic and public responsibilities or a collaborative approach to making family decisions, these kinds of healthy family behaviors are countercultural. In heterosexual partnerships, the male-female power dynamic assigned by a patriarchal culture will find its way into the marriage relationship unless it is actively resisted by both partners. This is the first (and very difficult) task for marriages. In addition, as discussed above, if women bring poor problem-solving skills, spouse-specific unassertiveness, beliefs in the destructive power of disagreements, and the need for mind reading into the relationship, there is a high risk for depression. Also, if there is violence in the relationship, there is again a very high likelihood of depression.

What this means is that depression is often resisted best by women when part of the counseling involves working within the primary relationship to address these issues. Much of the literature suggests that combining interpersonal counseling with cognitive counseling is an effective approach to counseling women struggling with depression. I believe that narrative counseling can combine these two approaches very helpfully.

A fourth insight from our explorations is that depression in women is an embodied experience. This means several things. Not only do women experience depression at a variety of physical levels (sleep and eating habits, muscle aches and pains, sense of being slowed down in movement, etc.), but caring for those physical dimensions can help ease depression. Many people report that when they are able to exercise appropriately, for example, they experience a decline in depressive symptoms. Those symptoms, however, are often what takes away one's motivation to do what might be "good for" oneself. In addition, women who are struggling with depression should be encouraged to get a good physical examination (hopefully by a feminist or profeminist physician) since some illnesses can create symptoms that mimic depression. A woman's body is the site of her depression, which should never be denied as strategies of resistance are developed.

Another aspect of depression shows that it is an embodied experience at the biochemical level. This is where much of the current media conversation about depression is focused. Many theorists suggest that depression is primarily a biochemical reality, a problem with neurotransmitters that can be addressed through the use of antidepressant drugs. There is much debate about the use of antidepressant medication for women among feminist and womanist scholars. Many feminist and womanist scholars have appropriate suspicion about the use of prescribed chemicals to mask women's (or other marginalized groups') awareness that something is wrong or to control their various forms of protest against the status quo. History supports their caution. Mitchell writes:

> By some accounts we have become a Prozac nation, popping the popular antidepressant (as well as many others) as if they were vitamins. But while the rest of America has embraced antidepressants, Black America most decidedly has not. Only 34% of African Americans polled in the National Mental Health Association survey said that they would take antidepressant medication if their doctor prescribed it.[51]

Many women reflect the sentiments above. Whereas antidepressant medication can literally be a lifesaver for some who are struggling with depression, for others it removes the symptoms that indicate the necessity of generating resistance to unjust and damaging power structures. It has become very difficult to trust the appropriate assessment of these two situations. For one thing, today's "miracle" antidepressants, which inhibit the uptake of the neurotransmitter serotonin (or one of the other key neurotransmitters) in the brain so that appropriate levels of the chemical are present, work to enhance pleasure in a variety of contexts, not just in those struggling with depression. Prozac has been used for treating low self-esteem, chronic fatigue syndrome, migraine headaches, drug and alcohol addiction, premenstrual syndrome, obesity, anorexia, bulimia, phobia, anxiety and panic disorder, and behavioral and emotional problems in children and adolescents.[52] In other words, the use of antidepressant medication no longer can serve as a means for differential diagnosis for biochemically based depressions. As Peter Roger Breggin writes,

> Ever since antidepressants were discovered, it has been assumed that they work because of their effect on nerve transmission in the brain. It has also been assumed that, because they work, there must be something wrong with the nerves they affect. This assumption is commonly used as the major reason for searching for a biochemical cause of depression and other psychiatric disorders. It goes like this: The drugs work, the drugs affect the brain, so there must be something wrong with the brain. But this is faulty

and unscientific reasoning. Many known drugs, such as caffeine and alcohol, affect the mind and brain in the absence of any underlying defect in the brain.[53]

But the larger problem, in my opinion, is the way that the pharmaceutical companies in the United States are selling antidepressants directly to the public through their marketing strategies. We are always eager for "quick fixes" and the drug companies are willing to cater to that. Greg Critser has explored the relationship of the pharmaceutical industry to the health care industry with some very disturbing discoveries. Pharmaceutical companies began to aggressively market serotonin reuptake inhibitors (SRIs) antidepressants to psychiatrists but moved quickly to the health maintenance organizations (HMOs). As Critser writes,

> In the case of antidepressants, which were traditionally dispensed by the nation's small corps of psychiatrists, the industry desperately needed to broaden its base of distributors. To do that, Lilly, Pfizer, and a number of other manufacturers targeted health-management groups and HMOs which are charged with the dual responsibilities of providing therapy and cutting costs. For them, Prozac was a panacea. Almost immediately, the average number of insurer-paid visits to talk therapists fell dramatically while drug-therapy numbers soared. By the late Eighties, of nearly sixteen million patients who visited doctors for depression, seventy percent ended up in drug therapy. And slowly but surely, non-psychiatric physicians were brought into the prescribing fold. Lilly and other manufacturers underwrote "mental health days" for area medical groups. The events were marketed as "educational" forums; they functioned as subsidized marketing for the company and for the physicians. . . . Today, the American patient is inexorably being transformed into his/her own pharmacist. The trend is most apparent in the pages of magazines [and now the Internet], with their weirdly text-heavy ads. Less obvious are the marketing fests taking place in the nation's doctors' offices and emergency rooms. There one inevitably hears the cheery, insistent voices of the local "health care" cable station prattling on about how you can have "a better fuller life" if you just fill out the self-diagnostic chart about depression that's sitting right there by your chair.[54]

Aggressive marketing (and research) by pharmaceutical companies, along with their appeal directly to the potential consumer, and their competition with other kinds of health care options (like counseling), must make us cautious. This is especially true when we put these realities alongside the history of overmedicating women who demonstrated resistance to the status quo. We, as feminist and profeminist pastoral counselors of women, need to be much more rigorous in making decisions about referrals—when we will make them and to whom—rather than assuming a beneficent health care/pharmaceutical system for women. Again, this is not to say that antidepressant medication is never helpful. It is only to say that we have tended to be gullible consumers even when women's best interests are again at stake. It also challenges pastoral counselors (and other psychotherapy providers) to find ways to engage in counseling with women that are effective and efficient in helping them resist the life-threatening realities of depression.

Finally, the literature on women's experiences with depression suggests that depression both causes and is aggravated by a tendency toward social isolation. This tells us that the counseling relationship between pastor and counselee is a very important one. At its best, it should be an embodiment of hope and community. In addition, the pastor represents the hope of their shared faith even when a woman experiencing depression can't find any access to God for herself. The well-boundaried, wholistic, woman-centered, and competent pastoral counselor can make a connection that serves to re-member the community of support for a counselee who has found herself withdrawn from it. It is a very important role for the pastor given the pervasiveness of depression in women.

This tendency toward social isolation also suggests that one of the most important resources that a pastoral counselor can provide for a woman struggling with depression is a solid, feminist support or therapy group of women. There is no substitute for the healing power of this kind of countercommunity for a woman experiencing depression. All pastoral counselors should have knowledge about and access to these kinds of groups. If they don't exist in the immediate community, pastors can work to create them cooperatively with other churches or community centers. They are an indispensable part of resisting and defeating the threat of depression, and thus a high priority for the pastor's referral list.

Implications for Narrative Counseling

It seems to me that there are two major tasks for the pastoral counselor seeking to use narrative counseling to help a woman struggling with depression. The first task is to help her gain clarity about the problem she faces, with the purpose being to develop strategies to resist it. This identification of the problem is a very important first step for the counseling process and should never be skipped or shortchanged. It requires a great deal of careful listening and assisting the woman to come to voice. It also requires the judicious use of deconstructive questions in order to help introduce the possibility that neither the problem depression (or whatever it has been named) nor the narrative strands supporting it are necessarily truth. The pastoral counselor, operating from a position of not knowing where the story will go, listens for and inquires about things like what the problem looks like, feels like, acts like, and how it most often gains a foothold in her life. The question of how depression sneaks up on her and takes hold of her thoughts and feelings is an important one for her to consider. The counselor may be curious about things like what narrative strands, thoughts, beliefs, or activities make it more likely for depression to get underneath her defenses; what the family or partner narratives are or what behaviors team up with the problem/depression to strengthen its ability to harm her or her family; and what the community's or culture's narratives or actions are that make depression feel it has the right to attack her. These are the kinds of questions that help a woman struggling with depression to separate herself from the depression and observe its strategies. They give her ideas about how best to resist it or block its pathway into her life. The supposed "truths" of patriarchy in its variety of forms and locations are challenged by working to deconstruct and examine them. Clarity is thus possible.

The second task for the pastoral counselor and counselee is the development of counterstories or, to use Dunlap's term, resistance narratives. The point of the counterstories is to make it harder for depression to invade the person and her significant relationships. These counterstories can come from a variety of sources. They may come from her own unstoried experiences, stories of when she was able to resist depression even though it threatened her, or times when she was able to defy depression's mandate of hopelessness and helplessness. These are the exceptional narratives that are available to be storied if the hermeneutical lenses that have blocked them out have been adequately deconstructed.

The counterstories may come from her faith community—the traditions of liberation and empowerment that are at the heart of many of our foundational beliefs. The problem is that our faith communities may also hold stories that reinforce women's vulnerabilities to depression—stories of selflessness, self-sacrifice, secondary citizenship, or subordination. It is the pastor's responsibility to be able to be theologically critical in ways that allow the liberating and empowering stories to be woven into other resistance narratives in the counselee's life. The pastor hopefully has a proven track record of being a theologically astute and empowering religious leader and thus has credibility for the woman struggling with depression.

Counterstories may also emerge from other women and their experiences, especially as a counselee listens to women she has learned to trust as they explore their own struggles with depression and false truths. It is in these countercommunities that the most powerful and guiding counterstories may emerge. These countercommunities should have a central place in the community of faith.

It is important that the work of gaining clarity and agency is the work of the counselee, not the counselor, who could attempt to weld liberation onto her intact problem narrative. Gaining agency in this process is the key to being able to resist depression if it threatens in the future. Pastoral counselors can help provide frameworks and opportunities for these resistance narratives. They can help women remember their agency and prior strategies of resistance. They can help women remember their own responsibility for making meaning out of the experiences they encounter. They can help the counselee carry her new narrative with its central stories of resistance into important communities so that she is not known by her old story. These are the roles and functions of the pastoral counselor as she or he helps women struggling with depression to gain clarity and resist the threat of depression.

seven

Helping Women Make Choices

One of the key features of pastoral counseling, especially in the parish context, is that it is time limited. The purpose of engaging in a process of pastoral counseling is to address specific life problems with the goal of setting in motion the process of their resolution. A feminist-based pastoral counselor seeks to do three things: (1) empower the telling of the story the problem is rooted in, (2) assist in the process of clarifying the issues by seeing them through a variety of cultural lenses and employing appropriate deconstructive frames to better illuminate the real problems, and (3) empower the counselee to make choices that work to resist and transform the oppressive forces in her life and world. Too often counseling processes stop short of this choice- and change-making work. Sometimes people assume that it is enough to tell the story and get the relief of sharing that story with another. Indeed, as we saw in chapter 3, the storytelling and coming to voice are key dimensions of the liberating process. Without the support to make the new choices in light of the lies overturned and new truths found that occur in the clarifying process, however, no real transformation can occur. And choices, as we will see, have their own vulnerabilities that need clarification and support from the counseling process.

Choice is an important part of counseling. Sometimes choice making emerges as a natural consequence of clarification. In many cases, however, especially when the counseling has not been understood to be time limited, the counselor and counselee do not move to making choices but rather get stuck in the clarification phase. There is always more to know and to be clear about so it is easy to be seduced by ongoing clarification. Moving to choice, however, acknowledges that the counseling has a purpose—the purpose is to address the questions or problems, now relevantly framed and voiced, that brought the person into counseling in the first place. One of the most important questions to keep in the foreground during counseling is how the counselee and the counselor will know when they are finished. Having this question before them serves three purposes. First, it clarifies the nature of the counseling. Counseling is to address issues and problems that are causing distress. Knowing when the counseling is finished helps put boundaries around the counseling "contract," which is especially important when counseling is done in the parish context. Since parish ministry involves multiple roles, including the ongoing role of pastoral care, it is important for the beginning and end of this unique and time-limited relationship to be clear. Second, this question helps to generate images of what it would be like to "successfully" complete the counseling—what it would look like to resolve the distress. Having an image like this begins to break what is often a stranglehold of despair and helps to generate an attitude of hope. Hope can facilitate a move toward empowerment. If one can imagine new possibilities, one can begin to move toward them. Third, it puts the evaluative task mostly in the hands of the counselee. It is the counselee who is mainly responsible for setting the goals of the counseling when she and the counselor attempt to answer this question of the ending point.

People who come for pastoral counseling are usually experiencing considerable distress in their lives and are anxious for help in relieving that distress. Usually they have tried all of the logical or reasonable solutions that any counselor could suggest. Many women, especially those who are depressed, tend to use dichotomous thinking as they attempt to solve the problems in their lives, thinking that suggests that there are only two possible directions they can follow in their lives. This either/or limitation on alternatives usually means that people feel that either they can continue to live with the problem or they can engage in some opposite that is generally a reactive solution to the problem with numerous negative consequences. In both cases the problem continues to direct the person's life choices.

Because people who come for counseling have tried most or all of the reasonable solutions to their problems according to the limitations of the problem narrative, prescribing or advising more reasonable solutions is a poor approach to the counseling—it is ineffective and it reinforces the dynamics that created the problem in the first place. The feminist-grounded pastoral counselor is not about giving advice but rather is oriented to helping the counselee gain voice, agency, and perspective in such a way that a whole new set of options becomes available. The strengths and resources in the woman's life that have either been denounced as worthless by patriarchy or disregarded because they don't fit in her core narrative become available to her in the feminist narrative approach to counseling.

The phase of making choices thus needs to happen after coming to voice and gaining clarity for two reasons. First, in coming to voice and finding language the counselee is able not only to name the story accurately from her own core but also to feel entitled to have this story with all of its implications. This sense of entitlement is usually a key component to the counseling process. The counselee has developed an agency that she did not know she had, and resources become available to her for making new choices. Second, in gaining clarity the counselee has learned how to frame the issues through a variety of helpful and even revolutionary lenses that orient the original problem in a new direction. In the narrative counseling work, she has learned that those elements of her life that stood as contradictory to her problem narrative can be reclaimed and a new future story built around them. She has also learned that what she has thought of as her own problems, craziness, or hopelessness are largely held in common with many other women because of the way she and others have been trained and shaped in the culture. These two processes of coming to voice and gaining clarity do not necessarily eliminate the pain or even make the tensions easier to live with. Sometimes feminist-based pastoral counseling with all of its multivalent perspectives may create more chaos temporarily. But the process is able to give a sense of both hope and agency to the counselee. Whereas the woman counselee may have seen only hopelessness and futility for the problems she faced when she decided to come for counseling, by the time she has moved to the process of making choices in the counseling she generally feels renewed hope that the choices she will make will actually help her create a better life for herself without sacrificing those things that matter most.

The dimension of making choices comes in the context of new language, new frames, new agency, and a sense of hope. Choices can be made out of a real ownership of the person's or relationship's whole narrative. New and transformative choices where there can be real accountability are only possible when liberation has already begun. A helpful illustration of this is the chronology of the Exodus story where the people, who had been under oppression for a long time, needed to gain language and voice about their experience. They called to God for deliverance and through the leadership of Moses, Aaron, and Miriam came out of their slavery into the wilderness. Over the forty years of wandering in the wilderness the people began to clarify and understand what it meant to live free of slavery. Once they had experienced this community of empowerment, never perfectly, of course, they were called by God to a new kind of accountability, illustrated in the Ten Commandments. Choice and accountability came when oppression (internal and external) was being dismantled and the dismantling of oppression was furthered by the choices made.

Risks in Making Choices

Before we look at some models of helping women to make choices in pastoral counseling, it is important to be clear about the risks that women may face when they move to this phase of the counseling. Although the work of coming to voice and gaining clarity for many women in counseling is painful, disorienting, and frightening, it is often comforting and exhilarating. To be supported by someone who believes and validates a narrative that frequently has been dismissed and disbelieved is a powerful experience. And to gain separation from a set of "truths" that seemed inevitable and oppressive through the process of narrative externalization and feminist clarification gives a vision of possibility that has often been unimaginable. These phases of counseling have an almost immediate payoff in the lifting of burdens and the generation of energy.

When the counselor and counselee move to the primary phase of making choices, it is easy for the old narrative to regain its hold. Hopefully, throughout the process of externalizing the problem and generating alternative stories (counterstories and exceptional narratives), new options have moved into the foreground very naturally. When a counselee identifies times and strategies when she has resisted the power of depression or has been able to defeat the voice in her head that tells her she will never amount to anything, for example, new options for choices surface almost automatically as she seeks to reproduce those times when she has successfully triumphed over the problem narrative and the damaging situation. Yet those exceptional stories need to be reinforced by making deliberate choices to act in ways that consistently disempower the problem in her life. Those choices may feel (and be) very risky for a variety of reasons.

One of those reasons we have just been discussing. Often a counselee has been so disempowered by the strength of the problem that she is only able to see two choices. Even when more options begin to emerge through the process of generating alternative and exceptional stories, it is not easy to hold the habit of dichotomous thinking at bay. As the counselee begins making choices about her situation that will help her move in a new direction, the problem narrative often rears its head and threatens the dire consequences that it has always presented to her. It says things like, "Either you stay with your abusive partner or you will be lonely for the rest of your life," or "If you pay attention to your own needs, then everyone will recognize how selfish you are," or "If you leave your job and train for another career, you will lose everything you have worked so hard for." These examples of dichotomous thinking are typical of the voices that surface when choices are considered. The key to challenging the dichotomies is to keep remembering the variety of options that continue to be available when any choices are made and to have ways to evaluate choices so that agency is continuously experienced. These kinds of dichotomous and catastrophic responses to potential choices are symptomatic of an unstable agency. The counselor's job is to return agency to the counselee by being clear that all choices belong to her and by confronting the "truth" of the old set of consequences. If the counselor is able to help the counselee explore where she learned that these are the inevitable consequences of choices she makes and why she believed that they were accurate (in other words, are there exceptions that she knows from her or others' experiences?), then she can regain her agency.

A second risk that may emerge in the process of making choices is the reality of retribution. In chapter 2, I referred to Mary Ballou and Nancy W. Gabalac's paradigm of harmful adaptation as a five-stage paradigm to explain how women are shaped into playing their "appropriate roles" in patriarchy. The third phase of that paradigm is called "retribution." Retribution involves punishing women for breaking the rules of being female in our culture. The punishments vary—they can be overt or covert. They may involve physical or sexual abuse. They may involve name-calling and threats. They may involve being exposed to the exclusion and isolation of girls who "don't fit in." Retribution begins in early girlhood and continues throughout a woman's life unless she is able to break free of the harmful adaptation process. The purpose of retribution is to extinguish the desire of girls and women to break the rules of "femininity."

Fears of retribution may run all through the counseling process. Women have often learned that to name truths in their lives is dangerous. But when they begin to make choices that reveal their movement out of harmful adaptation into a way of being—being an agent— retribution becomes a very real possibility. One of the most extreme examples of retribution is demonstrated by the high percentage of battered women who are murdered after they have decided to leave their abusive partners. People and systems that have benefited from oppressed and depressed women may become overtly threatening when a woman begins to make life choices on her own behalf.

One of the most important aspects of pastoral counseling with women is the work of helping them make good and strong connections with other women. It is only in recognizing that a woman is not alone in her fears and doubts that she will be able to resist being lured back into false narratives that have largely defined her and her meaning making. Women need to be connected to other women who are also attempting to resist patriarchal definitions and oppressions so that they can reclaim agency with less fear. As Alfred Adler suggested, social interest, or the need to productively belong, is a basic human need. The key is to belong to a healthy community, a countercommunity, which serves as a source of resistance and hope for women's lives. This diminishes the risks of retribution.

Finally, a third risk of making choices is the reality that the counselee has been known by many others through the lens of her problem narrative. In other words, a woman may be engaged in rewriting her life and finding meaning and hope in that process, but when she goes to her family or work or friendships, she is also asked to be the character these other people have known in living out their own narratives. She is a character in their stories who has not been rewritten, as far as they know. When important people in the counselee's life assume her former narrative to be defining, it is easy for her to get drawn back into the problem narrative. The choices lose their grounding in the new narrative that only she and her counselor seem to know. This is a very real risk. New narratives must be built up over time in order to gain the richness, detail, and familiarity that the old narrative had. Exceptions to the old narrative need to be remembered and accumulated in ways that strengthen and reinforce the new. This takes time, time that usually extends well beyond the formal counseling process. While the new narrative is relatively fragile, the old problem narrative may wait in the wings for an invitation to reassert itself at center stage. This often comes from people and communities that have known the counselee by who she has been for them. As she makes choices that fit her new narrative and her new future story, those choices may look alien and out of context to her communities. Unless they have become both audiences of and characters in the new narrative, they are likely to undermine the choices she makes. Inviting meaningful members of the systems in which the counselee lives and works is central to the later processes of counseling. In fact, some theorists suggest that a narrative approach is only to be understood as a systems theory because of the importance of this aspect of narrative counseling.

Models of Choice Making

Given these risks of making choices, what models work best for helping women to make good choices for their lives—choices that give movement to the narratives they have been creating for themselves? First, it's important to say that women do not lose their whole narrative when they begin to rewrite those narrative strands that have been problematic. Many times, when women are restorying and counterstorying those dimensions of their lives that have been harmful or oppressive to them, it feels like they are turning themselves into entirely new people. A woman once said to me, "I feel like killing that woman I used to be now that I know the new me." It was important to help her look at how much of the "me" was still there—that, in fact, it was the me she had always known at some level that had been uncovered in the narrative work. She had been re-membered, pulled back together and made whole, as she had gained voice and clarity about the story she was living.

Valerie M. DeMarinis talks about the feminist hermeneutical process she calls "responsible scavenging" in her book *Critical Caring*. She suggests that scavengers have been thought of negatively—as those who take indiscriminately and uncaringly from others. She says, however, that "scavengers have the ability to investigate below the surface in order to make important decisions. . . . The responsible scavenger is one who is skilled at survival, one who knows how to search, salvage, purify, and transform the elements of the world into that which nurtures and sustains life."[1] Responsible scavenging means that women do not have to throw out all they have known about themselves. Instead, they have to search their experiences, their assumptions, and their visions for that which can be salvaged or transformed through the new lenses gained in the clarifying process. It's important that this reclaiming and scavenging work be done so that the woman experiences an integration of old and new. We cannot "kill" who we used to be when we discover new truths. We can only reclaim the power of the person who was threatened, sometimes even lost, under the weight of oppression, violence, and distortion. Responsible scavenging prepares us to make choices that re-member who we are in the world.

Along with the notion of responsible scavenging, Ballou and Gabalac's model of corrective action is a useful paradigm for helping women to make healthy choices. The paradigm of corrective action is set as a reversing and healing process against harmful adaptation. The first phase of corrective action is called "separation." This involves helping a woman become aware that the problem, at least in part, is outside of herself and that she is separate from the demands and definitions of patriarchal power systems. The narrative work of externalization and of coming to voice is directed toward this separation process. The second phase is called "validation." This consists of validating the experience and story of the woman as well as affirming the woman's value and strength. These are also achieved in the process of coming to voice and are a part of gaining clarity. It is the third and fourth phases of the corrective action model that are particularly useful as we look at the work of making choices. Ballou and Gabalac's third phase is called "association." They write that

association with other women, both the physical getting together for social or task purposes and the establishment of psychological contact between or among women is necessary to break down the barriers, the isolation, the fear of differences and mistrust built up during the retribution phase of harmful adaptation. During validation, women start to allow themselves to experience their feelings and thoughts without censoring out those incongruent with the power system messages. . . . They start to regard their own thoughts and feelings as being as valid as those of their power system superiors. . . . Without validation and the support of association, such data would be too dangerous, too guilt provoking for most women to assimilate. . . . [A woman's] perceptions may be clearer, but without the risk of seeking out and trusting other women through association, the truth has not yet set her free. Her isolation would continue to keep her in a relatively powerless position.[2]

One of the major roles of a pastoral counselor working with women is that of helping her make formal and informal connections with other women seeking to find counterstories in a culture of harmful adaptation. The power of support groups, consciousness-raising groups, reality-testing groups, truth-telling church circles, friendships, and so on cannot be overestimated in this process of empowerment. It is in those kinds of groups that retribution can be resisted and that choices can be tested and evaluated.

Ballou and Gabalac's fourth phase is also relevant to the choice-making process. They name this fourth phase "authorization." According to Ballou and Gabalac, "Once she is assured that her difficulties are not evidence that she is crazy, wrong, or unworthy, but are held in common by many women in our culture, she is ready to authorize herself to be her own agent, to prepare to advocate on her own behalf. This authorization of herself to be responsible for her life choices is diametrically opposed to the surrender of self to the direction of others required in the conversion step of harmful adaptation."[3] Authorization means that women are able to take responsibility for their own choices in ways they have not been able to before. When women feel that they have few choices or that they will be punished for making choices out of keeping with their place in the family or culture, then they cannot take responsibility for those choices even though they may well feel guilt or shame about them. When new options emerge for women through the process of gaining voice, clarity, and agency, then they also become moral agents in new ways. The choices they make will be evaluated on new terms—terms that take seriously the new lenses that have been created. And they will be evaluated by the woman herself. She will hold herself accountable for them and will let herself be held accountable by her communities of choice. This is very different from fearing retribution for choices never really made.

Ballou and Gabalac's fifth phase, called "negotiation," involves the testing out of a woman's new perspective and intentions in the world in which she must continue to live. In this phase of negotiation the audience to the new narrative is expanded as the counselee learns how to maintain a supportive community. As Ballou and Gabalac point out, the counselee has now become a healthy person in an unhealthy world, and she must find ways to maintain her health over the long haul.[4]

A Feminist Narrative Approach to Helping Women Make Choices

It seems to me that a feminist narrative approach to pastoral counseling with women takes the insights of the above models very seriously in helping women make choices. Thomas St. James O'Connor, a chaplain and family counselor, and his research team report that people "most often seek help from a therapist when they view their lives as problem-saturated and feel powerless to overcome their problems."[5] In other words, people seek out a counselor when they cannot make choices that get them free of the problems that are oppressing their lives. The real goal of the pastoral counselor (and indeed all counselors) is to help people make choices that open up a preferred direction that is healthy, moral, and hopeful.

Studies exploring the effectiveness of a narrative approach to pastoral counseling have demonstrated that people and families uniformly feel that the counseling has helped them to overcome the problems that brought them to the counselor. One of the most important aspects of narrative counseling that gets named by people who have been engaged in it is the sense of agency that they have gained in the process. O'Connor et al. write, "Personal agency is more noticeable to families than the external-izing conversation or the development of an alternate story. Somehow, families feel empowered by therapy as they come to recognize that they are able to make some change in the problem."[6] When counselees begin to realize that they do have choices and at least some power to make meaning out of their life experiences, they begin to have confidence in a future story that has value for them.

Before we discuss the narrative process in choice-making further, I want to raise a couple of caveats to this work. There is a risk in a counsel-ing approach like narrative that the counselor will want to move quickly to the stage of finding the exceptional or alternate stories with which to resist the problem narrative. It is very important that the counselee be very carefully heard in the fullness of her experience before moving to find pathways of resistance. This is true for two reasons. First, if a woman

who has had the frequent experience of not being heard and validated—
and this is true for most of the women who will come for counseling—is
rushed, even with the best of intentions, to attempting to find solutions,
she will sense that the dominant culture has just been replicated in terms
of imposing power upon her. This would not serve the primary goal of
feminist narrative work, which is the enhancement of effective agency in
the counselee. Second, if the counselor attempts to help the counselee generate exceptional narratives prematurely, she or he will be doing so out of
the problem narrative. Unless the problem is fully named and well described in the externalization process, it will be very difficult to develop
counterstories/exceptional narratives to resist it. My experience is that
people who are new to narrative counseling do not spend adequate time
hearing the story and naming and externalizing the problem.

The second caveat is similar. There is the risk that feminist-oriented
counselors, who generally have had their own experiences of consciousness-raising and liberation, may be eager to guide and direct the liberating process of the counselee. They may urge a counselee in a particular
direction, often the one the counselor has experienced for herself. Fortunately, the narrative approach to counseling provides a useful correction
to the tendency toward this form of false advocacy. Narrative theory in-
sists that the counselor operate from a position of not-knowing. The
counselor must be open to whatever directions the counselee chooses to
move in. Every woman, in her variety of particularities, has a unique narrative even as it is shaped in a culture that generally works against
women. A counselor cannot know what is best for the counselee, nor the
directions that will best accomplish her goals. The point is that there is a
"passionate disinterest" in the counseling outcome. The goals are to validate the counselee, deconstruct problem narratives so that new options
emerge, and enhance the woman's agency whenever possible.

Given these two caveats it is useful to look at the two most relevant
phases of narrative counseling for helping women to make choices. In offering these, I am assuming that the first two phases of the model proposed
in this book, coming to voice and gaining clarity, have been occurring and
that the counselee's choice-making has emerged from the process. Good
narrative counseling evolves naturally from externalizing the problem to
listening for exceptional narratives. As the counselor listens carefully to
the problem narrative, she or he also listens for hints of story lines of resistance and hope. When she or he hears those, the counselee is invited to

talk about those other stories (or the "invisible" story of possibility that usually is ignored). As narrative theorists point out, however, new narratives are very tentative and fleeting. They need lots of "thickening" and care as the counselee and counselor work together to strengthen the new narratives so that they become livable. The problem-saturated story and its attitudes and options are very detailed and familiar to the counselee and consequently the tendency will be to screen out or reject the new narrative because it doesn't fit well with the old one. One does not want to replace the old one—it is, after all, part of the whole story—but one does want to lay along side it a rich and detailed version of the new story so that it is available for generating new options and less pain.[7]

When we ask people to talk about an alternative strand of their story, we encourage them to relive that story. We ask for detail. We ask people to imagine themselves back in that situation. It recalls who they were during the exceptional moment so that they can remind themselves that that person is a person that they also are now, even if that person is hidden from view. The counselee begins living both the old story and the new story and its implications in the moment of recalling. It is re-enactment. When the people of Israel told the story of God's saving work in bringing them to safety, they re-experienced God's active and trustworthy presence in their lives. It wasn't just the telling of the story, it was the renewing of the certainty of God's active presence even though the context was different and worries and doubts may have been plaguing them. This is a similar understanding.

In the midst of this work it is important to connect past experiences to current time. So it is common in this kind of counseling to ask something like, "Who wouldn't be surprised by the way you have learned to stand up for yourself?" This kind of question takes the current story back into the past to demonstrate that strands of this story have always been present in the counselee, even if they hadn't been developed until recently. It is also important to take the story into the future, like "It sounds like you are preparing to take another step. Is something moving you toward that next step?" Stretching a preferred narrative through time will help strengthen it.[8]

This is the step prior to choice making. As a woman becomes clear about the problem she is resisting and how she might be able to resist it in such a way that a better life will be possible for her, new choices emerge almost automatically. It is important to help her look at what those choices might be and how she might consider their value for her. The counselor might help her imagine that she has made the choice and is now living with the consequences of it. Using imagination techniques, the counselor can help the counselee imagine in some detail whether the choice has turned out as she would like it. This also strengthens the counselee's grip on the preferred narrative and her sense of agency in achieving it.

Much of the counseling process is made up of this movement from problem identification, narratives of resistance, the emergence of counterstories, and choice making to further developing those counterstories and resistance stories in the life of the counselee. The process continues until a preferred future story can realistically be imagined and acted upon. At that point, the counselee often faces some larger choices that both symbolize and implement the new sense of self and narrative that has emerged in the counseling process. These are the choices that need criteria for evaluation, both in the decision-making process and as the person is living with those decisions down the road. One of the most helpful things that the counselor can do with the counselee at this point is to help her develop some criteria for this evaluation process. Having a structure and meaning system for evaluating choices increases a woman's sense of authority. She no longer has to look to the power structures—in fear or in hope—for their evaluation of her life choices. She instead turns to herself and her communities of accountability for the evaluative process. At the moral level, she claims responsibility for her actions, and lives with the consequences for good and for ill.

Criteria for Making and Evaluating Choices

Choices, of course, can take endless shapes and go in endless directions. Consequently, it is helpful to have some criteria by which to judge the helpfulness of choices made in the counseling process. The criteria that go into assessing the helpfulness of these choices might vary considerably based on the counselee's and counselor's theology, on each of their visions of a just world, on their priorities for health, and on their particular life contexts—especially that of the counselee. I suggest the following seven evaluative questions as useful criteria for assessing the helpfulness of choices made during the pastoral counseling.

First, does this choice address the real issues involved as revealed in the coming to voice and gaining clarity dimensions of the counseling? In other words, if the other two phases of counseling have not been adequately achieved, there is the risk that the choices will emerge from the framework of the problem narrative. Other questions that may help explore this might include: Is the counselee making choices out of a sense of the new possibilities revealed to her through the gaining clarity process? Is she operating with a reasonable sense of agency generated by her acknowledgment of feeling empowered? Have the problems been externalized enough so that her decisions are not being driven by the internalized sense of responsibility for the problems that brought her into counseling? Is she clear about what needs to be resisted and how this choice will enable her to continue disempowering the oppressiveness of her presenting and identified problems? In short, the choice needs to reflect a response to the problems as they have been framed by her new clarity and agency.

Second, does this choice empower the counselee in a nondestructive way? In other words, does this choice take seriously the complexities of her life or does it sacrifice those things that are valuable to her for the sake of some idealized direction? When Mary said to me, "If I get healthy, I'll lose my family," that had to be taken seriously in the choices that she made. There are few perfect choices with perfect consequences that come out of a counseling process. All choices need to be made with all of the counselee's important values in mind, even if those don't perfectly fit the counselor's value system. While making her choices in the counseling process, the counselee must know that she had agency in making them and is able to take responsibility for them.

Third, does this choice reverse or reframe damaging patriarchal values in such a way that the reversing or reframing will continue to provide a means toward ongoing clarity for the counselee? Further, has the counseling process integrated the unique and personal story of this counselee with the larger cultural milieu she has developed and continues to live in? Is she able to perceive the deceptions of patriarchy and the lies about power and value that permeate the culture around gender, race, class, sexual orientation, able-bodiedness, and age? Has she developed adequate counterstories and discourses of resistance to maintain an acceptable degree of health and awareness? And, does she feel that she has the tools with which to continue deconstructing and dismantling those forces in the

culture that work against her and against other people and groups desig-
nated as less valuable? The assumption here is that she needs those tools
in order to maintain a sense of her own agency and hope.

Fourth, does this choice enhance the possibility of healthy relationships and support the healthy relationships that are already in the counselee's life? As Adler and many others since have suggested, human beings
have a deep need to be in relationship. Theologically, we affirm that God
created us to be in relationship with one another and with God. Some
even suggest that the meaning of the *imago dei* in humans is their ability
to be in profound relationship.[9] The point is that being in relationship is
central to life. Some feminist authors suggest that relationality is even
more important in women's lives than in men's for a variety of reasons,
including their developmental patterns and their gender training.
Whether or not this is true, we do know that isolation makes women
more vulnerable to the oppressive power dynamics of the culture. The
choices a woman makes in counseling need to support her relationality
and her relationships.

Fifth, does this choice fit with the counselee's (and counselor's) understanding of God's ongoing calls for love and justice? Have issues of spirituality been raised and addressed in the pastoral counseling process? Is
the counselee clear about what she believes spiritually and morally about
the directions for her life? Does she understand herself and her vocation
in spiritually congruent ways? Does she have a sense of spiritual agency in
her life? In pastoral counseling there needs to be an awareness that our religious traditions have served both as discourses of harm against women
(and others) and discourses of resistance and transformation. Has the
counselee, then, gained the ability to evaluate her religious life critically
and make appropriate choices in light of it? Has she, to use DeMarinis's
metaphor, developed the ability to be a responsible scavenger of the religious traditions that are a part of her life? And is she adequately involved
with a community of faith that will support these directions in her life?
Sometimes, for better or worse, these are some of the hardest questions to
address adequately in the pastoral counseling process. There are times
when the pastor herself or himself is too caught up in the religious traditions and faith communities to be a good role model of either critical
evaluation or responsible scavenging. If so, it is the pastoral counselor's
responsibility to take these issues seriously for herself or himself to avoid
doing harm in the pastoral counseling process.

Sixth, is there adequate support for the ongoing implications of this choice or these choices? This has been addressed to a large extent above. The need to bring important relationships into the new narrative—developing the audience, as narrative theorists say—must be central if the counselee is to be able to continue strengthening this preferred story line. Often, it is important to do family counseling as a part of this process to make sure that the whole central system of the counselee's life is involved in rewriting the problem narrative that has affected everyone. The difficulty that I see in always making the whole counseling process a family approach is that for many women (especially women who are struggling with depression), there is such an inequity of power in the primary relationship that she is unable to negotiate or be heard in the family. It is important that women who are experiencing an inequity of power in their primary relationships are able to be helped to come to voice and to begin the clarification process without having to play the family power games for survival. As her sense of agency and entitlement grow and she experiences adequate support, it may be very important to encourage her to invite her family into the counseling process. In that way she can participate in holding the whole system (including herself) accountable for its role in the problem narrative and its responsibility to mutually resist it.

Finally, the seventh question asks if there is a method and a plan for ongoing evaluation of the consequences of this choice or these choices. It is important that a counselee be able to take her knowledge and skills with her out of the counseling office. Especially in a short-term counseling situation, as the parish must be, these skills must be intentionally honed so that the work can continue. Methods of ongoing evaluation might involve a check-in session with the counselor, regular family discussions to see how new behaviors are working, a support group or certain friendships in which the members serve as a community of accountability, and so on. It is important that the counselee have a clear and external method of checking on the success and health of the choices she has made so that they can be renewed, changed, or abandoned as appropriate.

These evaluative questions may not all be answered positively, but when any are answered negatively, consequences of the negative answers need to be carefully considered. The purpose of these criteria is to give the counselor and the counselee a way for putting insights into action and maintaining health for the future.

The Personal and Political Nature
of Making Choices

As the evaluative criteria suggest, there is always a dynamic tension in making choices when counseling is done from a feminist pastoral perspective. The tension may be thought of as the familiar personal and political dialectic or it may be thought of as the pastoral and the prophetic dialectic. Emilie M. Townes suggests that the pastoral and the prophetic always belong together in the ethics of ministry. Without that tension the pastoral can become too individualized and uncritically accepting, and the prophetic can become harsh and disconnected from the real lives of people.[10] Pastoral care and counseling in general have been much more in sync with the pastoral side of ministry and not as able to draw on the prophetic. We have had trouble holding people and systems accountable for the harm they do. We have had trouble preparing our counselees to reach out as prophetic agents into the world that has harmed them and to work to dismantle unjust structures of power and oppression. The work of the feminist pastoral counselor can't be limited to helping a woman challenge the discourses of harm in only her own life without also helping her to perceive and take action against the kyriarchal structures in the culture that harm so many. This empowerment is necessary for a counselee's own ongoing agency as well as for the sake of her participation in the justice making of God's realm.

The prophetic themes in our own religious traditions are of help to the pastoral counselor who seeks to hold together the personal and the political, the pastoral and the prophetic. Rosemary Radford Ruether suggests that four themes are central to the liberating prophetic traditions. They are (1) God's defense and vindication of the oppressed, (2) a critique of the dominant systems of power, (3) the vision of a new age to come, and (4) a critique of the ideology that sustains the unjust order.[11] How counselors carry out these prophetic principles changes depending on the context, but the themes of this prophetic tradition rightly belong at the center of a feminist-based pastoral counseling theory and they belong in the pastoral counseling process itself.

In helping women to make choices in pastoral counseling, counselors need to pay attention to these prophetic issues if the counseling is to be truly transformative to both a person and a culture in distress. We must acknowledge in both the theories and the practices that making choices of this nature is not an easy process. Making choices against a system, even a destructive one that has been deeply internalized as truth and that is persistently presented in culture as part of the natural order, is a frightening enterprise. These choices cannot be made without a great deal of personal and relational deconstructive work. And the choices (and their healthy consequences) cannot be maintained without communities of support and communities of shared prophetic mission.

eight

Making Choices
in the Context of Aging

There are numerous challenges in exploring the issue of making choices in the context of women's aging. For one thing, defining the term *aging* for our purposes is difficult. We are all aging from the moment we are born. Even if we understand that we are using the term to mean that we are discussing women who are older, *aging* is still a relative term. Women who are the same age are highly diverse in the ways they have responded to the passing of the years. There is more diversity among older people of the same cohort than there is for any other life stage. Carroll Saussy suggests that it is very difficult to talk about life stages in any group, especially those of old age. She writes,

> There are at least three reasons why it is difficult to categorize people according to chronological stages. First, norms for what one calls childhood, adolescence, adulthood, and old age are always shifting. Second, increased longevity lengthens the period that has been called old age to one-third, and for some as much as one-half, of a normal lifetime—too long an epoch to be considered one stage. Third, it is difficult for writers to project themselves into anything more than their immediate futures; they simply lack firsthand experience and their imaginations fail.[1]

So it is very difficult to talk about "aging women" as a category and have a common understanding. For the purposes of this chapter I will talk about women who are exploring issues that come in the second half of life, issues like retirement, launching children, and widowhood.

"Aging women" will be defined both by chronological age (past midlife) and by the kinds of tasks and issues that women face in their later years.

Another problem with talking about women and aging is that there is a complex weave of stereotypes about women in their later years that emerge out of ageism, sexism, and, to some extent, ableism that are hard to untangle. In some ways, the sexism that has plagued women throughout their lives may, in the face of ageism, give women the momentum they need to become more true to themselves and their own needs. On the other hand, sexism is cumulative and its effects hamper women as they move into later life. We will explore these paradoxes throughout the chapter. One of our first tasks, however, will be to explore women's experiences, still keeping in mind that we are making generalizations that falter in the face of each woman's uniqueness, in an attempt to unveil sweeping stereotypes that our culture tends to perpetuate about older women.

Obviously, older age is a context that is somewhat different from the contexts of violence and depression. For one thing, all women who live long enough will experience it, whereas there is some chance, albeit small, that they will not experience depression or violence. Nonetheless, the purpose of this chapter is to explore some of the experiences and contexts of older age so that the pastoral counselor better understands the issues when an older woman seeks counseling. The point is not to portray older age as a problem in and of itself but as a context in which issues may well arise that require choice making. It is important for the pastoral counselor to have challenged her or his own stereotypes and misinformation so that she or he can best be prepared to collaborate in re-authoring problematic narratives.

Older women generally face a variety of transitions that require a re-examination of their identity narratives for the sake of integration. There is probably no other life stage that requires the work of narrative integration as dramatically as that of older age. The pastoral counselor has to be able to recognize cultural stereotypes of aging so that they can be examined, critiqued, and responsibly scavenged as part of the pastoral counseling process. This chapter is about making choices in that context.

Challenging Ageist and Sexist Stereotypes

Despite many dominant cultural stereotypes, most elderly women report high life satisfaction and are strong and active people. In fact, 95 percent of the elderly (aged sixty-five and older) live in ordinary community settings and only 5 percent are institutionalized. Even for people in the eighty-five plus range, the majority rate themselves to be in good health and high in life satisfaction.[2] Why, then, are images of elderly women so often negative? Robert C. Atchley, a well-known gerontologist, suggests that part of the problem is that the frail elderly catch our attention and the healthy, vigorous elderly are invisible to us. But, he suggests, the ideas that older men and women are frail and disabled and that they mostly have been abandoned by families remain in the common folk knowledge even though both ideas are false. Part of this, he suggests, is that we have reduced the general incidence of death in our society and thus concentrated the experience of death in the elderly population. When we see frail older people, they remind us that death comes not at any possible moment, but it comes when we get old. We closely associate death with aging and then attempt to deny aging and thus deny death.[3]

As part of the research process, I began to listen carefully to older women and groups of women, who often spontaneously began to talk about aging. The kinds of images and experiences I heard from older women included the seeming contradictions of fears of and experiences of loss, a general acceptance of the changes of the life cycle, and a genuine gratitude for the various freedoms that aging can bring to women. Some examples I uncovered during my "listening research" included:

- a woman on a bus as she struggled to get up and out saying to me, "Don't get old, dear, it's not worth it."
- a woman in a group of friends who were talking about physical aging said, "I really like my gray hair—it feels so much more like me than my brown hair did."
- a churchwoman who was invited to do some pastoral counseling work said, "It's really too late for me to look at all my feelings. I feel like I would be opening Pandora's box and wouldn't be able to close it again."
- a thirty-five-year-old seminary student in a small group said, "I really don't want to get ordained now—I think that I would be forced to go

along with everyone's expectations. I would like to be ordained in twenty-five or thirty years when I could be a feisty old preacher woman and tell the truth to the congregation."

As an additional part of my research, I asked eighty master of divinity students from two different seminaries I was visiting, most of them in their twenties or early thirties (and so heirs to the insights of the women's movement), to imagine what perceptions they would have and how they would feel if they had just been appointed or called to be the pastor of a particular church that was described as being made up of a large number of elderly women. They were to write their images and feelings down in a paragraph that they turned in to me. Their responses were interesting. About 20 percent gave responses that indicated some emotional or cognitive understanding of the gains and the losses, the strengths and the needs, the possibilities and the limits of older women. Often, there were still stereotypes attached to these understandings, but at least there was some complexity in the portrayal. Approximately 20 percent gave responses that indicated an idealization of the older woman. These statements included phrases like, "women with unlimited, untapped potential," or "strong, salt-of-the-earth leaders," "women who are absolutely committed to one another," and "hardworking, wise, and wonderful." All of them probably contained elements of truth but missed the real complexity of older women— probably, again, as a flip side of their own fears of aging—and may have had to do with expected interviewer bias.

About 60 percent of the students, though (and they were all in pastoral care or counseling classes) gave exclusively negative emotional responses and images. In fact, the first ten paragraphs that I looked at all said something about "little, gray- or white-haired old ladies." Ministry expectations in all of these cases were almost exclusively perceived as giving needed or demanded care to these women without any sense of what they might be offering back to the church. Statements on their papers included: "I see a dying church," "I feel cheated and devalued to go to a church like this," "These are women very set in their ways, who all sit together, and criticize everything around them," "Powerless, needy, bridge-playing, withered, babies, depressed, confused, dominating, fault-finding, complaining, fragile, and weak." These were the dominant images from more than forty-five master of divinity students who were in advanced pastoral care and counseling courses. Several said that they feared for the church if this was to be the population. And the dominant ministry in which they would engage, they often said, would be to pay less than normal attention to the congregation and seek to evangelize younger people.

So it is interesting to note that even though the majority of elderly women are strong, satisfied, and active, most of the images didn't include this population. What does it mean that these women are invisible? Barbara F. Turner and Lillian E. Troll distinguish between phenomenological age and social age. Phenomenological age is how people see themselves and their aging. Most older people, both male and female, tend to see themselves as younger than their chronological age. There are no gender differences in that. Social age, however, which is the perception others have about those of older age, is significantly gender biased. Turner and Troll write that "social age differs markedly for men and women. To give but one example, in this country people think that women become middle-aged and old at younger chronological ages than men, despite women's greater longevity. Women, however, differentiate age boundaries for the sexes less than men do."[4] So, although older women are largely healthy and productive, they are often dismissed as a group because stereotypes about them are stronger than reality.

There are at least four dimensions to aging: the biological, the psychological, the spiritual, and the social, and each person has aspects of self that age at different rates and with different positive or negative consequences. We end up in trouble if we try to generalize aging in either all-negative or all-positive ways. We must be willing to tolerate the ambiguity of the different realities and dimensions of the aging process and the varieties of images that help us live with and minister out of that ambiguity. And we have to be willing to dismantle the stereotypes that prevent us from exploring and understanding the complexities of people with their variety of experiences as they age.

I believe this to be especially true with aging women, about whom our society has given consistently negative messages. Typically, people's image system has more negative stereotypes about older women than about older men, as indicated by Turner and Troll's statement about social age perceptions. In studies of recent television shows, considerably more older women are portrayed as unsuccessful than are older men. In addition, whereas a man may be seen as dignified with his gray hair and facial character lines, a woman is encouraged to fight nature and maintain her youthful (and valued) appearance.

Ageism and Sexism

It is important to explore the demographics of aging women in our culture, as well as the personal and cultural narratives that provide their contexts, because it is in these contexts of aging women's lives that the seeming contradictions become more evident. It's worth noting here that there is limited literature on the topic of women and aging. As we seek to discover what sociologists and psychologists can tell us about this part of women's life span, we find that much of the literature on this topic does not make gender distinctions. When it does make those distinctions, the research perspectives and methods are still often tinged with sexist assumptions and thereby ask the kinds of questions that do not provide relevant information for understanding aging women. Much still needs to be done in this area of research.

Nonetheless, it is important to explore the research that does exist. As I introduce some of the negative realities that older women face, it's important to put them into the context of sexism and ageism. As we have seen, the "isms" (things like racism, classism, ableism, sexism, ageism, and so on) have certain things in common. They represent a cultural value decision whereby a particular group of people is accorded more worth than another group based on a set of rather permanent characteristics. The consequence of the assignment of cultural devaluing is loss of cultural power. There are multiple dimensions and ramifications of power loss in economic, legal, employment and labor, familial, social, and service realms, to name a few. One certainly sees these dynamics in exploring the experiences of older women.

Although sexism is clearly at work in the lives of older women, there is some evidence that ageism has even more influence than sexism on older women and that there is less sexist pressure on women as they age. Nonetheless, in a life-span approach, all that has gone before in women's lives has an impact on their present experience. We must be careful not to oversimplify the relationship between ageism and sexism or between any of the isms. Ageism is the cultural practice of attributing less worth and power to older people (in the third developmental phase of life—maturation, maturity, and aging) than to younger people (meaning mostly people in the maturity phase). Out of this valuing system certain stereotypes emerge that support the denial of power and esteem to this group of people. The most common stereotype is the notion of age as only decline and loss. I have alluded to this as I looked at typical images associated with aging.

The Importance of Studying Women and Aging

When we understand the complexities of women's life-cycle development in the contexts of ageism and sexism, it becomes clear that we need as much accurate information as possible about women's lives. And yet very little research on aging and women has been done—and almost none exploring aging women, ethnicity, and race. The research issues about aging have been considered, for the most part, to be issues of men. The issues associated with women that have been addressed up until about twenty years ago were stereotypically "women's issues" and were researched with sexist assumptions. For example, researchers assumed that empty-nest syndrome was one of the major crises of women's lives, and society developed a variety of myths around this life phase. Women faced empty nest and men faced retirement. Few people studied women's retirement (and there has always been a large number of women in the workforce). Research into older women's life experience is necessary for at least three reasons.[5] First, there is a demographic imperative. In 1990, 13 percent of the population was elderly, with women outnumbering men about three to two. About 10 percent of that population was above eighty-five. By 2050, conservative population projections estimate that we will have gone from the elderly making up almost 13 percent of the population in 1990 to the elderly making up 23 percent of the population, and the gender gap looks like it will continue.[6]

The second reason for study is that there is a considerable lack of research in terms of the specific experiences of older women. What little research there is has focused on things like menopause, depression, widowhood, and empty-nest syndrome. The research underlying theories of aging has often not included women at all. J. Dianne Garner and Susan O. Mercer point out that as recently as the 1970s older women were basically invisible within the population of women *and* within the population of the elderly. The women's movement has tended to focus on young to middle-age women even though the leadership of the first wave of feminism was in large part older women. At the White House Conference on Aging in 1981, for the first time in its thirty-year history, there was a special section for older women.[7] At that conference a bill of rights emerged claiming the right of older women to self-esteem, freedom from the stigma of living alone, sexual expression, economic support and equal employment opportunities, an adequate level of health care, positive representation in the media, and ridding oneself of dependence on others. It is interesting that this bill of rights is very similar to the Women's Declaration of Independence passed by United States feminists in Seneca Falls, New York, in 1848.[8] There *are* gender differences in aging, despite aging having been seen as an experience that minimizes gender difference. When I was working on this chapter, I asked a colleague who has done work in aging about gender-specific resources. His response was that gerontology was one of the few places that had been able to "maintain its freedom from gender polarization." When difference in experience is seen as polarization, it is no wonder that there is fear to pursue gender-specific research, even after gender differences have been identified.

This is the third reason for study: women's problems as they age (and the unique strengths and resources they bring through their aging) are not just the result of growing older. They are also the result of the various historical and current patterns of socioeconomic and gender stratification in our culture. Gender differences in aging reflect deeply embedded sexism. Those gender differences, according to Lois Grau, include women living longer than men do and tending to be poorer and less healthy than men who survive into old age. Women's social roles and relationships in old age differ from those of men in terms of marriage, family connections, friendship networks, church participation, and so on.[9] Elizabeth Midlarsky adds that women and men have very different psychosocial stressors, which include for women the experience of social powerlessness associated with both ageism and sexism, the multiplicity of role changes over the life cycle, different foci around retirement, different realistic expectations of poverty, likelihood of unsatisfactory and unsafe housing, widowhood, social isolation, boredom, fear of disability due to longevity, particular kinds of health threats like osteoporosis, higher rate of Alzheimer's disease and other forms of dementia, fear of relegation to custodial institutions due to outliving potential caregivers like spouses, patronizing attitudes in the various social and medical service arenas, and in the church if we can trust the images that emerge from my seminary students and many pastors with whom I have spoken.[10]

Living with and Escaping from the Culture's Sexist and Ageist Messages

Mary Wollstonecraft wrote a piece near the end of the eighteenth century in which she quoted an anonymous man who said, "I wonder what possible use a woman over the age of forty has on this earth." He wasn't expressing an idiosyncratic thought but was expressing a set of interlocking beliefs about women that persist even now. A recent advertisement in a feminist magazine had a woman suggest that she wasn't going to give in to aging gracefully, she was going to fight it every step of the way—of course the way to do this was through expensive cosmetic assistance. And it is not atypical that this was in a feminist magazine. The second wave of the women's movement has been made up primarily of young white women, and women of color and older women often have felt closed out by it. Even when the women's movement became aware of its narrowness and entered into closer dialogue with women of color, changing methods and assumptions in the process, older women still often felt excluded.

Because of the powerful messages that the culture sends about where women's value is located (youth, beauty, and reproductive ability), women's first trauma regarding aging often isn't a physical disability or an economic hardship but the dismay that results from observing the first gray hair, the facial wrinkles, or the added weight that frequently comes with normal aging. Since acceptance of the aging process is highly correlated with life satisfaction in elderly people, these various sexist messages about diminished worth when reproductive capacity and traditional sexual beauty are lost are closely tied to the potential for women to experience threatened life satisfaction.

Fortunately, the messages indicating a loss of worth are balanced to a certain degree by women's realization, often for the first time, that the rules inculcated into them by a patriarchal culture can't be followed. When a woman realizes that she no longer is able even to pretend to be all those things that society demands of her in order to be valued (young, traditionally beautiful, reproductively accessible, and so on), then she often begins to question the need to play by the rules of patriarchy at all. Midlarsky says that "in many respects, the aging woman may be free of earlier burdens and stresses; for example, rigid sex role expectations, intense demands for nurturance, conflicts between gratification of one's own needs and the like."[11] Many of the women to whom I spoke about their experiences of aging—and most of these women were fairly "traditional" women—made comments about their sense of freedom to be themselves for the first time in their lives. Atchley reports that a 1976 study discovered that "'traditional' women (nurturant and conventional conformists) showed a steady pattern of personality growth from adolescence to middle age, while 'independent' women (ambitious, unconventional, and gaining satisfaction from self-development rather than from attachment to others) found the traditional roles constricting and conflictual in their 40s, although by their 50s the social responsibilities of the independent women were more in tune with their possibilities."[12] In other words, both traditional women and independent women found themselves empowered by the reduction of sexist stereotypes on their lives, mostly because these women had in many ways "outgrown their usefulness" to the patriarchal culture and could be their own persons.

There are other measures of this, although much of the interpretation of meaning is speculative. For example, whereas suicide rates are considerably higher for older men than for younger men, women's suicide rates peak and plateau when they are in early adulthood and drop when they are older. And in studies of older women's sex-role identity, "androgynous" women (those who rate high in both stereotypically masculine and stereotypically feminine traits) score higher levels of life satisfaction than do "feminine" women; and "masculine" women score higher levels than either "feminine" or "androgynous" women in terms of self-esteem. Having the freedom to disregard patriarchy's rules seems to enhance self-image, freedom, and possibilities for older women. This means that although sexism sends messages of devaluation to older women, those very messages often allow women to become more fully themselves because the risks of breaking the rules have been reduced. This is one of the clearest areas of paradox in the realities of older women.

Risks and Benefits of Aging for Women

Let's move to some of the other areas of risk and harm for older women. Many of these have to be taken as central in our pastoral care and counseling ministry to this population.

Economics

Women's economic situation as they age has to be carefully understood. Many older women face poverty. This is for a variety of reasons, but it is mostly tied to:

- role expectations, consequent work patterns, and resulting pensions;
- longevity and predictable widowhood even though women are taught to expect that they will be cared for by their husbands through old age as part of the complementarity of marriage roles;
- social policies like Social Security that still operate on the assumption that men are workers and women are housewives.

Nearly 50 percent of African American older women, 25 percent of Hispanic older women, and 15 percent of European American older women live below the poverty level. White women tend to live considerably longer and so they make up the largest numbers of the elderly poor. Fifty percent of all single women over sixty-five and 80 percent of women over eighty have incomes below the poverty line. The poverty rate for an older woman is 60 percent higher than for an older man.

Many of these women are newly poor—they didn't expect or anticipate poverty in middle age because of their marital and class identity. With the high incidence of widowhood, as well as divorced, never-married, and displaced homemakers, however, women can expect that poverty is likely. Very often for newly poor women, poverty occurs when they feel the most vulnerable in other ways, such as when they face widowhood. The poverty rate for elderly women living alone is 30 percent. In every major American racial and ethnic group, the median income of the male is approximately one-and-a-half times as much as that of the female. And the rate of poverty is almost twice as great for elderly women as for elderly men.[13] So, although older Americans in general have experienced a dramatic increase in income in the past thirty years, many elderly women continue to be poor.

Why is this? Naomi Gottlieb suggests that the pivotal message for women is that their family role is the most important one and that all other roles are secondary.[14] Thus, women are expected to work without pay in the home and to be paid poorly for the work they do outside the home that is greatly sex segregated. Seventy-five percent of women work in only ten jobs that can mostly be seen as carrying out the work of the home in the larger world (office clerk, secretary-typist, manager-administrator, sales worker, machine operator, food service worker, janitor/maid, teacher, nurse's aide, and registered nurse). Only two of those jobs have a high probability of a private pension (teachers and nurses).[15]

Since the work world of women is organized around sex-role expectations and around women's primary domestic responsibilities, especially for the current cohorts of older women, the kinds of retirement or later life income available for them is minimal. According to Atchley, "pension entitlement is the single largest gender difference in retirement. Women's discontinuous work histories and higher likelihood of part-time employment decrease the probability that they will become entitled to adequate retirement pensions."[16] A 1988 study found that retired women had monthly pension benefits only 60 percent as large as those men received. And since women live considerably longer, their savings become depleted and their ability to stay even with the cost of living is minimal. In addition, since women generally outlive their spouses, their savings are often depleted by the husband's time of illness and the surviving spouse is left without adequate means to live.

These are significant issues for pastors to understand when ministering to elderly women. Worrying about having enough money to live on is one of the top three concerns for older women and obviously that worry has a strong negative correlation with life satisfaction. The pastor must stay alert to issues of survival with older women in the congregation, although women will not volunteer the information of economic hardship very often. Many older women have a strong need to maintain a sense of independence and to keep information about their neediness to themselves. Obviously this varies from person to person, but the literature indicates both increased reticence among older women and an increased desire for independence as threats to independence become greater.

Employment and Retirement

Although older women are currently more likely to have had a job rather than a career, there is increasing evidence that the role of work in older women's lives is and has been of considerable value. According to Mercer and Garner, surveys in both the United States and Europe indicate that women have a strong preference to keep working compared to attitudes of men in the same age group. This pattern remains consistent even if the women (middle-aged and older) felt they could afford to retire.[17] The recent studies in women and work have demonstrated how important work outside the home is to most women. For example, in studying depressed women, one of the most crucial factors that contributes to resisting depression was working outside the home. This held true even when the job was a menial or an unchallenging one. Consequently, it might not surprise us that retirement is often a significant crisis for older women. Until twenty years ago, however, the issue of women's retirement from the workforce was an uninvestigated topic. It was assumed to be a nonissue because women's primary vocation was seen to be in the home and, after all, when women retired they could return to that satisfying primary vocation to a large extent. Even when gerontologists began to study women's retirement they found that women tended to be more positive about retirement than men.[18] Every study I have encountered that was done by women or written about from a feminist perspective, however, has indicates that retirement is a significant problem for most women. For example, Hedva Lewittes suggests that the study of women and retirement has been hampered by sexist assumptions about women's work. She says that not only has women's labor force participation been overlooked but the role of work in women's self-concept has been ignored.[19] And Ruth Formanek writes that "despite unsupported views to the contrary, women do not enjoy retirement as much as men and take longer to adapt to the retirement transition. Moreover, women who approach retirement with a negative attitude seem unable to adjust to it even after a long period of time, feeling useless and lonely, missing social contacts and the satisfactions derived from work. In general, women worry more about their financial state after retirement, and are more anxious about retirement than men."[20]

It is clear, then, that recent research shows that retirement is a significant life event for women. The significance varies depending on the woman and her history and it often revolves around issues of self-concept, sense of vocation and contribution, and the threatened loss of social network and relationships. Women's work relationships are often a significant part of their sense of meaning. And frequently retirement comes at a time when there are other relationship losses, such as widowhood, for which the average age is fifty-six.[21] Both Midlarsky and Jean Coyle suggest similar findings in their research. Midlarsky says that studies indicate that women are more likely to experience a significant increase in feelings of uselessness than men do at retirement. Other studies show that women are more likely to have psychiatric difficulties after retirement than men.[22] Coyle's research and review of the literature also show contradictory findings between historical attitudes toward women's retirement and recent studies from women's perspectives. She says that women are less likely than men to be positively oriented toward retirement and are more likely than men to express apprehension about the effects of retirement. They also wish to remain employed longer than men do, although part of this may be that women have to remain employed longer than men in order to have an adequate retirement income.[23]

We must recognize that this is still a vague area of research and be careful when working with women approaching retirement to explore the meaning that they give to the event. We must be very cautious about making assumptions in either direction and thus again missing the multiple dimensions of this event for retiring women. It is also important to take note of what else is simultaneously occurring in the life of the retiring woman—aging parents, caretaking responsibilities, ill health in herself or her partner, and so on, all of which affect the retirement experience.

The predictors of retirement satisfaction in women have begun to take shape. For women working outside the home, the factors that emerged in a study by Laura Hubbs-Tait were, in order of importance, (1) perceived quality of health over seven years, (2) amount of loneliness, (3) degree of involvement in civic organizations and in church, and (4) number and quality of contacts and acquaintances. When Hubbs-Tait studied the homemakers who were experiencing retirement through their spouse and through their own shifting homemaking responsibilities, she found that the four factors for a successful transition were (1) a low amount of loneliness, (2) the ability to engage in continuing education, (3) a perception of current good health, and (4) an increase in the number of acquaintances over the past seven years.[24]

These findings have clear implications for pastoral ministry to older women. They also caution us not to lump all women's experience into the same categories. Women who are retiring from the labor force may need different things than do women who are retiring from homemaking responsibilities. The main difference that emerged in these studies (both groups need social contacts, reasonable health, and the avoidance of loneliness) was that women leaving the labor force need to be actively involved in the public realm, whether that is in civic activities, church life, or in some other way that gives her the opportunity to express her sense of vocation. Women who were retiring from active parenting and homemaking as their primary vocation indicated that they needed to be more involved in continuing education. These are, of course, generalizations. The point is that when women experience a shift in those things that give identity and meaning in their lives, they need to find something equally meaningful to replace them. All people, no matter what their life stage, need a future story that has meaning.

One other issue related to retirement deserves some discussion here. It is important to raise the issue of the empty nest since it has been one of the most popular mythic constructs about women as they face aging. The myths about empty-nest syndrome are based on the unquestioned belief that women find their primary meaning in the rearing of children and that the culture's value of them depends on that role. Again, it is important to say that, for many women, maybe even for most, the movement of the children out of the home full-time into their building new homes for themselves is at least a significant life-stage moment. There may well be grief, restlessness, and longing for the "good old days." It is important to be able to respond pastorally to the many dimensions of this experience.

On the other hand, researchers find that there are factors not generally considered by those who uncritically accept the empty-nest syndrome theory. For one thing, children do not generally leave home all at once anymore. Because children often engage in a longer process of preparation for adulthood, they may return to the home several times. In addition, parenting shifts in focus but doesn't end just because children are launched. Studies also indicate that middle-aged women who had not yet launched their children reported fewer positive self-concepts than those who had already had their children leave home. Women very often see their time after the children are gone as a chance for more freedom and new opportunities for things like education and work. Their negative feelings more often come from a worry that the child has not been adequately prepared for adulthood (her own sense of inadequacy), but their positive feelings come from the sense of accomplishment and new opportunities for her own life. Again, we must be careful not to oversimplify and say that women feel either devastated or relieved when their children leave home. Several reactions to the event are generally present. And most researchers now conclude that the last child's leaving home is a significant event, but not a traumatic one. Women's mental health at midlife does not seem to be negatively affected by the "empty-nest syndrome."[25]

Widowhood and Loss of Relationships

There is great ambiguity around women's experience of widowhood. Since pastors frequently encounter older women at this life crisis moment, it is important to look at the various dimensions of the experience. In the United States, the majority of older women are widowed or otherwise single and the majority of older men are married (for all races). Sixty percent of older women are widowed and 23 percent of older men are widowed. There are eight million older women widows and one-and-a-half million older men without spouses. One of the many things this means is that most older men can rely on their spouses for care and support, but most older women must rely on other sources of support. Fortunately, women are often well able to build strong and satisfying friendship networks, and these, along with relationships with daughters, are reported to be their primary (and most satisfying) support system.

Older women tend to see widowhood as normal, which makes sense given these demographics. There is a social identity for older women who are widowed (as opposed to younger women who are widowed). There are, however, a number of serious losses for widows.

Women grieve the loss of a spouse differently than men do. Women tend to experience a sense of abandonment and fear that they are not prepared to manage their lives—especially things that they have been "protected from" learning. Women tend to express grief over a longer period of time than men do and yet they are also more able to return to work and make use of their social networks than men are.

Very often, women lose a great deal with the loss of a spouse in addition to the often devastating loss of the particular person. First, they lose their opportunity to be in an intimate relationship with a male. Since most men marry younger women and since women live considerably longer than men, remarriage is unlikely for older widows. Two-thirds of widows live alone from the time of their husband's death until their own death. They lose the person who shared their history and who offered a variety of kinds of support. Their risk of loneliness, poverty, social discomfort (in a coupled world), and the loss of ties with in-laws is increased. In addition, they experience a number of secondary losses such as the loss of identity and prestige (being "Mrs. Someone" in a world that encourages borrowed power for women), the loss of access to certain social or business connections, or even access to the public world, the potential loss of their home, and the loss of one who might well have done the tasks that she does not know how to do.

Since the average age of widowhood is fifty-six, women may end up alone for a great number of years. And yet society expects that women will live with and be protected by a male spouse throughout their lives. When one looks at the number of never-married heterosexual women and divorced women along with widows, it is clear that a great majority of older women are single. Not only do our social policies, insurance plans, and social arrangements not reflect that reality, but often our churches don't either.

Adjustment to widowhood seems to occur better if women can maintain or build a network of friends, especially widowed friends, that can provide a restructuring of their social world. In addition, the presence of at least one confidante seems to make a significant difference in life satisfaction for widows. It is interesting that for men the presence of a confidant or close friend may actually exacerbate widowerhood, but for women it is an essential component of health. In fact, in one particular study widows with a confidante were better adjusted than married women without a confidante.[26]

This leads us into the other side of the picture for widows, and again both sides must be held together. Very often widows, within a few months after bereavement, experience a sense of freedom and relief. Particularly if they have an adequate social network of friends and family (usually daughters and sisters more than sons), women experience an increase in the amount of life satisfaction due primarily to increased socialization. Very often women have been restricted in their social and public lives because of expectations within the marriage. Some of the differences between women and men, and married and widowed women, are interesting. Whereas the death of a husband may allow an elderly woman to spend more time with friends, the death of a wife is likely to deplete an elderly man's social network (often she has been responsible for his social network). Widowed men fare worse than widowed women in terms of both health and social network. Widowed women, however, fare much worse than widowed men in terms of income and finances. Married women report many more physical ailments than do widowed women. Married men have fewer physical ailments than widowed men. Married women are the most physically distressed of the entire elderly population. And friends are the greatest stress buffers for widowed women and are predictive of life satisfaction scores. It is interesting to note that almost half of elderly married women report having no close friends, which may well be tied to their greater number of physical ailments. One other significant help to widowed women is their amount of church attendance and the importance of religious beliefs, which are important in the adjustments women make to widowhood.[27]

It is very important to see that widowhood, like the launching of children, may bring grief, restlessness, sadness, and great deprivation at the same time that it may lead to an increased sense of freedom, opportunities, social life, and better health. It is important over time to invite a widow to let herself experience this whole variety of possibilities, or whichever ones surface in response to her life context. Many women experience guilt and a sense of failure when they sense the relief and the freedom of widowhood. The rules of society suggest that women are to carry the image of their dead husband as central in their lives after widowhood. Since women generally internalize cultural messages, even those detrimental to their well-being, they may need some pastoral support for dealing with their ambivalent responses to grief.

It is also important to discuss some of the particular issues for lesbians who lose their partners. Very often this is a very complicated loss. Due to heterosexist assumptions in the culture, the lesbian couple may not have had a great deal of social support for their relationship. In addition, some lesbians are prevented from moving through final illnesses with their partners. Hospitals often operate with narrow understandings of family and lesbians may not have had any emotional or legal support for their relationship. There is rarely a well-developed support system or mutual help group to assist with the adjustment issues of grief. In addition, there is little preparation for lesbian widowhood because of the assumption that each partner will live as long as the other. Lesbians may also lack the support of the church during funeral rituals and grieving processes. As Gary Whitford and Jean Quam state, "The death of a lifelong partner is rarely recognized in society with the same sympathy that is afforded to heterosexual couples who lose a spouse."[28] Also, going through the dying and grief process with a lesbian partner may necessitate a coming-out process to children or grandchildren when the relationship has been at least partially closeted. The couple may also have to come out to the medical staff and experience fear of inadequate care. Whitford and Quam quote one lesbian who said, "I'm afraid of not getting good care if the doctor knew . . . my biggest fear about getting older is that I will be mistreated when I am too weak or sick to fight back."[29]

All of these issues must be considered when pastors are offering pastoral support to older lesbians. It is important to note that, on the whole, elderly lesbians have among the highest levels of life satisfaction. The majority of lesbians look forward to their later years and those who worry do so about the same kinds of things that nonlesbians do—poverty, loneliness, and so on.[30] Lesbians generally have the skills needed to live a single life if they need to because they have been less role-bound. They also seem to have devoted more time to leisure activities over their lives and thus are able to use retirement time more effectively. And lesbians have had to live with labels of deviance and lack of social support in many settings, so the stigma of age may be less of a threat to them than it is to heterosexual older women. They have already learned about the lies of a heterosexist patriarchy. Again, the multiple dimensions of images and needs for older lesbians need to be seen in their complexities so that pastoral counselors can provide appropriate ministry to them.

Health Issues

The greatest area of stress and the greatest predictor of low life satisfaction for older women is that of ill health. Although women live a long time in general, they tend to have numerous health problems. The average number of chronic health problems for elderly women—the vast majority of whom live at home—is three. The medical system has a strong bias of cure over care. When older women experience long-term chronic health problems that require indefinite care but do not readily respond to a cure orientation, they have problems getting their health care needs met. In addition, many studies report ageism (and sexism) in the medical profession, where less value is placed on the care of the elderly. Interestingly, there was a study done of medical students and their attitudes toward the care of the elderly. Upon entering medical school, their attitudes toward the elderly were generally strong and positive. Upon graduation from medical school, however, those attitudes had shifted to being generally negative and somewhat demeaning toward the elderly. When the process was analyzed, it became clear that the greatest influence on the shift in attitude was not the educational material to which the medical students were exposed, but the negative attitudes of their instructors—a challenge to all of us who have responsibilities for educational ministries.

Pastors often encounter older women in health care situations. While it is not the purpose of this chapter to discuss women's health crises at length, I will just name a few of the leading health care problems for older women. It is in the midst of these health care crises that women must often make important choices and integrate life-changing circumstances into their core identity narratives.

Heart disease is the leading cause of death in women over age sixty-five. African American women are at greater risk for heart disease after age forty-five and European American women after age fifty-five. Women are more likely than men to die of heart attacks in nearly every age group, and if she survives her first heart attack, a woman is two to three times more likely to suffer a second heart attack within five years. Also, women do not seem to benefit from the use of aspirin or from the procedure of bypass surgery to the degree that men do.[31]

Cancer is the second leading cause of death in women ages fifty-six to seventy-four and the third in women over age seventy-five. There has been considerable debate about possible sexism in the research priorities of cancer studies in terms of the slowness of progress in the treatment of specifically female cancers.[32]

Hypertension and stroke are another major cause of death in elderly women. By age sixty-five, 66 percent of European American women and 82 percent of African American women suffer from high blood pressure. Stroke-related illness accounts for the vast majority of the use of health care resources and is a major cause of disability in elderly women.[33]

Finally, osteoporosis is also a serious problem for elderly women. By the age of sixty-five, one-fourth of all women have osteoporotic fractures, although they may not have been diagnosed.[34]

In addition to these particular health problems, women face a variety of health care choices as they age. These range from decisions about taking calcium and other kinds of supplements to making major decisions about whether to take hormone replacement therapy in menopause and perimenopause, to how to proceed when breast cancer is discovered. It is beyond the scope of this book to do more than mention these critical health care issues, but it is important to say that when pastors and pastoral counselors are asked to help women work through these decisions, they need to avoid projecting their own decisions and conclusions onto the counselee. There is much disagreement about many of these topics. Hormone replacement therapy, for example, is the subject of hot debate in the feminist and medical literature, and there are significant risks and benefits to any of the possible decisions. Generally, women should be exposed to all sides of these debates so that they can make informed health care decisions with a sense of their own agency, a caveat similar to that raised in the chapter on depression in regards to choices about antidepressants. It is important to remember that there has been a tendency to medicalize and pathologize women's experiences—whether those are the experiences of domination and disempowerment or the life-cycle experiences of menstruation, childbirth, and menopause. While hormone replacement therapy may well be the right choice for particular women, many feminists are calling upon women to resist the universalizing of menopause as a disease and the normalizing pharmacological treatment of it.[35] Women need help making choices that reflect their own experiences and meanings, not those of the counselor or of a highly medicalized and sexist culture.

In terms of mental health, there has been considerable debate about health and elderly people, especially where depression is concerned. Research results are still mixed, but some interesting studies are emerging that suggest that the conflicting research results have occurred because there are different syndromes that look like depression. For younger women, depression is a serious problem. Somewhere between two and six times as many women are depressed as men. There is quite a bit of evidence, however, that depression in older women is considerably less than in younger women and that the gender differences for depression disappear in older age. What older women do seem to experience is what has been named a "depletion syndrome," which has a similar symptomatology to depression. The three most frequent patterns of depletion syndrome in elderly women are sleep disturbances, loneliness, and enervation (lack of energy). Some of the other characteristics of depletion syndrome are feelings of being down, difficulty sustaining effort at tasks, lack of interest in things, lack of appetite, feelings of worthlessness, and feelings of hopelessness. Depression has more focus on appetite disturbances, sense of guilt and self-blame, thoughts of dying, no vision for the future, and periods of weeping. One of the serious consequences of depletion syndrome is social withdrawal and, as we have seen, this can have a very negative effect on women's ability to deal with stress, health maintenance, and crisis. In addition, depression syndrome for women seems related to problematic relationships, whereas depletion syndrome seems related to loss of relationships. This gives added incentive to the pastor to make sure that there are social and friend resources available for older women in the congregation.

There are two other common mental health problems for older women. The first is generally labeled dementia and includes Alzheimer's disease, senility, and chronic brain syndrome. Dementia is one of the most dreaded aspects of aging in the older population. Midlarsky reports on a study done in the late 1970s that suggested that various psychosocial factors can stimulate dementia-type symptoms. Those included stresses like poverty, abuse, and loss of valued roles. In addition, boredom or lack of mental stimulation can cause irritability, impaired thinking, depression, and even hallucinations (even in young people).[36] Very often, elderly people living alone have an environment that is less than adequately stimulating, and that should go into our assessment of pastoral needs.

Alzheimer's disease accounts for about 75 percent of dementia among the elderly.[37] It is a crippling, irreversible organic brain disorder marked by loss of recent memory, personality and behavioral changes, and intellectual deterioration. Women are somewhat more likely to be the victims of Alzheimer's, probably because of their longevity. Since Alzheimer's is a chronic and degenerative condition, it also has a high secondary victimization rate among family caretakers, most of whom are women. It is important to note that the vast majority of caregivers for the elderly (spouses, parents, parents-in-law) are women, often women in their fifties and sixties. These women are spending large quantities of energy on caring for others at the same time that they are facing issues of their own aging. These factors need to be taken seriously by pastoral caregivers as they facilitate choice making for women.

Prescription drug abuse is the other major health problem that elderly women face. First of all, women are more likely to be handed a prescription upon a visit to a physician's office. Second, they are more likely to have multiple prescriptions for different conditions, often not monitored carefully by the specialist physicians. Third, older women may get confused or forgetful about taking medication and accidentally overdose on a chronic basis. And fourth, sometimes prescription drug abuse is a passive way to solve the multiple stresses that women are experiencing. When women show signs of dementia, possible chemical abuse (including alcoholism) should be looked into.

In terms of pastoral care for elderly women experiencing health problems, knowledge about the various kinds of likely health crises is important. The pastor needs to be able to help a woman who frequently suffers multiple chronic health limitations to integrate that reality into her larger sense of identity and meaning. The stories have to merge in some way for her to experience adequate acceptance and life satisfaction. As has been discussed throughout this text, these challenges to personal narratives mean that the pastor needs to be able to facilitate the sharing of stories and the exploration of meaning, which often takes considerable pastoral care time. Hospital and home visitations should seek to invite this kind of sharing and integration.

It is very common for older people not to have access to psychotherapists. First, there is considerable ageism in that field, with few specialists in the mental health needs of the elderly (to say nothing of elderly women). Second, access to a weekly, hour-long talk-oriented session is limited for many elderly people in need. And third, cost is often prohibitive. Clergy, however, can be available to serve this population of women who need counseling help.

Issues of Religion and Spirituality

It has long been known that people tend to become more religious with age. Various studies have indicated that people pray more, read the Bible more, and even attend worship services more often as they grow older. According to Harold G. Koenig, Director of Duke University's Center for Religion/Spirituality and Health,

> approximately three-quarters of persons over age sixty say that religion is
> very important to them. At least half of all older Americans attend church
> or synagogue weekly or more often, the highest percentage for all age
> groups, despite having more chronic illness and greater difficulty getting

to church. One-third to one-half of all older adults engages in personal prayer (apart from meal times) at least several times per week. No less than twenty-five percent of adults age fifty or over read the Bible every day, twice as frequently as persons under age fifty. In fact, sixty percent of persons age fifty or over in America believe that the Bible is either the literal or inspired word of God and contains no errors. Religious television is viewed several times per week by over forty percent of older Americans, particularly those with disability that prevents church attendance. It is clear, then, in terms of prevalence of belief and activity, that religion has an enormous impact on the lives of older adults in this country.[38]

Studies also reveal significant gender differences in the religiosity of older people. When asked in an open-ended way what has helped them to cope with difficult life events, 45 percent of participants in a particular study named religious resources. Approximately 66 percent of women, however, gave religious responses, compared to about 33 percent of men. When only men are surveyed, as in one study done at a Veterans Administration center, about 25 percent of them gave religious responses. And, as Koenig reports in a study of low-income elders in Georgia, 51 percent of African Americans and 28 percent of European Americans claimed religious resources as important in facing life crises.[39] It is important to note, then, that many older women frequently use religious resources when they make meaning in their later years. Many women rely on worship services, Bible reading, and prayer for their daily sustenance. This has clear implications for the pastoral visitation of the older adults in the church who can no longer travel to corporate worship services. Congregations need to decide how they will continue to re-member and integrate their older members into the spiritual life of the community.

An interesting paradox emerges in the literature about women and aging, though. Many of the older women who have experienced empowerment and liberation in their lives do not reflect this same increased religiosity in their older years. Carroll Saussy, in reflecting on a "high-powered" group of older women who met at the Esalen Institute in 1991 to discuss issues of gender and aging, notes that almost no mention was made of spirituality or religious interests. She writes, "Perhaps these twenty-six women are thoroughly secular. Perhaps the churches, synagogues, and mosques are too patriarchal for them. This group of successful women of the world might illustrate what is called 'the culture of disbelief.' . . . None of the Esalen women . . . gave evidence of religious belief." She goes on to say, "I think, too, of Esalen participant Cecilia Hurwich's work with women over seventy. Were not any of these people, all passionately engaged in something outside of themselves, motivated by religious faith?"[40] Also, in her article about women in their seventies and their sources of fulfillment and satisfaction, Lisa Greenberg notes that "none of the subjects mentioned religion as a source of satisfaction."[41] It is hard to know how to interpret these two contradictory pieces of data. It seems to me, however, that it adds weight to the priority of helping women deconstruct and responsibly scavenge their religious traditions throughout their life span's so that empowering and supportive spiritual resources are fully available to them as they face older age.

Helping Older Women Make Narrative Choices

Pastors often encounter older women in care and counseling ministry. As Melvin A. Kimble writes, "It is estimated that older adults represent a disproportionately large percentage of members in most faith communities—from twenty to forty percent—and that half of the clergy's pastoral work is directly related to this population. Clergy have the pastoral responsibility to be helpful and supportive guides in the older adults' exploration of the uncharted territory of living out their vocation in a longer life that continues to have meaning and purpose."[42] Although they may not directly seek pastoral counseling for the changes and choices confronting them, older women will be needing pastoral care and pastors/pastoral counselors need to be prepared to offer the most effective and empowering kind of care and counseling available. I have attempted to make the case that narrative counseling is a most helpful approach.

According to Erik Erikson, the major life task for older people is that of narrative integration. Older age is the time, according to this developmental theory, when people need to look back over their lives and assess its meaning and value. Ongoing life review is a core process in the lives of older people. The choices that need to be made in the face of the major losses and transitions of older age require integration into the larger life narrative. Often these losses, like the loss of a life partner, retirement, a change in primary roles, and so on, are deeply challenging to the core identity of a person. In addition, older women are facing these losses and transitions in the context of cultural ageism—ageism that sends powerful messages about the loss of worth and value in women because of their aging. From advertising for age-defying cosmetics to the medicalization of women's aging processes to myths about empty-nest syndrome, older women are constantly forced to make meaning out of their lives in the context of a social narrative that works against their healthy integration of aging.

A narrative approach to counseling with older women listens carefully to narrative strands that contain resources for positive meaning making in the face of some of the challenges of aging. As women lose relationships that have given their life primary meaning or they lose bodily strength or functions that have given them a sense of agency, there is a risk that those experiences will overpower a more positive sense of self. Given the cultural narrative that tends to reinforce the negatives of aging in women, a woman can be cast into a sense of helplessness or hopelessness when she encounters key losses. Narrative counseling seeks to help women remember positive images of who they have been or who they desire to be that help them resist the narratives of devaluation emerging from the culture and from key losses. As a woman seeks to make choices that come from the transitions associated with aging, she needs help in resisting a loss of agency and vision so that her choices can help her move toward a preferred future story. Pastoral counselors need to facilitate choice making, which works both to resist debilitating personal and cultural narratives and helps a woman move into her future in positive ways. The internal world of the older counselee cannot be seen as separate from the external realities in which she lives. Relationships with family, fears about health problems or becoming dependent, worry about the increase in robberies of older women, grief about a child who died forty years before—all of these become the threads and the contexts through which to bring healing. No counselor can content herself or himself with just being a good listener. The counselor of an older woman must be willing to be an informed and active resource person for that counselee, as well as one who can help deconstruct problematic narratives and reconstruct narratives of hope and possibility.

Researchers propose various things that help women maintain a strong sense of self and future as they age. For example, women need to allow themselves to recognize the strengths and possibilities of aging, and not just its challenges. Aging often helps a woman recognize that she does not have to be bound to patriarchal rules about how to be female. The freedoms that can come from that recognition often help a woman claim a more authentic and energized self. Feminist literature is full of poetry and prose about the power of becoming a crone, or "wearing purple" and breaking rules.[43] This literature and the support and company of other women who are working to resist the complexities of sexism and ageism can be very helpful to women as they attempt to make meaning out of the transitions of aging.

One of the most powerful resources for the elderly that is available to the pastor is support groups. Considerable research has been done demonstrating the extreme usefulness of counseling, support, and education done in the group context.[44] Especially for women for whom friendship and social networks are particularly important, a group can serve a variety of functions. First, it can speak to the needs that many older women have for continuing education. Groups that focus on topics of concern or interest, in which group members pursue those topics through reading and/or discussion, can be especially helpful. They can also help elderly women recognize their ongoing value in the creative process of generating ideas for contemplation and for change. Especially in terms of a feminist method, groups can help women learn about areas that have a direct effect on various dimensions of their lives. Health care policies for older women, tax laws, sexism in medicine, myths about aging, and so on can all be appropriate topics for this kind of group.

Second, there can be groups oriented around self-help and mutual help. This has long been a tradition in women's lives, although often at an informal level. These are groups where women listen to each other (and often thereby to unknown aspects of themselves) and offer care, nurture, and resources in times of stress and crisis. As mentioned earlier, these groups must take seriously the differences in need that different groups of women might have—for example, a retirement group of women from the outside labor force might very well need to be different from a retirement group for homemakers. Self-help and mutual help groups might be oriented around coping with loss, stress reduction, managing chronic pain, dealing with changing roles and relationships, and so on.

A third kind of group is one in which there is skill training of various kinds. This often falls into the category of preventive care. For example, one of the most effective kinds of training groups for older women is a training group in assertiveness. This builds confidence and helps women find ways to articulate and find resources for their needs—something women are not traditionally taught in a sexist culture. One of the transitions that many older women face is the need to gain satisfaction from within themselves more than from the roles and relationships in their lives.[45] A group that works on skills of self-care and assertiveness can be very helpful with this. A skills group might also focus on learning the processes of group dynamics, or how to teach classes, or even self-defense techniques.

A fourth kind of group is the counseling group. This kind of group might be especially for women who are experiencing depletion syndromes where the stimulation of relationships, the stimulation of group activity, and the nurturing of the group members may very well alleviate debilitating symptoms. This group might focus on storytelling, the process of reminiscence that has proven to be so helpful in the lives of older people, validating each other's life experiences, granting each other the authority to continue to grow and change as older women, and learning to negotiate the new life phases in which they are engaged.

A fifth group type could operate around the development of older women as lay caregivers. One of the most difficult experiences that older women report is a lack of mutuality in their lives. Much of women's worth, for better or worse, comes from being caregivers of others. Often, as women get older they experience themselves as the focus of care, without any expectation that they have something to give back. Frequently, older women need care during particular crises but not on a permanent basis. For these women, training in lay caregiving where they become the givers of care to others in temporary or chronic need of pastoral care can help to make it more acceptable to receive care when necessary. In addition, older women very often have experience and insights that make them effective at pastoral caregiving when they are offered appropriate training.

Finally, there might well be a group offered for preventive care to women who are just entering their later years and who are often engaged in caregiving to older relatives or to seriously/chronically ill husbands. Women are most often the caregivers to older generations in need—whether they are daughters or daughters-in-law, they are the ones expected to provide the physical and emotional support. Seventy-two percent of the caregivers of the frail elderly are female relatives.[46] There is often considerable sacrifice involved in this caretaking relationship, although it often also has very satisfying and need-meeting dimensions for the caregiver. It is common for the relationship between a frail elderly mother and a daughter-caregiver to be a precious, though not unconflicted, one. Caregivers of the elderly often need help in three areas: (1) increasing their own confidence in problem solving and being able to manage the challenges of the caregiving, (2) redefining difficult situations so that they don't seem unmanageable or hopeless, and (3) gathering appropriate social support.[47] All three of these needs can be met through a group for caregivers of elderly family members. And this may well provide resources and skills that will be useful when these women themselves reach later stages of aging.

There are a variety of challenges before us in terms of ministry to the aging woman. We need to understand the deeply internalized ageist and sexist biases of our culture, of our education, and of ourselves. In order to do that, we have to allow ourselves to form new images of older women that adequately represent the paradoxes and ambiguities in their lives. We need to sort through the particular crises that older women experience and become knowledgeable about their dynamics and the resources that we can make available. We need to be creative in the various forms of ministry that are useful and effective to older women and teach not only ourselves but our congregations how to best engage in those ministry forms. And we need to face our own fears of aging and of dying so that we are unafraid to move through the process with others.

Theological Concerns

There is one more serious challenge before us and it is theological. We have seen that often the church is a very important place for older women. In fact, it is one of the major predictors of life satisfaction and high morale for most currently older women. Yet the theology we find in our churches has deep sexist and ageist biases. As pastors, it is important for us to look at our theological resources with as much clarity and honesty as we look at our psychological and sociological resources. Like the culture in general, religion has also tended to perpetuate low (spiritual) self-esteem in women. It is through religion that we raise and explore the fundamental questions in our lives. We try to understand the purposes of our lives, our relationships with God and with creation, the meanings of our vocations, and who we are at our deepest levels. As religious people, our spiritual inquiries are at the heart of our search for meaning.

Women have not fared well for the most part in traditional theology. Most church doctrine is also strongly embedded in patriarchy. In addition, much theology is strongly ageist. Popular theology operates with certain assumptions regarding purpose, vocation, and value. That theology has tended to be goal-oriented—geared toward future transformation. When working with the elderly, this focus on future and goal directedness needs to be balanced with a focus on the present moment and on the richness of the now. Much theology has tended to focus on growth with an assumption of unlimited possibility, which needs to be balanced with a focus on integration: the pulling together of life strands and the joy of weaving together past, present, and future—all of which belong to a spirituality of aging. There also has been a theological focus on doing—on the fruits of the spirit. And, at least in Western culture, God's favor seems to rest on those who can "do" (and the word again has Western connotations) and not on those who can "be." In my pastoral counseling work with older people, this has been one of the greatest faith crises they face—the inability to find value in themselves or perceive the value God places on them because they see their limitations in actively carrying out their vocations. Related to this, much theology has focused on an implicit reward system for valued behavior (despite our spoken emphasis on grace). And both God and the church have been seen to reward those who follow the rules. This has both sexist and ageist implications since following the rules tends to preserve a status quo that is unjust. This focus on rewarded behavior needs to be balanced by a focus on the trustworthy and constant value God finds in all of creation and on the delight that God finds in our being.

Finally, the focus in much theology has tended to be on the individual, despite our conversations about the body of Christ being central. Our systems of salvation, of spiritual development, and of connection to God have all had an individualistic emphasis. For all of us, but particularly for elderly women, the power of relationship and the interdependency of the community are valuable and essential realities. The value of the individual must be balanced with the power of interdependency and the rhythms of connection that are also part of our faith traditions. Christian theology has all of the resources needed to guide an enriching and empowering spirituality of aging. Unfortunately, we have tended to prioritize and interpret theology in light of a sexist and ageist hermeneutic. The work of responsible scavenging and critical interpretation is before us as we engage in ministry with aging women.

As pastoral caregivers, we have to claim our own accountability in these issues and work to bring an appropriate critique of the damaging sexist and ageist assumptions to our theological positions. We need to reaffirm God's creative and redeeming presence along with God's love for all people, found often in its most profound forms among those who have been dispossessed. God's people have always been called to recognize those who have been oppressed, even in the name of religion, and to empower and bring liberation to them. We need to listen to those who we know have been hurt by the sexism and ageism in our traditions and renew our theological resources accordingly. We need to confront how we profit by maintaining ageist and sexist theology with its oppressive myth system. In addition, we must help older women learn to name their experiences of God and to claim those experiences as holy. It is important to help older women learn to tell their spiritual stories. The theological tradition is virtually devoid of images born of women's experience, especially that of older women. According to Mary Daly, as women reach out to name God and the reality of creation, they also name themselves. This is the necessary theological work before us as we develop effective and empowering methods of pastoral counseling with older women.

nine

Conclusion:
Helping Women Stay Connected

This book has been organized around three commitments. First, it is organized around the methodological spiral that characterizes pastoral theology—one that begins in particular and cultural experience and then uses that experience to both critique and utilize the traditions and theories of pastoral theology. From that dialogue between experience—understood broadly—and theory, new and relevant pastoral practices are generated. Those practices are brought into the pastoral care and counseling process with particular individuals and situations to see if they are, indeed, useful for offering liberating, empowering, and healing directions for the people who have come for help. We might define this process in the following way: Using the tool of empathic engagement, we engage in the methodological spiral that begins in the human story (in which the divine story is also partially embedded), moves to engage theological and other traditions, engages in reconstruction, and, out of practical wisdom and judgment, generates practices and performance of practices that are then brought to the particular story. The creative engagement of that encounter raises new questions and the spiral begins again. This becomes a practice of theology.

This book has used this method, at least as much as a theory-building text can do so. We began with two framework chapters. The first chapter explored the contexts in which women live in a dominant Western culture and the kinds of issues that emerge out of those contexts. The second chapter explored personality theory and theological frameworks that would be used in exploring the issues and contexts of women's lives. These two chapters represent the beginning places in the pastoral theology methodological spiral. The third, fifth, and seventh chapters proposed a counseling framework that helped bring the cultural contexts of women, the issues that bring women into counseling, and the traditions in which we have been formed into dialogue with each other for the purpose of generating useful pastoral practices. The fourth, sixth, and eighth chapters looked at how that proposed counseling framework operated in the midst of specific pastoral crises, those of intimate violence, depression, and aging—again for the purpose of generating liberating and empowering pastoral counseling practices.[1] The purpose of publishing a book like this is not only to make these theoretical and theological dialogues and pastoral practices available, it is also to continue the methodological spiral. The practices proposed in this book will be tested, I hope, in the real lives of women who come for pastoral counseling, and in that testing they will be refined, radicalized, or rejected.

The second organizing principle for this book is the proposed four-phase feminist pastoral counseling framework. This framework suggests that pastoral counseling with women should begin with helping women come to voice in a world in which women's voices are consistently discouraged, silenced, denied, and controlled. Helping women come to voice is not simply a matter of listening carefully, although this is an indispensable part of the process. It requires theological shifts and theoretical challenges to the traditional norms of pastoral counseling. As Riet Bons-Storm writes,

> My experience of working together with women who are afraid to speak their minds in their communities of faith has taught me that, first of all, these women quite literally have to become used to raising their voices. They have to hear the sound of their own voice in groups or in conversation with another person to whom they give authority. We practice speaking out, the act of "raising one's voice," in a safe context. The second step is more difficult. A woman has to become convinced that she has something to contribute. To arrive at this point she has to work through the effects on her sense of self of the traditional roles assigned to her in her socialization in a patriarchal society and church. . . . These insecurities have to be taken seriously and not laughed off with cheap words of encouragement. She needs new stories that give her the authority to speak. Practical theology should uncover these new stories. A woman needs an image of the Divine which will encourage her to raise her voice.[2]

Helping women come to voice requires actively resisting all of the cultural forces that work against women finding their voices, and using their "local knowledge" to change themselves and their contexts.

The phase of this counseling framework that follows coming to voice is helping women to gain clarity. The primary premise of this phase is that knowledge has been organized and truth has been named for the interests of those people, groups, and institutions that have dominance in the culture. The knowledge and truths of nondominant groups tend to be discounted and distorted and, thus, made unusable for the benefit of women and their communities. This counseling approach has advocated a search for women's experiences that can be understood—through reframing and restorying—as means for resistance and transformation of oppressive forces. A woman's forgotten or suppressed knowledge is attended to and re-integrated into her guiding narratives.

Sharon D. Welch, using Michel Foucault's work, talks about one dimension of this work in her discussion of genealogy. She says that "genealogy is the method that Foucault uses to examine resistance to dominant forms of power and knowledge."[3] Although Welch is talking primarily about larger communities, her liberationist method is also appropriate for this phase of pastoral counseling with women when she says that "the first two elements of genealogy, the memory of conflict and the expression of alternate knowledges, are not complete without the third element: the struggle of those knowledges against dominant forms of discourse. It is in fulfilling this task that the strategic rather than the merely speculative nature of genealogical thought becomes apparent."[4] When helping women to gain clarity, the pastoral counselor assists her to re-member and remember experiences and knowledges that contradict the oppressive or damaging narrative that limits her options and her hope. Only by coming to voice and gaining clarity is a woman then able to make choices that are relevant for her and for which she can hold herself accountable.

Thus, the third aspect of the pastoral counseling framework is helping women to make choices. Making choices for which a woman can claim relevance and accountability is not an easy part of the counseling process. For one thing, when women make choices for themselves that are based on subjugated knowledge and new counterstories, they are at risk of retribution from others and enormous self-doubt within themselves. At this point, women have the capacity to make healthy choices in a culture that is often unhealthy for them. Thus, women need communities where both support and challenge are available.

This brings us to the fourth phase of the counseling framework, that of staying connected. "Staying connected" was originally named "staying healthy," but a colleague pointed out that staying healthy was a stagnant concept and what I had described was the active and dynamic process of connection and relationality that are necessary for the maintenance of counterstories and for the ongoing work of resistance to and transformation of dominant and oppressive forces.

The third organizing commitment for this book is narrative counseling theory. Narrative theory is based on postmodern philosophies that include the assumption that our interpretation of reality *is* reality and that this reality is socially constructed. Realities, according to this theory, are organized and maintained by stories that are personal, familial, and cultural. Thus, a major part of the work of narrative counseling is to help people generate new language and new interpretive lenses and thus create new realities. How people engage the experiences they have and the contexts in which those experiences occur is central to the way they move forward in life and build their future stories.

Narrative theory acknowledges that not only do people create stories and plots in which they live and make meaning, but they are also characters in the stories and plots of other people, systems, and cultures. Changes in the plotline or interpretive lenses of any of these (individuals, systems, and cultures) mean the potential for the transformation of all. The personal is political and the political is personal in narrative counseling. Thus, narrative counseling theory works to help people remember stories, descriptions, and experiences that can serve as positive resources for them in generating options, resisting oppressive forces, and transforming their lives and relationships. These remembered stories, which previously did not have a place in a counselee's guiding narrative, are integrated into that core narrative in such a way that they provide a richer description of the counselee and her possibilities. This richer self-knowledge, combined with new possibilities for seeing the ways that knowledge has been negatively constructed by a dominant culture, offers both hope and positive strategies for the counselee's life. Narrative theory is a useful cognate theory for a pastoral counseling approach that emphasizes resistance, liberation, the construction of knowledge, power analysis, and new possibility. It is a counselee-driven approach that de-centers the counselor and, thus, empowers mutuality and healthy boundaries. It is well suited for a liberationist pastoral counseling method.

These three commitments—pastoral theological method, a feminist four-phase counseling framework, and narrative theory—have guided the organization of this book. They have worked together to generate practices of counseling that attempt to help women resist and transform the negative effects of living in a woman-unfriendly culture and to capitalize on the kinds of strengths and resources that women have available to them, although these strengths have often been forgotten or unstoried. One of these primary strengths or resources is healthy relationality, and it is that to which we now turn.

Helping Women Stay Connected— Women and Relationality

Feminist theorists have always been interested in the notion of relationality in women. I use the term *relationality* rather than *relationships* because I want to focus on the origin, function, nature, and role of relationships and relating in women's lives. Some of the earliest work in feminist theory, like that of Carol Gilligan, began to study women's tendency to evaluate life decisions in the context of their relationships. As feminist theorists began to reframe male-based evaluations of women's deviance and weaknesses, one of the areas of women's experience to be reclaimed was that of relationality. For example, women's unique tendencies toward and skills at building and maintaining relationships now can be seen as morally valuable and familially necessary, rather than being grounded in a lower developmental level and a more male-linked autonomy.

This focus on women's ability and tendency to be committed to cooperation, care, and the nurture of relationships has been important to reclaim for the valuing of women's lives and culturally given roles. Reclaiming women's behaviors and roles as strengths, however, can also get in the way of analyzing their sources and risks. Women often get caught in what Ellyn Kaschak calls "compulsive and compulsory relationality," feeling responsible and being held responsible for maintaining family and cultural harmony.[5] Skilled relationality may be as much a gender-trained service for a patriarchal culture (with its significant costs for women and for men) as it is a valuable orientation in women's lives. How we, as a culture and as pastoral counselors, appreciate women's relational abilities without exploiting them is the question for helping women to stay connected.

This tension between women's orientation to the care and nurture of relationships and cultural demands for women to be relationally oriented differently than men are is a difficult one to negotiate as we think about the necessity for women to be connected as they seek to develop strategies of resistance and transformation. If women are going to participate in communities of resistance and solidarity in ways that give them (and the culture) new options for justice and empowerment, they need to be clear about what kinds of relationships are healthy and positive and what kinds are exploitative and destructive. Carol Hess talks about the necessity for women to have relationships of "hard dialogue and deep connection."[6] These relationships require honesty and authenticity in order to provide communities of real care and transformation. Pastoral counselors need to help women evaluate the nature of their own relational tendencies and the relationships in which they engage. Walking the line between the nurture and mutuality of authentic relationships and the cultural demand to be available to anyone, especially men and children, requires new hermeneutical lenses and countercultural narratives.

The Importance of Community for Women in Pastoral Counseling

It is important for women to be in groups that help them resist and re-shape destructive personal and cultural narratives. Without the support and challenge of healing communities, re-membered and reframed narratives are often too fragile and too "thin" to be sustained when a woman takes them into the dominant discourse of culture and, often, family. Communities and groups that work to hear and elaborate the new and more positive narratives help a woman to make this new narrative a viable part of her life story. With this stronger narrative strand, a woman is more likely to continue gathering evidence that will support the preferred story rather than to allow the problem story to take over her life again.

Narrative counseling theory uses community as a primary tool. Members of a group can listen carefully to emerging preferred narratives so that they can retell to the counselee what riches and resources they heard in the telling. Then the counselee describes what she heard from the group members as they described what they had heard from her. This threefold telling of a preferred narrative helps to strengthen and "thicken" it. In addition, because the group members describe the strengths they have heard in connection with their own life experiences, the telling and retelling process begins to form bonds of commonality between group members. Members of the group might also be asked to talk about how they have been able to resist problem-saturated story lines (both cultural and personal) in their own lives as a way to join forces with the counselee in a shared struggle. These group processes are essential for building and strengthening narratives that are able to resist dominant and destructive cultural themes. In some ways, they are similar to the counterstory groups described in chapter 5. They allow for differences between people and stories while at the same time affirming the shared struggles and oppressive cultural discourses.

The church is a natural partner for helping to develop and sustain these kinds of communities of care if it takes its heritage of prophecy and justice seriously. As women engage in pastoral counseling, it is very appropriate that they do so in the context of group care either as the primary medium for the counseling or as an adjunct to it. In any kind of support or counseling group these kinds of re-enacting conversations can take place so that preferred narratives can be voiced and strengthened. The focus is always on the strengths, the resources, and the invisible and positive narratives that will help a person to resist the problem narrative.

Communities of care for women who are working to resist personal and cultural narratives of oppression and harm need to provide three resources. First, they need to provide a safe place where new ideas and reframings of long-assumed truths can be explored. Often this requires the kind of group that deeply understands the debilitating and disempowering discourses of a sexist, racist, classist, ageist, and heterosexist culture. Developing narratives of resistance and hope requires engagement with a network of supportive people who can reality-test ideas and perceptions without judging them by the norms of the dominant culture. This is a network of mutuality where people who are engaged in a common struggle for personal and communal transformation and liberation can encourage, support, and challenge one another appropriately. The seductive and coercive strategies of the dominant culture are too strong for anyone to resist. George Orwell once wrote that insanity is a minority of one. Solidarity and support are the sine qua non of staying healthy from a countercultural perspective.

Sharon Welch references Mary Daly in terms of the power of this kind of community.

> Mary Daly describes the interaction of political liberation in the experience of sisterhood. As women share stories of their own lives, a common experi-

ence of oppression and of resistance is recognized. This politicizing gives women the courage to persist in resistance, recognizing that their difficulties have not only an individual basis but a social and political basis as well. Fear of moving beyond accepted definitions of behavior is not definitively allayed, but the self-affirmation and hope that comes from the affirmation and community of sisterhood gives courage and enables creative resistance.[7]

I, too, interpret the experience of sisterhood as an experience of resistance and liberation, an affirmation of an identity different from that imposed by the dominant patriarchal social structures. The experience of resistance is itself a denial of the necessity of patriarchy; it is a moment of freedom, the power to embody an alternative identity. This affirmation serves as the ground for political resistance to social structures.

These kinds of groups may require a certain amount of "sameness" depending on how new the women are to challenging destructive cultural forces and to validating their own experiences and voices. When talking about these kinds of groups in the Netherlands, Bons-Storm says that

> in Woman and Faith groups, for instance, women talk freely about their life, their doubts, their ideas about the Divine. The situation is safe; no men are present, neither are there "real" theologians, ministers, or priests. Black women in the Woman and Faith movement often opt for an all-Black group. The power-rendering factor of "being White" gives White women hidden privileges and an unconscious conviction of a greater authority than that of Black women. Black women feel safer and speak their minds more freely in an all-Black group. This is very difficult for White members of the Woman and Faith movement who still have to learn how to handle their hidden privileges. Persons with only a few power-rendering factors and thus shy to speak about their personal knowledge of the Divine, can learn to share in the dialogue of faith.[8]

So one of the tasks of caring communities is to provide a safe place with few enough challenges that women can begin to gain confidence in their new strategies of resistance and empowerment.

Clearly, however, there is a danger in this kind of group. It risks becoming another exclusive and even oppressive force if doesn't have adequate diversity. So a pastoral counselor has to find ways to allow both the intracultural connections that allow important dimensions of sameness to generate solidarity and the intercultural (culture used broadly here) connections that provide adequate challenges against new forms of power and false universalizations. This is the second resource that communities of care must provide. It is necessary intentionally to seek out this kind of broad-based community since cultural separatism is a norm for Western culture and is often even a norm of homogeneous, liberation-seeking groups (like white feminists). Without this kind of commitment to communities of diversity, even liberation-based groups are in grave danger of repeating the exclusivist patterns of currently dominant groups.

Hess makes an interesting distinction when talking about a group in which she participated. This particular group generated its own project to break out of its sameness and seek the riches of diversity. Hess states that

> in reflecting on this spiraling politics of difference, I was prompted to expand my understanding of justice by making a distinction between a "community of solidarity" and a "life-style enclave." Life-style enclaves were denounced by Robert Bellah . . . for being "segmental" groupings which celebrate the "narcissism of similarity." Such enclaves "involve only a segment of each individual, for they concern only private life, especially leisure and consumption. And, they are segmental socially in that they include only those with a common life-style." As opposed to genuine "community" which attempts to "be an inclusive whole" celebrating a variety of life styles, enclaves are comfortable and protected gatherings of the like-minded who prefer not to be in the company of those who do not share the same life style. Communities of solidarity, however, are sometimes needed. These are gatherings of persons who share a common oppression, who protest against that oppression, and who attempt to construct alternative understandings of themselves as human beings.[9]

Eventually, the goal in pastoral counseling with women is to create groups that can be effective communities of both care and solidarity that are also both safe and diverse. Hess concludes that "just as solidarity groups nurture the voices of those who speak out against domination, so too must they invite different voices within their own solidarity grouping. It is important that prophetic communities not become ideological strongholds, or else they become increasingly more like life style enclaves. A leader helping a just community to be born will continually encourage it to attend to those on its own margins."[10]

The third resource that communities of care must provide is the ability to generate counterstories. Counterstories were discussed at some length in chapter 5 and yet it is important to remind ourselves here that communities of care are for the sake of helping women to come to voice (safety), to gain clarity (diversity and challenge), and to develop and thicken narrative strands that can offer effective strategies of resistance and transformation to personal and cultural narratives of harm (counterstories). Bons-Storm reminds us that

> living in this world with one's eyes open spells dread and despair. The brokenness of life in all its aspects cannot be ignored. To be faithful one needs stories that go against the grain because they do not gloss over the dread and despair but give a vision of hope. To be faithful one needs to have imagination, to imagine a different order, a new earth. . . . Hope, trust, and faith give people courage to look at themselves and the world critically, honoring the values as ascribed to the Divine in the Christian tradition and living accordingly.[11]

For women to be able to develop new ways of describing themselves, their experiences, their place in the culture, and the hope with which they will live, they need to be in communities of care that generate these kinds of stories that "go against the grain." In order to develop, maintain, and use those stories, we need the support, care, and challenge of one another.

Welch gives us helpful words to understand the role and power of the kinds of connections we have been describing. She writes,

> "The symbolic language of grace is appropriate at this point: the ability to love and to work for justice is something that we are given through the power of community. An attempt to bring justice does not make sense as an abstract imperative or judgment outside of this communal context. Within a liberating faith we find social structures that mediate the divine and enable solidarity, rather than an abstract call to justice. The imperative of justice is motivated not by guilt or duty but by love, by the power of relatedness.[12]

Women need to be able to use their relational abilities to join together in communities of truth telling, or, using Hess's words, communities of "hard dialogue and deep connection." Pastoral counselors need to re-member that the Christian tradition in which we work has, despite its significant collusion with oppressive cultural forces, a strong tradition of justice, prophetic voice, and solidarity. As Welch writes, "The truth of Christianity is also understood in terms of solidarity. Solidarity breaks the bonds of isolated individuality and forgetfulness—the bondage of sin—and enables the creation of community and conversion to the other. The Christian message is interpreted as the hope of universal solidarity and the Christian faith is remembered and celebrated as a vehicle of that solidarity."[13] It is our task as pastoral counselors working for justice and liberation to participate in these communities of solidarity, even in our pastoral counseling work. Allowing counterstories of resistance and new narratives of hope and transformation to surface in the context of the church helps us to embrace the deepest truths of our faith, transforming the world even as we assist individuals and groups to find healing and possibility.

Notes

Chapter 1

1. Candace West and Sarah Fenstermaker, "Doing Difference," in *Race, Class, and Gender: Common Bonds, Different Voices*, ed. Esther Ngang-Ling Chow, Doris Wilkinson, and Maxine Baca Zinn (Thousand Oaks, Calif.: Sage, 1996) 357–84.

2. Quoted in Chow, Wilkinson, and Zinn, *Race, Class, and Gender,* xxi.

3. Christie Cozad Neuger, ed., introduction to *The Arts of Ministry: Feminist Womanist Approaches* (Louisville: Westminster John Knox, 1996).

4. Rebecca S. Chopp, *Saving Work: Feminist Practices of Theological Education* (Louisville: Westminster John Knox, 1995) 86.

5. An earlier version of this material is found in Christie Cozad Neuger and James Poling, eds., *The Care of Men* (Nashville: Abingdon, 1997) chap. 1.

6. Elaine Graham, *Making the Difference: Gender, Personhood, and Theology* (Minneapolis: Fortress Press, 1996) 31.

7. Ibid., 24.

8. Paula Rothenberg, ed., *Race, Class, and Gender in the United States,* 2nd ed. (New York: St. Martin's, 1992) 6.

9. Neuger and Poling, *The Care of Men,* chap. 1.

10. Hannah Lerman, "The Limits of Phenomenology: A Feminist Critique of the Humanistic Personality Theories," in *Personality and Psychopathology: Feminist Reappraisals,* ed. Laura Brown and Mary Ballou (New York: Guilford, 1992) 15–17.

11. Philip Sheldrake, "Spirituality and Sexism," in *Who Needs Feminism? Men Respond to Sexism in the Church,* ed. Richard Holloway (London: SPCK, 1991) 91.

12. Rosemary Radford Ruether, "The Liberation of Christology from Patriarchy," in *Feminist Theology: A Reader,* ed. Ann Loades (Louisville: Westminster John, 1990) 138.

13. Jacquelyn Grant, *White Women's Christ and Black Women's Jesus* (Atlanta: Scholars, 1989) 216.

14. See Neuger and Poling, *The Care of Men,* chap. 1.

15. Mary Potter Engel, "Evil, Sin, and Violation of the Vulnerable," in *Lift Every Voice: Constructing Christian Theologies from the Underside,* ed. Susan Brooks Thistlethwaite and Mary Potter Engel (San Francisco: Harper and Row, 1990) 155.

16. Ibid.

17. Ibid., 156.

18. Richard Hokenson, *Donaldson, Lufkin, and Jenrette Newsletter*, May 3, 1996, 13.

19. Chow, Wilkinson, and Zinn, preface to *Race, Class, and Gender,* xiii.

20. Cynthia Costello and Anne J. Stone, eds., *The American Woman, 1994–95: Where We Stand, Women and Health* (New York: Norton, 1994) 281.

21. Ibid., 309

22. Paulette Thomas, "Success at a Huge Personal Cost," *Wall Street Journal,* July 26, 1995, B1.

23. Wu Xu and Ann Leffler, "Gender and Race Effects on Occupational Prestige, Segregation and Earnings," in Chow, Wilkinson, and Zinn, *Race, Class, and Gender,* 120.

24. Robert Farmighetti, ed., *The World Almanac and Book of Facts, 1996* (Mahwah, N.J.: World Almanac, 1995) 152.

25. Sam Roberts, "Women's Work: What's New, What Isn't?" *New York Times,* April 27, 1995, B6.

26. Ibid.

27. Thomas, "Success at a Huge Personal Cost," B1.

28. Peter Kilborn, "For Many in Work Force, Glass Ceiling Still Exists: White Men's Fears for Barrier, Study Says," *New York Times,* March 16, 1995, A22.

29. Wu and Leffler, "Gender and Race Effects," 114.

30. Ibid., 112.

31. Ibid., 113.

32. "The Leading Indicator Starts to Lead Again," *Inferential Focus Briefing,* January 29, 1996, 1–6.

33. Farmighetti, *The World Almanac and Book of Facts, 1996,* 152.

34. Costello and Stone, *The American Woman, 1994–95,* 328.

35. Farmighetti, *The World Almanac and Book of Facts, 1996,* 152.

36. Costello and Stone, *The American Woman, 1994–95,* 143.

37. Nijole V. Benokraitis and Joe R. Feagin, *Modern Sexism: Blatant, Subtle, and Covert Discrimination* (Englewood Cliffs, N.J.: Prentice-Hall, 1986) 7.

38. Chow, Wilkinson, Zinn, *Race, Class, and Gender,* xxiii.

39. Sara E. Rix, ed., *The American Woman, 1990–91: A Status Report* (New York: Norton, 1990) 33.

40. Benokraitis and Feagin, *Modern Sexism,* 42.

41. Carol Tavris, *The Mismeasure of Woman* (New York: Simon & Schuster, 1992).

42. Hokenson, *Donaldson, Lufkin, and Jenrette Newsletter,* 13.

43. Margi Laird McCue, *Domestic Violence: A Reference Handbook* (Santa Barbara: ABC-CLIO, 1995) 81.

44. Ibid.

45. Patrick Langan and Christopher Innes, "Preventing Domestic Violence against Women," *Bureau of Justice Statistics—Special Report,* August 1986, 1.

46. McCue, *Domestic Violence,* 77.

47. Costello and Stone, *The American Woman, 1994–95,* 121.

48. Marianne Zawitz, "Violence between Intimates," *Bureau of Justice Statistics* (Washington, D.C., November 1994) 2.

49. McCue, *Domestic Violence,* 77.

50. Zawitz, *Violence between Intimates,* 4.

51. Linda Brookover Bourque, *Defining Rape* (Durham, N.C.: Duke Univ. Press, 1989) 11–12.

52. Tom Hester and Tina Dorsey, "National Crime Victimization Survey: Criminal Victimization 1994," *Bureau of Justice Statistics* (Washington, D.C.: April 1996) 2.

53. Bourque, *Defining Rape,* 12.

54. Dianne Herman, "The Rape Culture," in *Women: A Feminist Perspective,* ed. Jo Freeman (Palo Alto, Calif.: Mayfield, 1984) 32.

55. Women's Action Coalition, *Stats: The Facts about Women* (New York: New Press, 1993) 49.

56. Rix, *The American Woman, 1990–91,* 43.

57. Benokraitis and Feagin, *Modern Sexism,* 59.

58. Catharine A. MacKinnon, *Feminism Unmodified: Discourses on Life and Law* (Cambridge: Harvard Univ. Press, 1987) 51.

59. Herman, "The Rape Culture," 23.

60. E. Sue Blume, *Secret Survivors: Uncovering Incest and Its Aftereffects in Women* (New York: Wiley, 1990) 10.

61. McCue, *Domestic Violence,* 84.

62. Daniel Linz, Edward Donnerstein, and Steven Penrod, "Sexual Violence in the Mass Media: Social Psychological Implications," in *Sex and Gender,* ed. Philip Shaver and Clyde Hendrick (Newbury Park, Calif.: Sage, 1987) 114.

63. Ibid., 107.

64. Ibid., 115.

65. Dolf Zillman and Jennings Bryant, "Pornography, Sexual Callousness, and the Trivialization of Rape," *Journal of Communication* 32 (1982) 10–21.

66. Benokraitis and Feagin, *Modern Sexism,* 10.

67. Women's Action Coalition, *Stats,* 50.

68. Ibid., 49.

69. Benokraitis and Feagin, *Modern Sexism,* 18.

70. Women's Action Coalition, *Stats,* 18–19.

71. Jean Kilbourne, "Beauty and the Beast of Advertising," in Rothenberg, *Race, Class, and Gender in the United States*, 349.

72. Kilbourne, "Beauty and the Beast," 348.

73. "The Leading Indicator," 6.

74. Tom Dorsey, "Girls Searching for Role Models Get Little Help from Television," *Courier Journal* (Louisville) July 22, 1996, D3.

75. Rothenberg, *Race, Class, and Gender,* 322.

76. Costello and Stone, *The American Woman, 1994–95,* 119.

77. Ibid.

78. Wu and Leffler, "Gender and Race Effects," 120.

79. Quoted in Tavris, *The Mismeasure of Woman,* 311.

80. Tavris, *The Mismeasure of Woman,* 24.

Chapter 2

1. Carol Tavris, *The Mismeasure of Woman* (New York: Simon & Schuster, 1992) 40.

2. Laura Shapiro, "Guns and Dolls," *Newsweek,* May 28, 1980, 62.

3. Joanna Rohrbaugh, *Women: Psychology's Puzzle* (New York: Basic Books, 1979) 424.

4. Helen Collier, *Counseling Women: A Guide for Therapists* (New York: Free Press, 1982) 28–29.

5. Miriam Greenspan, *A New Approach to Women and Psychotherapy* (New York: Guilford, 1987) chap. 2.

6. Carol Plummer, "Refusing Co-dependency," *MCC Women's Concerns Report* 91 (July–August 1990) 11.

7. Tavris, *The Mismeasure of Woman,* 197.

8. Alfred Adler, "On the Origin of Striving for Superiority and of Social Interest," in *Superiority and Social Interest*, 3rd ed., ed. Heinz Ansbacher and Rowena Ansbacher (New York: Norton, 1979) 34–35.

9. Quoted in Dorothe N. Rigby-Weinberg, "A Future Direction for Radical Feminist Therapy," in *A Guide to Dynamics of Feminist Therapy,* ed. Doris Howard (New York: Harrington Park, 1986) 195.

10. Quoted in Rigby-Weinberg, "A Future Direction," 195.

11. Gerald Monk, John Winslade, Kathie Crocket, and David Epston, eds., *Narrative Therapy in Practice: The Archaeology of Hope* (San Francisco: Jossey-Bass, 1997) 26.

12. Nijole V. Benokraitis and Joe R. Feagin, *Modern Sexism: Blatant, Subtle, and Covert Discrimination* (Englewood Cliffs, N.J.: Prentice-Hall, 1986) 10.

13. Rachel Hare-Mustin, "The Problem of Gender in Family Therapy Theory," in *Women in Families: A Framework for Family Therapy,* ed. Monica McGoldrick, Carol Anderson, and Froma Walsh (New York: Norton, 1989) 63.

14. *Statistical Abstract of the United States of 1989* (Washington, D.C.: Bureau of the Census, 1989).

15. Grace Jantzen, "Who Needs Feminism?" *Theology* 93 (September/October 1990) 341.

16. Margaret Anderson, *Thinking about Women: Sociological Perspectives on Sex and Gender,* 2nd ed. (New York: Macmillan, 1988) 248.

17. Mary Ballou and Nancy W. Gabalac, *A Feminist Position on Mental Health* (Springfield, Ill.: C. C. Thomas, 1987) chap. 4.

18. Michael White and David Epston, *Narrative Means to Therapeutic Ends* (New York: Norton, 1990) 10

19. Wendy Drewery and John Winslade, "The Theoretical Story of Narrative Therapy," in Gerald Monk et al., *Narrative Therapy in Practice,* 34–35.

20. Gerald Monk, "How Narrative Therapy Works," in Gerald Monk et al., *Narrative Therapy in Practice,* 28.

21. Jill Freedman and Gene Combs, *Narrative Therapy: The Social Construction of Preferred Realities* (New York: Norton, 1996), 69.

22. Monk, "How Narrative Therapy Works," 3–31.

23. Bill O'Hanlon, "The Third Wave," *Family Therapy Networker* 18 (November/December, 1994) 6.

24. Christie Cozad Neuger, "A Study in Women's Spiritual Growth Using Psycho-Imagery Techniques" (Ph.D. diss., School of Theology at Claremont, 1987).

25. Larry Kent Graham, *Familiar Strangers: Learning about God from Gays and Lesbians* (Louisville: Westminster John Knox, 1997) chap. 8.

Chapter 3

1. Riet Bons-Storm, *The Incredible Woman: Listening to Women's Silences in Pastoral Care and Counseling* (Nashville: Abingdon, 1996).

2. Serene Jones, "Women's Experience between a Rock and a Hard Place: Feminist, Womanist, and *Mujerista* Theologies in North America," in *Horizons in Feminist Theology: Identity, Tradition, and Norms,* ed. Rebecca S. Chopp and Sheila Greeve Davaney (Minneapolis: Fortress Press, 1997) 34.

3. Linell Elizabeth Cady, "Identity, Feminist Theory and Theology," in *Horizons in Feminist Theology,* ed. Chopp and Davaney, 20–21.

4. Ibid., 23.

5. Dale Spender, *Man Made Language*, 2nd ed. (London: Routledge and Kegan Paul, 1980) xiii.

6. Jean Baker Miller, *Toward a New Psychology of Women*, 2nd ed. (Boston: Beacon, 1986) 47.

7. There is considerable literature on this topic in both culture and church. For example, Casey Miller and Kate Swift, *Words and Women*, rev. ed. (New York: HarperCollins, 1991); Spender, *Man Made Language*; Mary Vetterling-Braggin, *Sexist Language: A Modern Philosophical Analysis* (Philadelphia: Littlefield, Adams,

1981); Keith Watkins, *Faithful and Fair: Transcending Sexist Language in Worship* (Nashville: Abingdon, 1981); Brian Wren, *What Language Shall I Borrow?: God-Talk in Worship: A Male Response to Feminist Theology* (New York: Crossroad, 1989).

8. Nelle Morton, *The Journey Is Home* (Boston: Beacon, 1985) 127. This phrase has been important to many inside and outside the church. The sense of collaboration—of giving birth to one another's ability to speak truth—is at the essence of empowerment.

9. Miriam Greenspan, *A New Approach to Women and Therapy* (New York: McGraw-Hill, 1983) 233.

10. Sandra Lipsitz Bem, *The Lenses of Gender* (New Haven: Yale Univ. Press, 1993) 138.

11. Miller, *Toward a New Psychology of Women,* 11.

12. Laura Brown, *Subversive Dialogues: Theory in Feminist Therapy* (New York: Basic, 1994) 155.

13. Carter Heyward, ed., *God's Fierce Whimsy: Christian Feminism and Theological Education* (New York: Pilgrim, 1985) 134.

14. Susan Brooks Thistlethwaite, "Theological Language," in *Language about God in Liturgy and Scripture: A Study Guide*, ed. Barbara Withers (New York: Geneva, 1980) 17.

15. This is a well-known quote by Nelle Morton, *The Journey Is Home,* 52.

16. Mary Daly, "Why Speak about God?" in *WomanSpirit Rising: A Reader in Religion,* ed. Carol Christ and Judith Plaskow (San Francisco: Harper & Row, 1979) 212.

17. Joan Bolker, "A Room of One's Own Is Not Enough," *Tikkun* 9, no. 6, 51.

18. Casey Miller and Kate Swift, *Words and Women* (Garden City, N.Y.: Anchor, 1977) 22.

19. Karen Adams and Norma Ware, "Sexism and the English Language: The Linguistic Implications of Being a Woman," in *Women: A Feminist Perspective,* 5th ed., ed. Jo Freeman (Mountain View, Calif.: Mayfield, 1995) 331.

20. Gerald Monk, John Winslade, Kathie Crocket, and David Epston, eds., *Narrative Theory in Practice: The Archaeology of Hope* (San Francisco: Jossey-Bass, 1997) 43.

21. Bons-Storm, *Incredible Woman,* 63.

22. Carol Gilligan, "Women's Psychological Development: Implications for Psychotherapy," in *Women, Girls, and Psychotherapy: Reframing Resistance,* ed. Carol Gilligan, Annie Rogers, and Deborah Tolman (New York: Harrington Park, 1991) 14.

23. Carol Gilligan, "Hearing the Difference: Theorizing Connection," *Hypatia* 10, no. 2 (1995) 124.

24. Ellyn Kaschak, *Engendered Lives: A New Psychology of Women's Experience* (New York: Basic, 1992) 89.

25. Ibid., 84.

26. Ibid., 97.

27. Ibid., 112.

28. Ibid., 124.

29. Lyn Mikel Brown and Carol Gilligan, *Meeting at the Crossroads: Women's Psychology and Girls' Development* (Cambridge: Harvard Univ. Press, 1992) 216.

30. Maria Harris, "Women Teaching Girls: The Power and the Danger," *Religious Education* 88, no. 1 (winter 1993) 56.

31. Tracy Robinson and Janie Victoria Ward, "A Belief in Self Far Greater than Anyone's Disbelief: Cultivating Resistance among African American Female Adolescents," in Gilligan, Rogers, and Tolman, *Women, Girls, and Psychotherapy,* 87–103.

32. Beverly Joan Smith, "Raising a Resister," in Gilligan, Rogers, and Tolman, *Women, Girls, and Psychotherapy,* 144–45.

33. See Patricia H. Davis, *Beyond Nice: The Spirituality of Adolescent Girls* (Minneapolis: Fortress Press, 2000).

34. Bons-Storm, *Incredible Woman,* 73.

35. Joan Martin, "The Notion of Difference for Emerging Womanist Ethics," *Journal of Feminist Ethics* 9, no. 1–2 (spring/fall 1993) 43.

36. bell hooks quoted in Martin, "The Notion of Difference," 43.

37. Bolker, "A Room of One's Own Is Not Enough," 54.

38. Ibid., 55.

39. Sue Campbell, "Being Dismissed: The Politics of Emotional Expression," *Hypatia* 9, no. 3 (summer 1994) 49.

40. Bons-Storm, *Incredible Woman,* 72.

41. Audre Lorde quoted in Campbell, "Being Dismissed," 52.

42. Bolker, "A Room of One's Own Is Not Enough," 52.

43. Carol Lakey Hess, *Caretakers of Our Common House: Women's Development in Communities of Faith* (Nashville: Abingdon, 1997) 14.

44. Lori Stern, "Disavowing the Self in Female Adolescence," in Gilligan, Rogers, and Tolman, *Women, Girls, and Psychotherapy,* 115.

45. Gilligan, "Hearing the Difference," 124.

46. *Kyriarchy* is a term coined by Elisabeth Schüssler Fiorenza to mean "lordship" or the variety of hierarchical power arrangements based on essential traits like gender, race, class, and sexual orientation.

47. Hess, *Caretakers of Our Common House,* 183.

48. Kathleen D. Billman. "Pastoral Care as an Art of Community," in *The Arts of Ministry: Feminist-Womanist Perspectives,* ed. Christie Cozad Neuger (Louisville: Westminster John Knox, 1996)

49. Bons-Storm, *Incredible Woman,* 84.

50. This is Ballou and Gabalac's term for the therapeutic process of helping women undo the effects of harmful adaptation.

51. Wendy Drewery and John Winslade, "The Theoretical Story of Narrative Therapy," in Monk et al., *Narrative Therapy in Practice,* 43.

52. Ibid.

53. Ibid., 32.

54. Alan Parry, "A Universe of Stories," *Family Process* 30, no. 1 (1991) 44.

55. Bons-Storm, *Incredible Woman,* 145.

56. Mary Sykes Wylie, "Panning for Gold," *Family Therapy Networker* 18, no. 6 (November/December 1994) 44.

57. John Winslade and Lorraine Smith, "Countering Alcoholic Narratives," in Monk et al., *Narrative Therapy in Practice,* 174–76.

58. Jill Freedman and Gene Combs, *Narrative Therapy: The Social Construction of Preferred Realities* (New York: Norton, 1996) 50.

59. Drewery and Winslade, "The Theoretical Story of Narrative Therapy," 33.

60. Parry, "A Universe of Stories," 37.

Chapter 4

1. Ola W. Barnett, Cindy L. Miller-Perrin, and Robin D. Perrin, *Family Violence across the Lifespan: An Introduction* (Thousand Oaks, Calif.: Sage, 1997) 4.

2. Richard Hokenson, *Donaldson, Lufkin, and Jenrette Newsletter* (May 3, 1996) 13.

3. Patrick Langan and Christopher Innes, "Preventing Domestic Violence against Women," in *Bureau of Justice Statistics—Special Report* (Washington, D.C.: August 1986), 1.

4. Judith Lewis Herman, *Trauma and Recovery* (New York: Basic, 1992) 8.

5. Ibid.

6. Carol J. Adams, "'I Just Raped My Wife! What Are You Going to Do about It, Pastor?'": The Church and Sexual Violence," in *Transforming a Rape Culture,* ed. Emilie Buchwald, Pamela Fletcher, and Martha Roth (Minneapolis: Milkweed, 1993) 75.

7. Quoted in Larry Kent Graham, "Responding to Victims and Perpetrators of Abuse: Panel Discussion," *Pastoral Psychology* 41 (1993) 298.

8. Alberta Wood and Maureen McHugh, "Woman Battering: The Response of Clergy," *Pastoral Psychology* 42 (1994) 191.

9. Ibid., 192.

10. Carole R. Bohn, "Dominion to Rule: The Roots and Consequences of a Theology of Ownership," in *Christianity, Patriarchy, and Abuse: A Feminist Critique,* ed. Joanne Carlson Brown and Carole R. Bohn (Cleveland: Pilgrim, 1989) 107.

11. For more on atonement, see Christie Cozad Neuger and James Newton Poling, eds. *The Care of Men* (Nashville: Abingdon, 1997) chap. 1.

12. Annie Imbens and Ineke Jonker, *Christianity and Incest,* trans. Patricia McVay (Minneapolis: Fortress Press, 1992) 212.

13. Mary Daly, *Beyond God the Father: Toward a Philosophy of Women's Liberation* (Boston: Beacon, 1973) 77.

14. Imbens and Jonker, *Christianity and Incest,* chap. 5.

15. James Newton Poling, *The Abuse of Power: A Theological Problem* (Nashville: Abingdon, 1994).

16. Imbens and Jonker, *Christianity and Incest,* 215.

17. Marie M. Fortune, "Forgiveness: The Last Step," in *Violence against Women and Children: A Christian Theological Sourcebook,* ed. Carol J. Adams and Marie M. Fortune (New York: Continuum, 1995) 202.

18. Marie M. Fortune and James Poling, "Calling to Accountability: The Church's Response to Abusers," in Adams and Fortune, *Violence against Women and Children,* 453.

19. Larry Kent Graham and Marie M. Fortune, "Empowering the Congregation to Respond to Sexual Abuse and Domestic Violence," *Pastoral Psychology* 41 (1993) 340.

20. John Dominic Crossan, paper presented at the Gustafson Lecture Series at United Theological Seminary, November 1–2, 1999.

21. Paula Cooey, "Re-membering the Body: A Theological Resource for Resisting Violence against a People Called Feminine" (unpublished paper, 1997) 12.

22. David Tracy, *On Naming the Present: Reflections on God, Hermeneutics, and the Church* (Maryknoll, N.Y.: Orbis, 1994) 21–22.

23. Cooey, "Re-membering the Body," 27.

24. Fortune and Poling, "Calling to Accountability," 457.

25. L. J. "Tess" Tessier, "Women Sexually Abused as Children: The Spiritual Consequences," *Second Opinion* 17, no. 3 (January 1992) 12.

26. Lisa Goodman, Mary Koss, and Nancy Russo, "Violence against Women: Physical and Mental Health Effects. Part I: Research Findings," *Applied and Preventive Psychology* 2 (1993) 80.

27. Lenore E. A. Walker, *Abused Women and Survivor Therapy: A Practical Guide for the Psychotherapist* (Washington, D.C.: American Psychological Association, 1994) 30.

28. Tessier, "Women Sexually Abused as Children," 12.

29. Walker, *Abused Women and Survivor Therapy,* 6.

30. Maria P. P. Root, "Reconstructing the Impact of Trauma on Personality," in *Personality and Psychopathology: Feminist Reappraisals,* ed. Laura S. Brown and Mary Ballou (New York: Guilford, 1992) 229.

31. Ibid., 239–41.

32. Ibid., 241.

33. J. L. Herman, *Trauma and Recovery,* 36.

34. Barnett, Miller-Perrin, and Perrin, *Family Violence across the Lifespan,* 73–74.

35. Dianne Herman, "The Rape Culture," in *Women: A Feminist Perspective,* 3rd ed., ed. Jo Freeman (Palo Alto, Calif.: Mayfield, 1984), 32.

36. Susan Morrow and Mary Lee Smith, "Constructions of Survival and Coping by Women Who Have Survived Childhood Sexual Abuse," *Journal of Counseling Psychology* 42, no. 1 (1995) 27–30.

37. J. L. Herman, *Trauma and Recovery,* 114.

38. Buchwald, Fletcher, and Roth, *Transforming a Rape Culture*, 7.

39. Ibid., 8.

40. J. L. Herman, *Trauma and Recovery,* 63.

41. Walker, *Abused Women and Survivor Therapy,* 31.

42. Judith Worrell and Pam Remer, *Feminist Perspectives in Therapy: An Empowerment Model for Women* (Chichester, England: Wiley, 1992) 206–9.

43. Wood and McHugh, "Woman Battering," 193.

44. Ibid.

45. Marianne Zawitz, "Violence between Intimates," *Bureau of Justice Statistics* (Washington, D.C.: November 1994) 2.

46. Buchwald, Fletcher, and Roth, *Transforming a Rape Culture,* 78.

47. Walker, *Abused Women and Survivor Therapy,* 56.

48. Ibid., 79.

49. Worrell and Remer, *Feminist Perspectives in Therapy,* 247.

50. Walker, *Abused Women and Survivor Therapy,* 86.

51. Graham and Fortune, "Empowering the Congregation," 343.

52. Walker, *Abused Women and Survivor Therapy,* 402–4.

53. J. L. Herman, *Trauma and Recovery,* 213.

54. Marie M. Fortune, "Making Justice: Sources of Healing for Incest Survivors," *Daughters of Sarah* (September/October 1987) 9.

55. bell hooks, "Seduced by Violence No More," in Buchwald, Fletcher, and Roth, *Transforming a Rape Culture,* 351–58.

56. Adams, "I Just Raped My Wife!" 62.

Chapter 5

1. Jeffrey Zimmerman and Victoria Dickerson, "Using a Narrative Metaphor: Implications for Theory and Clinical Practice," *Family Process* 33 (1994) 242.

2. Riet Bons-Storm, *The Incredible Woman: Listening to Women's Silences in Pastoral Care and Counseling* (Nashville: Abingdon, 1996) 58.

3. Julia A. Boyd, "Ethnic and Cultural Diversity: Keys to Power," in *Diversity and Complexity in Feminist Therapy,* ed. Laura S. Brown and Maria P. P. Root (New York: Harrington Park, 1990) 164–65.

4. Mary Ballou and Nancy W. Gabalac, *A Feminist Position on Mental Health* (Springfield, Ill.: C. C. Thomas, 1985) 102–3.

5. Ibid., 104.

6. Alan Parry, "A Universe of Stories," *Family Process* 30, no. 1 (1991) 51.

7. Hilde Lindemann Nelson, "Resistance and Insubordination," *Hypatia* 10, no. 2 (spring 1995) 23.

8. Bons-Storm, *Incredible Woman,* 84.

9. Nelson, "Resistance and Insubordination," 24.

10. Nicola Slee, "Parables and Women's Experience," in *Feminist Theology: A Reader,* ed. Ann Loades (Louisville: Westminster John Knox, 1990) 42.

11. Donald Capps, *Reframing: A New Method in Pastoral Care* (Minneapolis: Fortress Press, 1990).

12. When I use the word *vocation,* I intend that to mean the call by God to authentic personhood and to use one's gifts and graces in the service of God's salvific kindom.

13. Joseph B. Eron and Thomas W. Lund, *Narrative Solutions in Brief Therapy* (New York: Guilford, 1996) 32.

14. Gerald Monk, "How Narrative Therapy Works," in *Narrative Therapy in Practice: The Archaeology of Hope,* ed. Gerald Monk, John Winslade, Kathie Crocket, and David Epston (San Francisco: Jossey-Bass, 1997) 27.

15. Wendy Drewery and John Winslade, "The Theoretical Story of Narrative Therapy," in Monk et al., *Narrative Therapy in Practice,* 43.

16. For more about this counseling situation, see Christie Cozad Neuger, "Feminist Pastoral Counseling and Pastoral Theology: A Work in Progress," *Journal of Pastoral Theology* 3 (summer 1992).

17. Mary Daly, *Gyn/Ecology: The Metaethics of Radical Feminism* (Boston: Beacon, 1978).

18. Thomas A. Droege, *Guided Grief Imager: A Resource for Grief Ministry and Death Education* (New York: Paulist, 1987) 6.

19. To read more about the use of imagination in pastoral counseling, see Christie Cozad Neuger, "Imagination in Pastoral Counseling," in *Clinical Handbook to Basic Types of Pastoral Care and Counseling,* ed. Howard W. Stone and William Clements (Nashville: Abingdon, 1991).

Chapter 6

1. Angela Mitchell, *What the Blues Is All About: Black Women Overcoming Stress and Depression* (New York: Perigee, 1998) 25.

2. Susan Nolen-Hoeksema, *Sex Differences in Depression* (Stanford, Calif.: Stanford Univ. Press, 1990) 3.

3. Mitchell, *What the Blues Is All About,* 33.

4. Ibid., 35–36.

5. Ibid., 37.

6. Nolen-Hoeksema, *Sex Differences in Depression,* 57.

7. Mitchell, *What the Blues Is All About,* 39.

8. Howard W. Stone, *Depression and Hope*: *New Insights for Pastoral Counseling* (Minneapolis: Fortress Press, 1998) 2.

9. Nolen-Hoeksema, *Sex Differences in Depression,* 3.

10. Ibid., 36.

11. Ibid., 194.

12. Ibid., 195.

13. Ibid., 75–76.

14. Susan J. Dunlap, *Counseling Depressed Women* (Louisville: Westminster John Knox, 1997) 2.

15. Cynthia Costello and Anne J. Stone, *The American Woman, 1994–95: Where We Stand, Women and Health* (New York: Norton, 1994) 119.

16. Mitchell, *What the Blues Is All About,* 4.

17. Ibid., 148.

18. Kay Rawson and Glen Jenson, "Depression as a Measurement of Well-Being in Women at Midlife," *Family Perspective* 29 (1995) 305.

19. Ibid., 308.

20. Marianne Zawitz, "Violence between Intimates," *Bureau of Justice Statistics* (Washington, D.C.: April 1994) 3.

21. Tom Hester and Tina Dorsey, "National Crime Victimization Survey: Criminal Victimization 1994," *Bureau of Justice Statistics* (Washington, D.C.: April 1996) 2.

22. Zawitz, "Violence between Intimates," 2.

23. Nolen-Hoeksema, *Sex Differences in Depression,* 91.

24. Jennifer Christian, Daniel O'Leary, and Dina Vivian, "Depressive Symptomatology in Maritally Discordant Women and Men: The Role of Individual and Relationship Variables," *Journal of Family Psychology* 8 (1994) 36.

25. Donald Meichenbaum, *A Clinical Handbook/Practical Therapist Manual for Assessing and Treating Adults with Post-Traumatic Stress Disorder* (Waterloo, Ontario, Canada: Institute Press, 1994) 70–72.

26. Xiaoqin Wu and Alfred DeMaris, "Gender and Marital Status Difference in Depression," *Sex Roles* 34, no. 5/6 (1996) 317.

27. Christian, O'Leary, and Vivian, "Depressive Symptomatology," 36.

28. Mitchell, *What the Blues Is All About,* 148.

29. Ibid., 155.

30. Miriam Greenspan, *A New Approach to Women and Therapy* (New York: McGraw-Hill, 1983) 300.

31. Linda Tschirhart Sanford and Mary Ellen Donovan, *Women and Self-Esteem: Understanding and Improving the Way We Think and Feel about Ourselves* (New York: Penguin, 1984) xiv.

32. Dunlap, *Counseling Depressed Women,* 36.

33. Sandra Guggisberg, "Etiological Comparisons between Depressed Men and Depressed Women" (master's thesis, Mankato State University, 1993) 34.

34. Charles Neuringer, "Suicidal Self-Destruction in Women," in *Women and Depression: A Lifespan Perspective,* ed. Ruth Formanek and Anita Gurian (New York: Springer, 1987) 241.

35. Ibid., 244.

36. Mitchell, *What the Blues Is All About,* 4.

37. Neuringer, "Suicidal Self-Destruction in Women," 241.

38. Moira Plant, *Women and Alcohol: Contemporary and Historical Perspectives* (New York: Free Association Books, 1997) 14.

39. Jahn Forth-Finegan, "Sugar and Spice and Everything Nice: Gender Socialization and Women's Addiction: A Literature Review," in *Feminism and Addiction,* ed. Claudia Bepko (New York: Haworth, 1991) 23.

40. Plant, *Women and Alcohol,* 136.

41. Forth-Finegan, "Sugar and Spice and Everything Nice," 28.

42. Deborah Bushway, "Chemical Dependency in Lesbians and Their Families: The Feminist Challenge," in Bepko, *Feminism and Addiction,* 168.

43. Sheila Blume, "Alcohol and Other Drug Problems in Women," in *Substance Abuse: A Comprehensive Textbook,* 2nd ed., ed. Joyce H. Lowinson, Pedro Ruiz, Robert B. Millman (Baltimore: Williams and Wilkins, 1996) 799.

44. Ibid., 797; Plant, *Women and Alcohol,* 115.

45. Blume, "Alcohol and Other Drug Problems," 797.

46. Plant, *Women and Alcohol,* 111.

47. Blume, "Alcohol and Other Drug Problems," 797.

48. Ibid., 800.

49. Nolen-Hoeksema, *Sex Differences in Depression,* 177.

50. Dunlap, *Counseling Depressed Women,* 42.

51. Mitchell, *What the Blues Is All About,* 192.

52. Peter Roger Breggin, *Talking Back to Prozac: What Doctors Won't Tell You about Today's Most Controversial Drug* (New York: St. Martin's, 1994) 4.

53. Ibid., 29.

54. Greg Critser, "Oh How Happy We Will Be," *Family Therapy Networker* (September/October 1996) 37.

Chapter 7

1. Valerie M. DeMarinis, *Critical Caring: A Feminist Model for Pastoral Psychology* (Louisville: Westminster John Knox, 1993) 13.

2. Mary Ballou and Nancy W. Gabalac, *A Feminist Position on Mental Health* (Springfield, Ill.: C. C. Thomas, 1985) 108–9.

3. Ibid., 115.

4. Ibid., 101–19.

5. Thomas St. James O'Connor, Elizabeth Meakes, M. Ruth Pickering, and Martha Schuman, "On the Right Track: Experience of Narrative Therapy," *Contemporary Family Therapy* 19 (December 1997) 480.

6. Ibid., 487.

7. Jill Freedman and Gene Combs, *Narrative Therapy: The Social Construction of Preferred Realities* (New York: Norton, 1996) 171.

8. Ibid., 180.

9. Larry Graham, "From Impasse to Innovation in Pastoral Theology and Pastoral Counseling," *Journal of Pastoral Theology* 6 (summer 1996) 23.

10. Emilie M. Townes, "Ethics as an Art of Doing the Work Our Souls Must Have," in *The Arts of Ministry: Feminist-Womanist Perspectives,* ed. Christie Cozad Neuger (Louisville: Westminster John Knox, 1996).

11. Rosemary Radford Ruether, *Sexism and God Talk: Toward a Feminist Theology* (Boston: Beacon, 1983) 24.

Chapter 8

1. Carroll Saussy, *The Art of Growing Old: A Guide to Faithful Aging* (Minneapolis: Augsburg Books, 1998) 15.

2. Robert C. Atchley, *Social Forces and Aging: An Introduction to Social Gerontology*, 6th ed. (Belmont, Calif.: Wadsworth, 1991) 33.

3. Ibid.

4. Barbara F. Turner and Lillian E. Troll, eds., *Women Growing Older: Psychological Perspectives* (Thousand Oaks, Calif.: Sage, 1994) 17.

5. J. Dianne Garner and Susan O. Mercer, eds., introduction to *Women as They Age: Challenge, Opportunity, and Triumph* (New York: Haworth, 1989) 7.

6. Atchley, *Social Forces and Aging,* 27.

7. Susan O. Mercer and J. Dianne Garner, "An International Overview of Aged Women," in Garner and Mercer, *Women as They Age,* 13.

8. Ibid., 14.

9. Lois Grau, ed., *Women in the Later Years: Health, Social, and Cultural Perspectives* (New York: Harrington Park, 1989) 1.

10. Elizabeth Midlarsky, "Feminist Therapies with the Elderly," in *Feminist Psychotherapies: Integration of Therapeutic and Feminist Systems,* ed. Mary Ann Dutton-Douglas and Lenore E. A. Walker (Norwood, N.J.: Ablex, 1988) 255–59.

11. Ibid., 255.

12. Atchley, *Social Forces and Aging,* 104.

13. Ketayun Gould, "A Minority Feminist Perspective on Women and Aging," in Garner and Mercer, *Women as They Age,* 203.

14. Naomi Gottlieb, "Families, Work, and the Lives of Older Women," in Garner and Mercer, *Women as They Age,* 218.

15. Ibid., 219.

16. Atchley, *Social Forces and Aging,* 167.

17. Mercer and Garner, "An International Overview of Aged Women," 30.

18. Atchley, *Social Forces and Aging,* 219.

19. Hedva Lewittes, "Just Being Friendly Means a Lot: Women, Friendship, and Aging," in Grau, *Women in the Later Years,* 143.

20. Ruth Formanek, "Depression and the Older Woman," in *Women and Depression: A Lifespan Perspective,* ed. Ruth Formanek and Anita Gurian (New York: Springer, 1987) 276.

21. Lewittes, "Just Being Friendly Means a Lot," 143.

22. Midlarsky, "Feminist Therapies with the Elderly," 257.

23. Jean Coyle, "Retirement Planning and the Woman Business Owner," in *Women as Elders: The Feminist Politics of Aging,* ed. Marilyn Bell (New York: Harrington Park, 1986) 54.

24. Laura Hubbs-Tait, "Coping Patterns of Aging Women: A Developmental Perspective," in Garner and Mercer, *Women as They Age,* 103.

25. Kay Rawson and Glen Jenson, "Depression as a Measurement of Well-Being in Women at Midlife," *Family Perspective* 29 (1995) 308.

26. Susan Gaylord, "Women and Aging: A Psychological Perspective," in Garner and Mercer, *Women as They Age,* 107.

27. James Lubben, "Gender Differences in the Relationship of Widowhood and Psychological Well-Being among Low-Income Elderly," in Garner and Mercer, *Women as They Age,* 168.

28. Gary Whitford and Jean Quam, "Older Gay and Lesbian Adults," in *Aging, Spirituality, and Religion: A Handbook,* ed. Melvin A. Kimble, Susan H. McFadden, James W. Ellor, and James J. Seeber (Minneapolis: Fortress Press, 1995) 381.

29. Ibid., 382.

30. Kristine Falco, *Psychotherapy with Lesbian Clients: Theory into Practice* (New York: Brunner/Mazel, 1991)

31. Barbara Pearson and Cornelia Beck, "Physical Health of Elderly Women," in Garner and Mercer, *Women as They Age,* 161.

32. Ibid., 162.

33. Ibid.

34. Ibid., 165.

35. For example, see Renate Klein and Lynette Dumble, "Disempowering Midlife Women: The Science and Politics of Hormone Replacement Therapy," *Women's Studies International Forum* 17 (1994) 327–43.

36. Midlarsky, "Feminist Therapies with the Elderly," 268.

37. Older Women's League, "The Picture of Health for Midlife and Older Women in America," in Grau, *Women in the Later Years,* 60.

38. Harold G. Koenig, "Religion and Health in Later Life," in Kimble et al., *Aging, Spirituality, and Religion,* 12.

39. Ibid., 13.

40. Saussy, *The Art of Growing Old,* 84.

41. Lisa Greenberg, "Old Wives Tales: Retrospective Views of Elderly Women," in Formanek and Gurian, *Women and Depression,* 290.

42. Melvin A. Kimble, "Pastoral Care," in Kimble et al., *Aging, Spirituality, and Religion,* 131.

43. See the poem "Crone" by Gert Beadle in Bell, *Women as Elders,* xiii, and "Warning" by Jenny Joseph in *When I Am an Old Woman, I Shall Wear Purple: An Anthology of Short Stories and Poetry,* ed. Sandra Martz (Manhattan Beach, Calif.: Papier-Mâché, 1987)

44. I have drawn many of the ideas for these types of groups from Toba Schwaber Kerson, "Women and Aging: A Clinical Social Work Perspective," in Garner and Mercer, *Women as They Age,* 135.

45. Greenberg, "Old Wives Tales," 292.

46. Toba Schwaber Kerson, "Women and Aging: A Clinical Social Work Perspective," in Garner and Mercer, *Women as They Age,* 131.

47. Ibid., 131–33.

Chapter 9

1. It is important not to imply that aging in and of itself is a "life problem." Rather, aging is a specific context for women that has frequently been made out to be a problem by the culture and thus deserves some particular attention.

2. Riet Bons-Storm, "Putting the Little Ones into the Dialogue: A Feminist Practical Theology," in *Liberating Faith Practices: Feminist Practical Theologies in Context,* ed. Denise Ackerman and Riet Bons-Storm (Leuven, Belgium: Peeters, 1998) 23.

3. Sharon D. Welch, *Communities of Resistance and Solidarity: A Feminist Theology of Liberation* (Maryknoll, N.Y.: Orbis, 1985) 19.

4. Ibid., 55.

5. Ellyn Kaschak, *Engendered Lives: A New Psychology of Women's Experience* (New York: Basic, 1992) 124.

6. Carol Hess, "Education as an Art of Getting Dirty with Dignity," in *The Arts of Ministry: Feminist-Womanist Approaches,* ed. Christie Cozad Neuger, (Louisville: Westminster John Knox, 1996) 64.

7. Welch, *Communities of Resistance and Solidarity,* 42.

8. Bons-Storm, "Putting the Little Ones into the Dialogue," 22.

9. Carol Hess, "Becoming Mid-wives to Justice: A Feminist Approach to Practical Theology," in Denise M. Ackerman and Riet Bons-Storm, eds., *Liberating Faith Practices: Feminist Practical Theologies in Context* (Leuven: Peeters, 1998) 72; Robert N. Bellah, William M. Sullivan, Steven M. Tipton, Richard Madsen, and Ann Swidler, *Habits of the Heart: Individualism and Commitment in American Life* (Berkeley: Univ. of California Press, 1985) 72.

10. Ibid., 72.

11. Bons-Storm, "Putting the Little Ones into the Dialogue," 15.

12. Welch, *Communities of Resistance and Solidarity,* 67.

13. Ibid., 45.

Index

257